Toward Spatial Humanities

D1615676

THE SPATIAL HUMANITIES
David J. Bodenhamer, John Corrigan, and Trevor M. Harris, editors

Geographies of the Holocaust, Edited by Anne Kelly Knowles,
Tim Cole, and Alberto Giordano

Locating the Moving Image: New Approaches to Film and Place,
Edited by Julia Hallam and Les Roberts

The Spatial Humanities: GIS and the Future of Humanities Scholarship,
Edited by David J. Bodenhamer, John Corrigan, and Trevor M. Harris

*Troubled Geographies: A Spatial History of Religion and Society
in Ireland,* Ian N. Gregory, Niall A. Cunningham, C. D. Lloyd,
Ian G. Shuttleworth, and Paul S. Ell

TOWARD SPATIAL HUMANITIES

HISTORICAL GIS AND SPATIAL HISTORY

EDITED BY IAN N. GREGORY AND ALISTAIR GEDDES

INDIANA UNIVERSITY PRESS   *Bloomington & Indianapolis*

This book is a publication of

INDIANA UNIVERSITY PRESS
Office of Scholarly Publishing
Herman B Wells Library 350
1320 East 10th Street
Bloomington, Indiana 47405 USA

iupress.indiana.edu

Telephone   800-842-6796
Fax   812-855-7931

© 2014 by Indiana University Press

∞ The paper used in this publication meets the minimum requirements of the American National Standard for Information Sciences–Permanence of Paper for Printed Library Materials, ANSI Z39.48–1992.

*Manufactured in the
United States of America*

*Library of Congress
Cataloging-in-Publication Data*

Toward spatial humanities : historical GIS and spatial history / edited by Ian N. Gregory and Alistair Geddes.
    pages cm
    Includes bibliographical references and index.
    ISBN 978-0-253-01180-0 (cloth : alkaline paper) – ISBN 978-0-253-01186-2 (paperback : alkaline paper) – ISBN 978-0-253-01190-9 (ebook) 1. Historiography – Methodology. 2. Geographic information systems. 3. History – Sources. 4. Historical geography – Methodology. 5. History – Data processing. I. Gregory, Ian N. II. Geddes, A. (Alistair)
    D16.T74 2014
    910.285 – dc23

                          2013037075

1 2 3 4 5 18 17 16 15 14

Contents

Acknowledgments · vii

Introduction: From Historical GIS *to Spatial Humanities:*
Deepening Scholarship and Broadening Technology
Ian N. Gregory and Alistair Geddes · ix

PART 1. DEEPENING SCHOLARSHIP: DEVELOPING
HISTORIOGRAPHY THROUGH SPATIAL HISTORY · 1

1. Railways and Agriculture in France and Great Britain, 1850–1914
Robert M. Schwartz and Thomas Thevenin · 4

2. The Development, Persistence, and Change of Racial Segregation
in U.S. Urban Areas, 1880–2010 · *Andrew A. Beveridge* · 35

3. Troubled Geographies: A Historical GIS of Religion, Society, and
Conflict in Ireland since the Great Famine · *Niall Cunningham* · 62

PART 2. BROADENING TECHNOLOGY: APPLYING
GIS TO NEW SOURCES AND DISCIPLINES · 89

4. Applying Historical GIS beyond the Academy: Four Use Cases for
the Great Britain HGIS · *Humphrey R. Southall* · 92

5. The Politics of Territory in Song Dynasty China, 960–1276 CE
Elijah Meeks and Ruth Mostern · 118

6. Mapping the City in Film · *Julia Hallam and Les Roberts* · 143

7. Conclusions: From Historical GIS to Spatial Humanities:
Challenges and Opportunities · *Ian N. Gregory and
Alistair Geddes* · 172

8. Further Reading: From Historical GIS to Spatial Humanities:
An Evolving Literature · *Ian N. Gregory* · 186

Contributors · 203

Index · 207

Acknowledgments

WE EXPRESS OUR SINCERE GRATITUDE TO ALL OF THE CON-
tributors for their efforts and speedy replies to our requests and queries.
The work was strengthened as a result of detailed anonymous review,
and we thank those involved in that process. The series editors – David
Bodenhamer especially – gave sagacious advice, and we benefited from
guidance of Darja Malcolm-Clarke, Dan Pyle, Robert Sloan, and Jenna
Whittaker, all at Indiana University Press. We are also very grateful to
Mary M. Hill for undertaking the copyediting. Others gave their support
and kindness unstintingly: Alistair would particularly like to thank Jen
and Robin Flowerdew.

The groundwork for this book came as a result of an Economic and
Social Research Council (ESRC) Seminar Series Grant, "The Historical
GIS Research Network" (RES-451-25-4307). Its completion benefited
from support from the European Research Council (ERC) under the
European Union's Seventh Framework Programme (FP7/2007–2013)/
ERC Grant "Spatial Humanities: Texts, GIS, Places" (agreement number
283850).

Introduction: From Historical GIS to Spatial Humanities: Deepening Scholarship and Broadening Technology

IAN N. GREGORY AND ALISTAIR GEDDES

WHEN GEOGRAPHICAL INFORMATION SYSTEMS (GIS) FIRST began to be used by academic geographers in the late 1980s, their use was nothing if not controversial. Proponents of the new field argued that it had the potential to reinvigorate geography as a discipline under a more computational paradigm.[1] Opponents argued that it marked a lurch toward an unacceptable form of positivism with no epistemology or treatment of ethical or political issues.[2] One thing on which they both agreed – or perhaps took for granted – was that GIS was a quantitative technology that was to be used in a social scientific manner (to its supporters) or a positivist way (to its antagonists).

When GIS first began to be used by historians it was not surprising that much of the early focus was also quantitative and social science based. It is no coincidence that the first special issue of a journal dedicated to historical GIS (HGIS), published in *Social Science History*, included essays on topics such as fertility, migration, urban history, and economic growth, all well suited to quantitative analysis.[3] In 2008, eight years after this issue was published, a conference devoted to HGIS was held at the University of Essex.[4] It attracted 125 delegates, with papers organized in 21 sessions. While some of these sessions were themed on topics that still had a strong quantitative bent – demography, urban history, environmental history, transport, and so on – there was also an increasing number of papers and sessions that concentrated on topics that were clearly qualitative and did not follow traditional social science paradigms. These topics included art, performance culture, literature, the Bible, and medieval and early modern history. What was happening

in the quantitative sessions was also interesting. Rather than concentrating on issues associated with database construction and potential
applications, many of these papers had developed to focus on conducting applied works of history – studies that developed the historiography by answering applied research questions. This was an indication
of two emerging trends within HGIS that have continued since: HGIS
is deepening from an applied perspective, and it is broadening from a
technical perspective. It is deepening in that it has reached a stage where
researchers apply it to scholarship that develops new knowledge about
the past. This must be the ultimate aim of the field, as it takes HGIS
beyond a narrow technical specialism and makes it relevant to a much
wider audience. HGIS is also broadening its technical scope in terms of
the ever-widening potential for its application to both qualitative and
quantitative sources. This means that GIS is thus able to expand beyond
social science history – a fairly narrow field – to be applicable to the discipline more broadly, and beyond that to spread outside the disciplinary
boundaries of history into other humanities disciplines.

GIS AND HISTORICAL RESEARCH

There are many different definitions of GIS and related terms such as
GISc (Geographical Information Science).[5] The emergence of new geospatial technologies such as Google Earth that do not fit traditional definitions only complicates these definitions. Originally, "GIS" was considered as the umbrella term for the field, and it is often still used in this
way. The more recent trend, however, has been to use "GIS" to describe
the tools offered, while "GISc" emphasizes the broader understanding of
how these tools can be developed, used, and applied.[6]

   To take this further, GIS can be thought of as a type of software that
provides a way of representing features on the Earth's surface and a suite
of operations that allow the researcher to query, manipulate, visualize,
and analyze these representations. The representations, or data models, combine two types of data: *attribute data,* which were traditionally
held in a table and tend – or perhaps tended – to be quantitative, and
spatial data, which locate each item of data using a point, a line, a polygon
(which represents an area or a zone), or a pixel. Points, lines, and poly-

gons are used to represent discrete features, and data in these formats are referred to as *vector data,* while pixels are used to represent continuous surfaces and are referred to as *raster data.*[7] In this way the attribute data say *what,* while the spatial data say *where.* Thus, from this perspective GIS is a type of software that allows the user to store, retrieve, visualize, and analyze data that are *georeferenced* to a location on the Earth's surface.[8] GIS allows researchers to ask questions about their topics or sources that stress the importance of location and thus geography. This emphasis on geography, combined with the tools to represent and explore georeferenced data, is what allows scholars to conduct their research in new ways.

This approach to defining GIS leads to the conclusion that a Geographic Information System is really a database for managing georeferenced data. Until recently this conclusion made a quantitative paradigm almost inevitable, as databases were, almost by definition, quantitative, holding either numbers or structured textual information such as is found in library catalogs. Recent developments in Information Technology (IT) mean that this paradigm is no longer the case. Increasingly, almost any type of data can be held within a computer system, including unstructured texts such as books and web pages, still images, moving images, and sounds. As long as a location can be found for these items, they can be held within a GIS-type structure. This means that the need for attribute data to be quantitative is increasingly disappearing.

While this is true of attribute data, it is not true of spatial data, which, although they tend to be represented graphically, are indisputably quantitative in nature. What appears to be a point on the map is actually a pair of numbers representing *x* and *y* or latitude and longitude. A line is a series of points joined together, and the boundaries of a polygon are made up of one or more lines. Despite the many critiques of maps, researchers are usually far more comfortable interpreting the crude quantitative abstraction of space created from spatial data than they have been interpreting the crude quantitative abstraction of society created from quantitative data.[9] For example, many humanities researchers would be happy with a map showing the locations of certain events as points but would be suspicious of a scatterplot showing the relationship between two variables such as the unemployment rate and the number of crimes in tracts around a city. In reality, the two have much in common. They both simply show dots whose location is determined using values of *x* and *y*, values that are typically expressed to a far higher degree of precision than the accuracy of their measurement can really support.[10] There are a number of possible reasons for this apparent inconsistency. These include the valid reason that measuring and interpreting statistics about characteristics of the population are more difficult than doing the same for locations on the Earth's surface. Less justifiable are a misplaced confidence in the authority of maps and, from the opposite perspective, a misplaced suspicion of quantitative approaches among some researchers in the humanities.

Using GIS in humanities research presents the researcher with two major sets of challenges. The first is to get the data into a GIS. GIS databases are usually vector data, which require that every item of attribute data be located using a precisely defined point, line, or polygon. Techniques such as using raster surfaces or networks have been used effectively in HGIS research to represent imprecision in location, but even these approaches usually require a precise point-based location to be given initially and do not solve the inherent uncertainties within the spatial data.[11] In some cases it may simply be impossible to get a source into a form suitable for GIS; however, as we will see, this does not mean that such a source cannot contribute to a study that is centered on a GIS database.

The second, and more important, challenge is to get information back from the GIS databases and turn it into new scholarship that advances our knowledge of the past. Once a GIS database has been created it is very easy to produce large numbers of maps, graphs, tables, and summaries. Going beyond this to produce new knowledge or an innovative narrative requires a different set of skills. Creating a GIS and analyzing the data that it contains requires technical GIS skills. Producing new scholarship requires the skills of the historian or other humanities scholar to turn the GIS output into a contribution to our understanding of the past. A key test of the effectiveness of historical research is that the work that it produces should be of interest not only to HGIS specialists but also to an audience of subject specialists who are more interested in the results of the research than in the methodology that was used to achieve these results.

These challenges show that there are certain principles that research-ers interested in GIS must consider. Clearly, there must be a geographi-cal dimension to whatever study is being undertaken, and, beyond this, the requirements and limitations of the vector and raster data models need to be understood. However, the fact that HGIS research is ulti-mately based on a software tool does not, as is sometimes claimed, force a positivist approach onto the researcher. As described above, GIS merely provides a platform on which research can be conducted. It does not impose any approach other than the fact that the data within the GIS database have to be represented using attribute and spatial data and that the spatial data must be in the form of points, lines, polygons, or pixels. How scholars turn these data into information about the past and then to humanities scholarship is their decision. They would start from their discipline's existing paradigms and add the more explicitly geographical. That said, as noted above, GIS does require locations that are usually ex-pressed with high degrees of precision – usually far more precision than it makes sense to express them to. This is not, of itself, positivism, which is concerned with using statistical approaches to define relationships between variables so that empirical generalizations can be made.[12] Early fears of GIS causing a return to "the very worst sort of positivism" were prompted by calls for GIS to reinvigorate the use of quantitative attribute data and statistical approaches rather than by fears about the accuracy of spatial data.[13] It is also worth noting that representing the location of a mountaintop or a city using a point whose coordinates are given submillimetric precision makes no more sense in the earth sciences or social sciences than it does in the humanities. The limitations of the vector data model mean that locations are expressed with this spurious level of precision. It is up to the researcher to interpret this precision and its consequences sensibly, which is not always as easy as it may seem; indeed, here the humanities may have an advantage over more empirical approaches. While in other fields coordinates are often used as inputs into statistical approaches where their overly precise nature becomes lost in summary statistics, in the humanities – where the emphasis is on close reading and careful interpretation – imprecision and ambiguity are actually easier to handle, as these limitations remain more transparent to the critical researcher.

It is not the intention here to discuss existing humanities paradigms, but it is worth discussing in general terms what adding the use of GIS has to offer to them. Traditionally, it has been argued that there are three main advantages in using GIS in historical research: GIS structures the data to allow them to be discovered and explored in ways that are explicitly spatial; it allows the data to be visualized using mapping and other approaches; and it allows the data to be analyzed in ways that are explicitly spatial.[14] A fourth advantage, and one whose importance is frequently underestimated, is the ability of GIS to integrate data from a wide range of apparently incompatible sources. As all of the data are georeferenced to specific coordinate-based locations on the Earth's surface, at a technical level at least, any dataset can be integrated with any other dataset to see how the locations within one dataset compare with the locations in another. This integration has potentially major benefits, as, for example, previously disparate and apparently incompatible sources can be brought together.

Thus GIS can be thought of as a tool that enables researchers to explicitly handle space and location. It is far from a perfect tool, as its data models are crude. It is, however, a highly effective tool with much to offer many subjects across the humanities as long as its limitations are understood and the patterns that it reveals are evaluated critically.

TRENDS IN HGIS

As mentioned above, the 2008 conference illustrated that HGIS was being taken in two directions. On the one hand, the more traditional side of the field – the quantitative, social science–based side – was moving away from its original technical emphasis to focus increasingly on answering research questions and developing new narratives. In this respect the field was deepening as it moved from the technical to the applied. This change is reflected in the fact that the term "historical GIS" – with its clear emphasis on technology – is increasingly being replaced with the term "spatial history," an expression that stresses doing a form of history that emphasizes geography.[15] A key point about this is that as research within the field has developed, it has become increasingly topic based rather than technology or data based. This deepening of the field also represents a widening and a move toward maturity, because the new results lead to it being of interest to a broad audience of historians.

At the same time as this deepening, the field is also broadening at a technical level to allow it to address a greater range of sources; to explore, analyze, and disseminate them in new ways; to develop new questions that could not previously be asked; and to move into new subject areas. This broadening is happening on the quantitative side; it also, to an increasing extent, has developed the use of GIS into qualitative sources. This exciting development means that, rather than concentrating on social science history, the field is broadening into history more generally and also into other humanities disciplines. At present the emphasis is still on technology, data infrastructure, and potential. This is understandable and does not represent a major criticism. All GIS projects experience long lead times as databases are built. Investigations into what the data and technology are capable of offering then have to be made before applied research can take place. The social science end of HGIS went through this process for a number of years before it began to turn into the more applied field of spatial history. The broadening of HGIS to include qualitative sources is leading to the development of "humanities GIS," a field whose techniques and approaches have the potential to be applied across the humanities. This in turn provides a foundation for "spatial humanities," a field using geographical technologies to develop new knowledge about the geographies of human cultures past and present.[16]

THE ESSAYS IN THIS VOLUME

In this volume we provide six essays that showcase the deepening and broadening trends discussed above. The volume is divided into two parts of three essays each. The first part focuses on the deepening of the field into the applied scholarship that develops historiography – the move from HGIS to spatial history. It includes three essays that are based on large quantitative HGIS databases but that conduct applied research on a variety of very different topics. Robert Schwartz and Thomas Thevenin explore how agricultural change in England and Wales and in France was affected by the development of the rail network. Andrew Beveridge explores the changing patterns of segregation in U.S. cities over the long term, and Niall Cunningham explores a variety of questions associated with long-term religious change in Ireland and the violence that has sometimes accompanied it.

The second set of three essays explores broadening the technology into new areas. Humphrey Southall explores a variety of ways in which the Great Britain Historical GIS can be applied beyond the traditional boundaries of history. There are similarities between his essay and the one by Cunningham that precedes it in that both explore the potential of large HGIS databases for Ireland and Britain, respectively. The major contrast is that while Cunningham's essay concentrates very much on social science history approaches, Southall approaches the topic far more broadly and explores themes as diverse as modern medical demography, environmental change, and commercial applications. The other two essays in this part are more firmly based on qualitative sources and the shift from traditional historical GIS toward humanities GIS. Elijah Meeks and Ruth Mostern look at a range of potential uses for a major gazetteer of places in Song dynasty China. Julia Hallam and Les Roberts present a much more focused essay that explores the potential for the use of an archive of amateur films to help historians understand the city of Liverpool in the 1950s. Each essay is described in more detail at the start of each part.

Together, the six essays cover a broad range of subjects and scales – ancient and modern, national and local, rural and urban – and cover the spectrum from topic-based work that answers specific research questions to source-led or data-led work that is concerned with the development of new approaches and their potential applications. There are, however, some key themes that run through them all. These are particularly associated with the fact that GIS allows historians to make extensive use of the geographical nature of their sources. This goes well beyond simple mapping. As stated above, one of the key advantages of GIS is that it allows data from disparate sources to be integrated. Schwartz and Thevenin integrate agricultural statistics with data on the transport network. Southall integrates census data and a wide range of other sources. Cunningham integrates multiple censuses for Ireland to explore change over time and also integrates this polygon-based census information with a major database of killings during Northern Ireland's Troubles to allow violent deaths to be compared with background social and economic variables. All of the authors show the importance of applying geography and location to their research topics, but all of the essays are based on a wide range of different approaches to history. These stretch from Beveridge's highly quantitative approach to the study of segregation in U.S. cities based on census data to Hallam and Roberts's study of films of Liverpool. Finally, as discussed above, all of the essays are based on adding GIS approaches to existing paradigms in topics as diverse as Schwartz and Thevenin's study of Victorian Europe and Meeks and Mostern's study of Song dynasty China.

GIS is therefore a technology that provides scholars with a tool to assist them with their research. It is not a tool that forces any particular academic paradigm onto researchers; indeed, as the essays in this book show, GIS can be used with a wide variety of different approaches to different topics. It is a tool that relies on researchers being able to represent their data in a particular way based around linking attribute information about locations to precisely represented spatial data, particularly points, lines, and polygons. Not all data can be represented in this way; therefore, not all data can be explicitly incorporated into a GIS-based analysis. A study that has GIS at its core, however, does not need to exclude other types of evidence. As a tool, GIS clearly encourages researchers to think about location and geography. As soon as researchers create their database, they will map it, and much of the subsequent research will involve manipulating, refining, enhancing, and interpreting the maps that the database produces.

However, maps rarely answer questions; far more commonly, they pose them.[17] Why is the pattern as it is? Why are things different over here compared to over there? It is up to researchers to answer these questions in a way that they choose – GIS does not force a paradigm onto them. This presents a challenge. The technology was developed for reasons that have little to do with the needs of academic researchers, particularly those in the humanities. The challenge for humanities researchers is to take these tools and modify, develop, and apply them in ways that are appropriate to the paradigm that they want to pursue. As the subsequent essays show, this process is not always easy, but it does provide new and exciting opportunities to develop new knowledge in a wide range of disciplines and topics that focus on the study of geographies of the past.

NOTES

1. See, in particular, the work of S. Openshaw, "Towards a More Computationally Minded Scientific Human Geography," *Environment and Planning A* 30 (1998): 317–32; and S. Openshaw, "A View on the GIS Crisis in Geography, or, Using GIS to Put Humpty-Dumpty Back Together Again," *Environment and Planning A* 23 (1991): 621–28.

2. See P. J. Taylor, "Editorial Comment: GKS," *Political Geography Quarterly* 9 (1990): 211–12; P. J. Taylor and M. Overton, "Further Thoughts on Geography and GIS – a Pre-emptive Strike," *Environment and Planning A* 23 (1991): 1087–90; and the essays in J. J. Pickles, ed., *Ground Truth: The Social Implications of Geographic Information Systems* (New York: Guildford, 1995).

3. G. W. Skinner, M. Henderson, and Y. Jianhua, "China's Fertility Transition through Regional Space," 613–52; I. Gregory, "Longitudinal Analysis of Age- and Gender-Specific Migration Patterns in England and Wales," 471–503; L. Siebert, "Using GIS to Document, Visualize, and Interpret Tokyo's Spatial History," 537–74; R. G. Healey and T. R. Stamp, "Historical GIS as a Foundation for the Analysis of Regional Economic Growth," 575–612, all in "Historical GIS: The Spatial Turn in Social Science History," ed. A. K. Knowles, special issue, *Social Science History* 24, no. 3 (2000).

4. See http://www.hgis.org.uk/HGIS _conference/2008/index2008.htm for details.

5. N. R. Chrisman, "What Does 'GIS' Mean?," *Transactions in GIS* 3 (1999): 175–86.

6. M. F. Goodchild, "Geographical Information Science," *International Journal of Geographical Information Systems* 6 (1992): 31–45; D. J. Wright, M. F. Goodchild, and J. D. Proctor, "Demystifying the Persistent Ambiguity of GIS as 'Tool' versus 'Science,'" *Annals of the Association of American Geographers* 87 (1997): 346–62.

7. Any good introductory textbook to GIS will discuss these definitions in detail. See, for example, N. Chrisman, *Exploring Geographic Information Systems,* 2nd ed. (New York: John Wiley, 2002); F. Harvey, *A Primer of GIS: Fundamental Geographic and Cartographic Concepts* (New York: Guildford, 2008); I. Heywood, S. Cornelius, and S. Carver, *An Introduction to Geographical Information Systems,* 4th ed. (Harlow, Essex: Prentice Hall, 2012); D. Martin, *Geographic Information Systems and Their Socio-economic Applications,* 2nd ed. (Hampshire: Routledge, 1996).

8. See, for example, Department of the Environment, *Handling Geographical Information: Report of the Committee of Enquiry Chaired by Lord Chorley* (London: HMSO, 1987); D. J. Maguire, "An Overview and Definition of GIS," in *Geographical Information Systems: Overview, Principles, and Applications,* ed. D. J. Maguire, M. F. Goodchild, and D. W. Rhind (Harlow, Essex: Longman, 1991), 9–20; and D. F. Marble, "Geographical Information

Systems: An Overview," in *Basic Readings in GIS,* ed. D. Peuquet and D. F. Marble (London: Taylor & Francis, 1990), 8–17.

9. For examples of critiques of maps, see M. Monmonier, *How to Lie with Maps,* 2nd ed. (Chicago: University of Chicago Press, 1996); J. B. Harley, "Cartography, Ethics and Social Theory," *Cartographica* 27 (1990): 1–23; J. Pickles, *A History of Spaces: Cartographic Reason, Mapping and the Geo-coded World* (London: Routledge, 2003).

10. I. N. Gregory, "'A Map Is Just a Bad Graph': Why Spatial Statistics Are Important in Historical GIS," in *Placing History: How Maps, Spatial Data and GIS Are Changing Historical Scholarship,* ed. A. K. Knowles (Redlands, Calif.: ESRI Press, 2008), 123–49.

11. For raster surfaces, see, for example, K. Bartley and B. Campbell, *"Inquisitions Post Mortem,* GIS and the Creation of a Land-Use Map of Medieval England," *Transactions of* GIS 2 (1997): 333–46; and D. Cooper and I. N. Gregory, "Mapping the English Lake District: A Literary GIS," *Transactions of the Institute of British Geographers* 36 (2011): 89–108. For an example of networks, see M. L. Berman, "Boundaries or Networks in Historical GIS: Concepts of Measuring Space and Administrative Geography in Chinese History," *Historical Geography* 33 (2005): 118–33.

12. See R. J. Johnston, *Philosophy and Human Geography: An Introduction to Contemporary Approaches* (London: Edward Arnold, 1983), chap. 2; and A. Holt-Jensen, *Geography: History and Concepts,* 2nd ed. (London: Paul Chapman, 1988), chap. 4.

13. The quote is from Taylor, "Editorial Comment," 211.

14. I. N. Gregory, K. K. Kemp, and R. Mostern, "Geographical Information and Historical Research: Current Progress and Future Directions," *History and Computing* 13 (2003): 7–24.

15. R. White, "What Is Spatial History?," http://www.stanford.edu/group /spatialhistory/cgi-bin/site/pub.php?id =29.

16. D. J. Bodenhamer, "The Potential of Spatial Humanities," in *Spatial Humanities: GIS and the Future of Humanities Scholarship,* ed. D. J. Bodenhamer, J. Corrigan, and T. M. Harris (Bloomington: Indiana University Press, 2010), 14–30.

17. See A. R. H. Baker, *Geography and History: Bridging the Divide* (Cambridge: Cambridge University Press, 2003), or, for a more applied example of how geographical thinking was far more important than a single map in John Snow's famous work on cholera in Victorian London, see S. Johnson, *The Ghost Map: A Street, an Epidemic and the Hidden Power of Urban Networks* (Penguin: London, 2006).

Toward Spatial Humanities

PART ONE

Deepening Scholarship: Developing Historiography through Spatial History

HISTORICAL GIS PROJECTS TYPICALLY GO THROUGH A NUMBER of phases of which perhaps three can be identified: database development, exploration and enhancement, and topic-led questions. The database development phase, in which the database is constructed, is usually the most time-consuming, which in turn tends to make it expensive in terms of both academic time and frequently the grant income required to make it happen. Perhaps ironically, it is also the phase for which the academic or academics concerned will receive the least credit, even though it frequently involves a major scholarly effort.

The exploration and enhancement phase has a number of aspects of which only a few may be relevant to a particular project. In most projects this phase will be concerned with producing initial results from the database using a data-led perspective in which the researcher discovers the information provided by the database. This stage may also involve developing new methods for enhancing the database, interrogating the data, or disseminating the data electronically, perhaps by putting the database on the Internet to allow other users to explore it.

In the third stage, research shifts from being concerned with the data and what can be done with them to taking a more traditional approach of choosing a historical topic and developing research questions about it. The GIS database is used as the main source with which to further develop the historiography concerned with that particular topic. In other words, at this stage the researcher moves from having to have the skills of a data analyst to being a more traditional historian. This is also, as we have seen, the most important phase for the long-term success

of the field, as its audience moves from being relatively narrow specialists – members of the HGIS community – to being historians in general
interested in a wide range of possible topics.

The three essays in part 1 belong in this final stage of conducting
spatial history. They cover three very different topics: railways and agriculture in Britain and France, racial segregation in the urban United
States, and religion and conflict in Ireland. Beyond this, however, there
are some clear similarities. First, as was discussed in the introduction,
these three essays all follow social science–based approaches to quantitative sources, reflecting the origins of HGIS and the length of time
that it takes for a large project to move to this third stage. Second, all
are based on very large, national-scale databases, but in all cases the
databases are only of passing interest, relevant only because they allow the subsequent research to take place. In several cases significant
methodological work has also taken place (e.g., to allow data that show
changing administrative boundaries to be directly compared), but again,
this process is only of passing interest in these essays. Instead, all three
chapters are concerned with a particular applied research question or set
of questions within their topic, and each topic has a distinct geographical focus. Schwartz and Thevenin are concerned with the importance
of the distance that farmers had to cover to transport their goods to
market as the railway networks developed in Britain and France. Both
Beveridge and Cunningham focus on the geographical segregation between different communities: black from white in urban America and
Catholic from Protestant in Ireland, respectively. Third, in approaching
these topics all three essays combine a broad geographical scope – all of
Ireland, Britain, and France and comparisons of major U.S. cities – with
a thorough exploration of the detailed geographical patterns revealed by
GIS-based analyses. All three also cover long time periods of between
half a century and two centuries. Beveridge and Cunningham bring their
work as close to the present as currently available sources allow. They
were able to do so because of the ability of GIS to integrate data from different sources, in most cases censuses from different dates. While there
are similar sources for different dates, Schwartz and Thevenin and also
Cunningham were able to integrate other sources that would seem to be
unrelatable to their main source because all of the material is located in

space. Schwartz and Thevenin were able to compare information on the location of railway lines and stations with local administrative areas, allowing them to explore the importance of distance from rural parishes to the main transportation network on agriculture. Cunningham was able to compare data on the locations of killings during Northern Ireland's Troubles with census information on the populations in which these killings occurred.

Thus, although these three chapters are concerned with very different topics, bringing them together illustrates the ways in which HGIS databases and techniques can be used to conduct applied works of spatial history.

ONE

Railways and Agriculture in France and Great Britain, 1850–1914

ROBERT M. SCHWARTZ AND THOMAS THEVENIN

Losses year after year and increasing competition indicate that the crops now grown are not sufficient to support the farmer. When he endeavors, however, to vary his method of culture, and to introduce something new, he is met at the outset by two great difficulties.... The first [is] the extraordinary tithe ...; the second is really even more important – it is the deficiency of transit....

It is not too much to say that three parts of England are quite as much in need of opening up as the backwoods of America. When a new railroad track is pushed over [American] prairie and through primeval woods, settlements spring up beside it. When road trains [in Britain] run through remote hamlets, those remote hamlets will awake to a new life.

RICHARD JEFFERIES,
"Steam on Country Roads," 1884[1]

AFTER REFLECTING ON AMERICAN AGRICULTURE AND RAILROADS, Richard Jefferies, an agricultural journalist, saw one thing clearly: Britain must catch up. Goods trains in agrarian America, he wrote, stopped not merely at stations but virtually anywhere along the line where there were grain and produce to pick up. The British farmer, alas, enjoyed no such convenience. To get crops and produce to market was a struggle.

First, he had to cart them to a railway station – a slow journey of up to ten miles. Then, at the station, he faced a long wait, eventually surrendering "to the middleman to get his goods to market."[2] British trains went from town to town, but they needed to go to the farms and the crops.

"Road trains," Jefferies argued, were the solution. These redesigned steam-powered trains would run not along rails but on country roads, stopping at each farm and "loading at the gate of the field."[3] Railways, he granted, would still be essential for long-haul shipments, but the road trains would bring much-desired change. With speedy transit at hand, farmers, he continued, would plant perishable fruits and vegetables on unused plots, the rural population would grow, and British farmers would recapture revenue that was going to the Continent and America for imports. To break open rural isolation, daily road trains for passengers would connect villages with market towns. Remote hamlets would spring to life.

Casting his eye across the Channel at old rival France was no consolation. France was moving ahead of Britain, too: "We have lately seen the French devote an enormous sum to the laying down of rails in agricultural districts, to the making of canals, and generally to the improvement of internal communication in provinces but thinly populated. The industrious French have recognized that old countries, whose area is limited, can only compete with America, whose area is almost unlimited, by rendering transit easy and cheap. We in England shall ultimately have to apply the same fact."[4]

Jefferies's lament takes us back to a period of crisis and adjustment in the international division of labor and sets the scene for something new: a comparative spatial history that bridges the gap between two research areas typically treated in isolation from one another, one on railways and the other on agriculture. What we discover is a better understanding of change over space and time between rail transport and agricultural production. Although rural rail service was a boon to farming by opening distant urban markets, it also pinched farmers where it hurt, bringing intensifying international competition in foodstuffs to the farm gate. Still, even as competition grew and the agrarian depression of the 1880s and 1890s struck agrarian economies, accessible rail transport

often helped farmers adapt to the new market conditions of the globalizing world of the late nineteenth century. Jefferies was unable to see
this, even though he accurately depicted the general crisis of confidence
in European farming.

HISTORICAL GIS AND SPATIAL HISTORY

Farmers of the period knew very well that their fortunes increasingly
depended upon railways and their freight charges. Today, few scholars
doubt that railways and agriculture were linked and interdependent, and
yet historians concern themselves almost exclusively with one or the
other subject. Rare exceptions to this offer valuable insights that we can
improve upon in several ways. GIS and spatial analysis make it possible to
study larger and more complex bodies of evidence at different scales and
over time. Here, our georeferenced evidence comes from large databases
on railways, population, and agriculture for Great Britain and France
from the 1830s to the 1930s. Another improvement is our use of a comparative approach to investigate patterns of change within and between
states the better to identify and explain both similarities and differences
in countries that had differing political economies, a difference reflected
in agricultural policy by British free trade and French protectionism. In
this period of globalizing markets, comparative history is all but indispensable for understanding the position of any geographical area and its
producers in its relation to the shifting international division of labor – a
need underscored by its absence in much of the literature on the agrarian
depression of the late nineteenth century.[5]

    Among historians of British agriculture there is a consensus that
the depression in Britain was not a "general crisis" in agricultural output
but one that varied by region and that struck the cereal-growing regions
of the south and southeast much harder than elsewhere in England and
Wales. Debate continues, however, as to whether or not British agriculture "failed" to meet the challenges of intensifying foreign competition.
"Pessimists" point to the demise of large, more productive farms, a lack
of innovation and entrepreneurial savvy, and the government's compla-
cent dependence on imports from the bountiful agricultural resources
of the United States and Britain's colonies.[6] As more regional research is

undertaken, "optimists" argue that *resilience,* not failure, characterized English farming in difficult circumstances.[7] The role of rural rail transport in response to the agrarian depression in this literature, whether it is optimistic or pessimistic, is usually absent or mentioned only in passing.[8]

The same is true in research on French agriculture in the second half of the nineteenth century. By and large, studies of agricultural performance and the depression in particular concern themselves with the national level alone, and studies of specific regions are only beginning to appear.[9] Meanwhile, debate over French agriculture echoes that over British farming. French pessimists marshal evidence old and new to demonstrate that French agriculture lagged behind Britain and most of western Europe.[10] Optimists respond with new data and arguments that the French system of small farming was more rational and productive than commonly thought.[11] Within France itself, a long-held generalization is that in agriculture – as in industry – the country was divided between the developed north and the less developed south. On the issue of regional disparities, new opportunities for comparative spatial history abound, thanks in part to Jean-Claude Toutain's work on regional variations in productivity growth from 1810 to 1990.[12] One major finding was that north-south disparities narrowed after 1860 and that growth rates in the two regions converged at the end of the nineteenth and early twentieth centuries, owing in large part to the increased productivity of the wine and market-gardening sectors in the south. Toutain's data and argument bring welcome attention to the issue of agricultural restructuring after 1850 and renew debate. One recent article, for example, argues, rather unpersuasively, that regional specialization of the kind that developed in Britain was largely absent in France from 1870 to 1914.[13] In fact, the issue calls out for further research. In our larger work we answer the call, showing that the geographic restructuring of French agriculture was much facilitated by railway expansion. Although we do not pursue the broader patterns here, our analysis of the Department of the Côte-d'Or in Burgundy illustrates our approach.

With our problem in its historiographical frame, we can now consider tools and methods. How can our questions about spatial relationships and changes over time be systematically addressed? Time was when studying the influence of proximity in social relations was a hard row to hoe, and one had to limit either the size of the study area or the sample of data. Today, GIS and geographically referenced data reduce these previous constraints and open new possibilities in spatial analysis using visualization, cartography, and spatial statistics.[14] In this case, encoding the geographic coordinates in each unit of analysis makes it possible to calculate many different aspects of distance, proximity, accessibility, and transport cost when joined with GIS data on the development of railways and rail stations from the 1830s to the 1930s. Using georeferenced information on agricultural production and land use attached to British counties, registration districts, and parishes and to the corresponding units of French administration – departments, cantons, and communes – gives us comparable data at these several scales of geographic resolution.

Now we turn to specific questions. Which communities in a given rural area were ten miles or farther from a railway station, the condition Jefferies characterized as lamentable? Over the years, which villages continued to fall into the "distant" category, as opposed to those that, with rail expansion, came to be "near" a station, having five miles or fewer to get their crops to a shipping point? Further, how was proximity to rail transport related to change in the use of agricultural land, to the shift from arable farming to livestock and dairy farming? The combination of GIS and spatial analysis brings the examination of these complexities within reach.[15]

BACK TO THE STORY: THE AGRARIAN DEPRESSION AND
THE RAILWAY SYSTEMS OF BRITAIN AND FRANCE

The Depression

Many of his contemporaries agreed with Jefferies's concerns about the inadequacies of Britain's rural rail transport services. British services were woefully outmatched by those in the United States and might be overtaken by those in France as well. This insufficiency seriously undermined the British farmer's ability to survive the agricultural depression and withstand intensifying international competition in foodstuffs from

America.[16] The signs of difficulties emerged in the mid-1870s, when a series of cool and rainy summers led to bad harvests and cattle diseases that reached a crisis point in 1879. In the same period the first wave of American grain exports arrived in Britain and other European countries, forcing the price of wheat in particular to lower and lower levels until a mild recovery began in the mid-1890s. From 1873 to 1882 American exports of wheat rose from 40 to 150 million bushels, displacing Russia as the chief exporter of cereal grains. The largest share came to Britain.[17] Well before then, English interest in American agriculture had produced an outpouring of articles and reports, a fair number having been written by authors who had observed American farming firsthand. Many reports were written by James Caird, a member of Parliament and the main force behind the establishment in 1866 of the annual collection of British agricultural statistics.[18] Touring America in 1858, he described the Midwest as "the greatest track of fertile land on the globe."[19] In 1881 a royal commission was set up to study the agricultural depression in England and Wales. Recognizing American imports as one of the causes of this depression, the report charged one of the commission's members, John Clay, to gather evidence in the United States and report his findings. His report lauded the workings of American wheat production and American rail, calling them at one point "miraculous."[20] Other Europeans from France, Germany, Austria-Hungary, and Russia who came to study the American system agreed with Clay.[21]

In France the Ministry of Agriculture's interest rose to new heights in 1889, when the agricultural displays at the Universal Exposition in Paris caused astonishment at the prodigious agrarian capacities of the United States and other New World countries. In an 1891 report the enviable efficiency of the American system was described in some detail. In the wheat trade, good yields on enormous acreages, cheap transport, and the American system of grain elevators worked harmoniously, like a gigantic, well-designed machine. The rail system alone was as huge as the country, and its growth was remarkable. With more than 160,000 miles in operation in 1890, the U.S. rail system "has more than 19 times as much railway line today as it did 30 years ago."[22] In 1890 the figures for the much smaller countries of France and Great Britain were about 23,000 and 18,000 miles, respectively.[23]

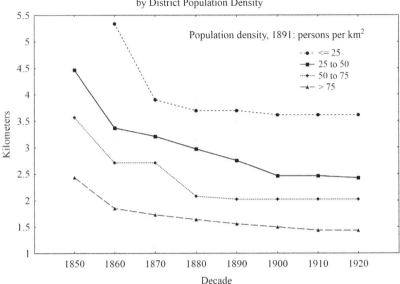

Distance from District Center to Nearest Station, 1850-1920
by District Population Density

1.1. a (*above*) and **b** (*facing*). Average accessibility of rail transport in (*a*) England and Wales, 1850–1920, and (*b*) France, 1860–1920.
a. Average accessibility in the registration districts of England and Wales.
Sources: Parish boundaries and associated population data from Ian Gregory; rail lines and stations taken from M. H. Cobb, *The Railways of Great Britain, a Historical Atlas,* 2 vols. (Shepperton: Ian Allan, 2003), as digitized under the direction of Jordi Martì Henneberg, University of Lleida, Spain.

Railways and Rural Transport

By 1890 railway expansion in England and Wales had developed more than Jefferies was willing to admit. At the end of the 1880s there were few rural registration districts – a market town and surrounding parishes – that lacked a station and some connection, however indirect, with the national system. Indeed, rail service began to reach the countryside in the late 1850s and 1860s, twenty years before Jefferies wrote "Steam on Country Roads." Using the HGIS data on British railways and population yields a more precise description in graphical and cartographical displays. After calculating the distance in kilometers from the center of each parish to the nearest railway station at a given date, a mean of the

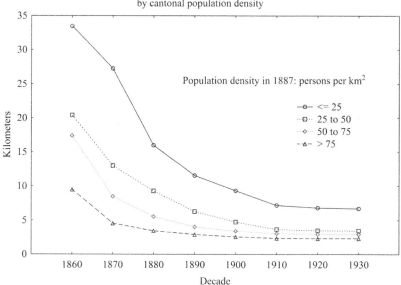

Distance from canton center to nearest station, 1860 to 1930, by cantonal population density

1.1. b. Average accessibility of rail transport in the cantons of France, 1860–1920. *Sources:* Population figures from the *Bulletin des lois de la République française* (1887): 204–48; rail lines and railway stations digitized from *Carte des chemins de fer français,* SNCF, 1944, Ge BB 368, Bibliothèque Nationale de France.

parish scores is calculated for each of 633 registration districts; then the district means for each date are classified by different levels of district population density. Figure 1.1 shows the pattern of increasing accessibility over the decades: except in the least populated districts, proximity to a railway station continued to increase until the turn of the twentieth century, especially for communities of modest population density (twenty-five to one hundred persons per square kilometer). Interestingly, Jefferies took this history so much for granted that he ignored it in his writings.

In Jefferies's assessment of the British system, a major deficiency was the long distance between the farmer's field and the railway station; Jefferies cited a journey of up to ten miles as not uncommon but regrettably inconvenient and outdated. Among the farmers he consulted, there were no doubt a goodly number who complained of this inconvenience.

Table 1.1. The growth of the main and secondary rail networks in France, 1870–1930

Years	1870	1880	1890	1900	1910	1912	1928	1930
Main lines (km)	17,707	25,759	34,878	38,261	40,214	40,696	n/a	42,400
Local lines (km)	293	2,187	3,515	7,612	15,347	17,653	20,291	20,202

Sources: Ministère des Travaux Public, *Statistique centrale des chemins de ferres français au 31 décembre 1932. France, voies ferrées d'intérêt local, tramways, services subventionnés d'automobiles* (Paris: Imprimerie Nationale, 1935), 5; Roget Price, *The Modernization of Rural France* (London: Hutchinson, 1983), 25; Association of American Railroads and Bureau of Railway Economics, *Comparative Railway Statistics of the United States, the United Kingdom, France and Germany for 1900 and 1909* (Washington, D.C., 1911). *Note:* n/a means data not available.

Still, had he traveled through French villages during the same period, he would have learned that the complaints of British farmers were small potatoes indeed. In fact, a comparative study of British and French rail networks suggests a more positive story of rural railway development in England and Wales than Jefferies would have us believe (see figure 1.1a and table 1.1).

In railway development France was a decade or more behind Britain. A county four times larger than England and Wales, France had a good deal more territory over which to lay down rails, to connect major cities and ports, and to reach country towns and the approximately thirty thousand rural communes in which the bulk of its population still lived and worked. Compared to Wales and the English Pennines, the uplands and mountains of the French south, the Pyrenees, and the Alps presented more formidable topographical and financial challenges. Moreover, the French pace of industrialization was relatively slow, agricultural productivity in two-thirds of the country was low by British standards, and the nation's defeat by Prussia in the war of 1870–71 had been a costly humiliation that siphoned off tax revenues to pay substantial reparations to the new German Empire.

In 1878, in the aftermath of defeat and the French state's desire to catch up with America and Britain, the government of the new Third Republic, much as Jefferies reported and praised, launched a huge project to expand the French rail system into the countryside. Named after

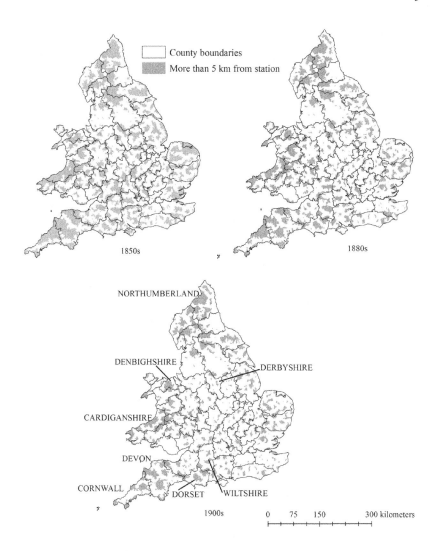

1.2. Proximity of railway stations in the parishes of England and Wales, 1850s–1900s. *Sources:* Parish boundaries and associated population data from Ian Gregory; rail lines and stations taken from M. H. Cobb, *The Railways of Great Britain, a Historical Atlas,* 2 vols. (Shepperton: Ian Allan, 2003), as digitized under the direction of Jordi Martí Henneberg, University of Lleida, Spain.

its chief proponent, the minister of public works, Charles Freycinet, the program, in addition to the expansion of main lines, included state subsidies to promote the growth of secondary lines designed to serve rural and agrarian communities.[24] A decade later, in the 1890s, the projected expansion of "lines of local interest" got under way, and the pace of construction quickened, culminating in the 1920s. Railway accessibility in the relatively vast territory of rural France lagged, accordingly, behind Britain, but the gap continued to narrow after 1870. By 1900 villages in moderately populated cantons (between twenty-five and fifty persons per square kilometer) were on average within three miles of the nearest railway station (see figure 1.1b).

Proximity to Railway Stations in Rural Britain
and France: Change over Time and Space

Turning to spatial analysis, first of Britain and then of France, we used the GIS data on railways and parishes to map the distance from parish centers to the nearest stations at the end points of three different decades: the 1850s, the 1880s, and the 1900s.[25] As shown in figure 1.2, British farmers had less reason to complain in the 1880s than before, and by the first decade of the twentieth century they had even less so, for by then there were only a few clusters of parishes where the nearest station was more than three miles away from the parish center – a good deal closer than the ten-mile isolation point mentioned by Jefferies. In other words, the majority of parishes in 1900 or earlier fell *within* what one farmer thought was a maximum distance: beyond three miles from a station, he remarked, is "agricultural death."[26] The high degree of accessibility held in Derbyshire and in the midlands and the south generally. Not surprisingly, in sparsely populated regions, accessibility was more of a problem. Around the periphery of the country – in Denbighshire and Cardiganshire (Wales), the southwestern counties of Dorset, Devon, and Cornwall, and the northern county of Northumberland – there were numerous parishes where convenient access to rail stations was in doubt. And yet, even in Wales and the southwest, such inconvenience as existed in 1850 had been much reduced by the eve of the Great War.

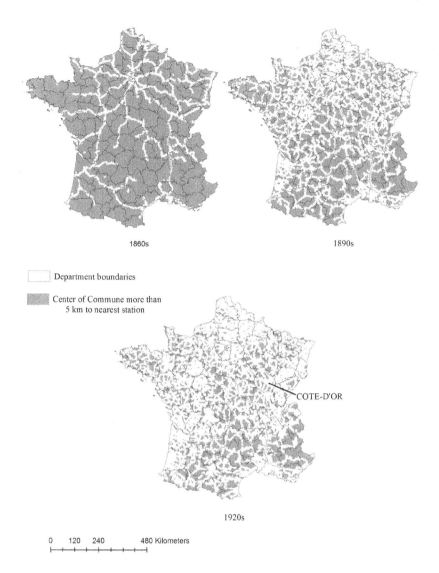

1.3. Proximity of railway stations in the communes of France, 1860s–1920s.
Sources: Population figures from the *Bulletin des lois de la République française*
(1887): 204–48; rail lines and railway stations digitized from *Carte des chemins
de fer français,* SNCF, 1944, Ge BB 368, Bibliothèque Nationale de France.
Habitation centers of communes and departmental boundaries provided
by Thomas Thevenin, Department of Geography, University of Burgundy.

Table 1.2. Wheat acreage in the United Kingdom, France, the United States, and Germany, 1867–1895

Country	Years						
	1867	1872	1877	1882	1887	1892	1895
UK	1,458,000	1,539,000	1,336,500	1,296,000	972,000	931,500	607,500
France	7,249,500	6,925,500	6,966,000	6,966,000	6,966,000	7,006,500	7,006,500
United States	4,991,500	8,464,500	10,651,500	15,025,500	15,228,000	15,633,000	13,770,000
Germany				1,882,500	1,903,500	1,984,500	1,944,000

Sources: France, Ministère de l'Agriculture. *Statistique agricole de la France: Résultats généraux de l'enquête décennale de 1892* (Paris: Imprimerie nationale, 1897), 94–95. Statistics from Maj. P. G. Craigie, Director of Statistics of the Board of Agriculture (Great Britain), originating from his "Communication faite au Congrès de l'Institute internationale de statistique" (St. Petersburg, 3 September 1897).

Proximity to a station, of course, was only one aspect of convenient shipping and passenger travel. Poor station facilities, high shipping rates and ticket prices, infrequent trains, delays, and inefficient connections from branch to trunk lines all produced higher costs and more aggravation for the farmer. In this respect, Jefferies was right on the money. But in terms of distance, the accessibility of rural rail service had improved substantially since the late 1860s, when Jefferies's career as an agricultural journalist was beginning.

In France improvement of this kind came later and at the different scale of a much larger territory. In the 1860s, when "iron roads" were reaching farther into the British countryside and opening remote mining and agricultural districts, the sound of a whistling locomotive was almost unknown in rural France. The major arteries of the national system were in place, but the modernizing benefits of rail transport in agricultural regions, so active in the minds of visionaries and government planners, had yet to materialize in most of the country. As shown in figure 1.3, the situation had changed for the better by the 1890s. Thirty years later, in the 1920s, the aims of the 1878 Freycinet program of railway expansion came to fruition, and the size of the main and secondary networks reached its zenith. There were regions in the southern uplands and mountains still not well served, but in two-thirds of rural France it was no more than half a day's walk to catch a train – less than that for horse-drawn wagons and, in the 1920s, even less for combustion-engine automobiles and trucks.

RAILWAYS AND AGRICULTURAL CHANGE

Gauging the benefits of rural railways for agriculture is a more complicated task. In Britain and France farmers were as convinced as was Jefferies that their increasing losses resulted from the intensified international competition in agricultural products. From 1867 to 1892 wheat acreage in the United States expanded threefold, while in the whole of the United Kingdom from 1872 to 1895 it declined by more than half in response to the falling prices caused mainly by American imports that arrived duty-free in open markets. Comparatively speaking, wheat production remained fairly stable in France and increased in Germany – two countries in which tariffs reduced foreign competition, as shown in table 1.2.[27]

As the profitability of wheat cultivation declined, British and French cereal farmers, in regions of suitable climate and ecological conditions, looked increasingly to cattle raising and dairy farming to minimize losses, transforming cropland to pasture and reducing their wage bills in the process. Profits from these activities were more likely in the offing because of the rising demand for meat, butter, and fresh milk in cities – a demand enlarged further as workers' rising real incomes permitted the consumption of higher-protein foods.[28]

Britain and Dorset County

Although railways, steamships, and telegraphy powered the globalization of foodstuffs and the increased competition that struck cereal farmers particularly hard, rail transit was nonetheless a crucial factor in the expansion and intensification of livestock and dairy farming. For dairy farmers in outlying counties such as Wiltshire, Dorset, and Derbyshire, rail transport permitted the shipment of fresh milk to London, Leeds, Manchester, and other cities. Similarly, cattle farmers in outlying counties stood to benefit because they could fatten their stock on-site and then ship the animals to market by train, avoiding the traditional and

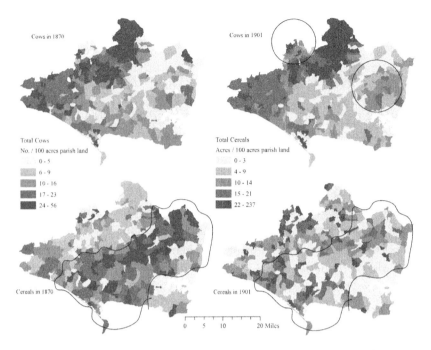

1.4. Changes in cattle raising and wheat farming, Dorset County, 1870 compared
to 1901. *Sources:* Ministry of Agriculture, Fisheries and Food and predecessors:
Statistics Divisions: Parish Summaries of Agricultural Returns, Dorset County,
1871 and 1901, M A F 68, National Archives, Kew; parish boundaries provided
by Ian Gregory, University of Lancaster.

less profitable practice of sending store cattle on foot to graziers in fat-
tening regions or to owners of feedlots. Four Welsh counties so affected
were Anglesey, Denbighshire, Flintshire, and Pembrokeshire.[29] Similar
patterns held true for France.[30]

If railways helped British and French farmers adapt themselves to
difficult circumstances during the agrarian depression of the 1880s and
1890s, then a review of specific evidence should help confirm or refine
this proposition. Selecting two cases from our existing data, we take up
the county of Dorset in England and the Department of the Côte-d'Or in
France.[31] In Dorset we used GIS data at the parish level from the returns
of the agricultural census in 1871 and 1901 to map the density of cereal
production and cattle at these two dates – the first before the agrarian
crisis, the second after its abatement. In both cases, the decline of wheat

Table 1.3. GWR regression of railway station proximity and mean terrain elevation on percent change in wheat acreage, 1881–1891

	Type of multiple regression analysis	
	Ordinary least squares	Geographically weighted
Cases to fit (N)	283	283
Adjusted r-square	0.017	0.62
Parameters	P-values	P-values
Intercept	Not significant (>0.10)	0.03
Distance from station (in meters)	0.01	0.00
Mean terrain elevation (in meters)	Not significant (>0.10)	0.00

Parameter	Minimum	Lower quartile	Median	Upper quartile	Maximum
	Parameters: five number summaries of regression coefficients				
Intercept	-89.91	-35.61	-18.91	-0.55	102.03
Distance from station (in meters)	-0.02	0.00	0.00	0.00	0.02
Mean terrain elevation (in meters)	-119.39	-1.63	0.19	1.81	49.14

Note: Wheat acreage is a smoothed rate calculated as a geographically weighted average in a moving window of ten parishes.

production stands out clearly. The intensification of dairy- and beef-cattle farming is less pronounced than might be expected when the returns for those two dates are used. The decline in wheat farming was dramatic. In the parishes of central and upland Dorset, wheat acreage estimated in 1871 had fallen by half or more in 1901, well in line with the national average. In the same period, the density of beef and dairy cattle remained stable overall and increased in two clusters of parishes noted on figure 1.4.

In Dorset we can dig deeper into the decline of wheat growing. There at the parish level, results from a geographically weighted regression (GWR) model estimate the degree of change in wheat acreage, the independent variable, explained by the interacting effects of the mean elevation of parish terrain and the distance from its center (centroid) to the closest railway station.[32] The results show that 62 percent of the variation in wheat acreage over the decade 1881 to 1891 can be accounted for by rail accessibility and mean elevation (table 1.3).

The effect of proximate rail service was varied and complex, for it carried a negative or positive influence on changes in wheat acreage de-

Spatially varying relationship of rail station proximity and change
in wheat acreage, 1881-1891, with terrain elevation below

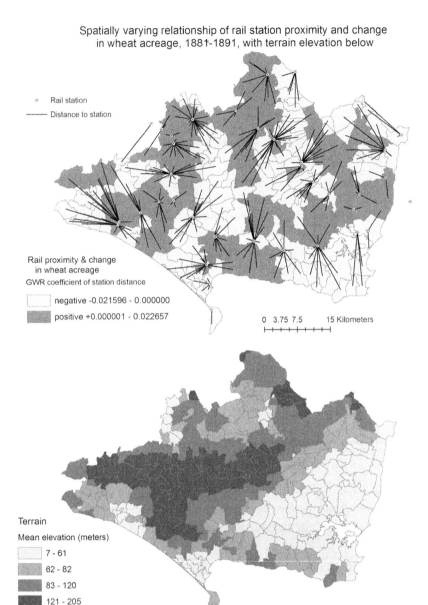

1.5. Spatially varying relationship between railway station proximity and change
in wheat acreage, 1881–91, with terrain elevation (*below*). U.S. Geological Survey
(USGS) Earth Resources Observation & Science (EROS) Center, Shuttle Radar
Topography Mission (2000), version 4 (2008) produced by the CGIAR
Consortium for Spatial Information, http://srtm.csi.cgiar.org/.

pending upon location and the average elevation of the location. Taking station proximity alone, the main tendency was for wheat acreage to decline slightly as the distance to the nearest stations increased. But when joined with the effect of terrain elevation, that main tendency was inflected. As shown in figure 1.5, the influence of station distance was negative in the areas shown in gray and positive in those shown in black. From 1881 to 1891 in upland areas where wheat production had been extensive, wheat acreage tended to increase or remain stable in parishes *farther* from stations; in the lowlands, in contrast, parishes *closer* to a station showed an increase in acreage compared to lowland parishes farther away. The evident complexity well reminds us that we are dealing with a complicated history of short- and long-term decisions by farmers of the period in the face of shifting markets, weather, and leasing conditions. This complexity calls for further study and the incorporation of other factors, such as travel distance or travel time along roads (as opposed to the straight-line Cartesian distance), numbers of cattle and other competing agricultural activities and crops, the varied farming ecologies of the county, the freight-handling capacity of stations, and so forth.[33]

What about changes in livestock? Somewhat surprisingly, our analyses – using ordinary least-squares regression, GWR, and other spatial statistics – found no significant effect of rail accessibility on changes in the size of cattle herds over two decades from 1871 to 1891. This suggests – in keeping with the patterns displayed for cows in figure 1.4 – that the expansion of cattle raising in Dorset *intensified*; it did not spread widely over the county. Further, this intensification was determined by factors other than rail proximity in the 1870s and 1880s. If the parish returns for those years had distinguished dairy cows from beef cattle, we would likely find an effect of rail accessibility and dairy farming, because the fresh milk trade depended upon railways to get products to major urban markets.

France: The Department of the Côte-d'Or

The French Department of the Côte-d'Or presents a story with similarities and differences. There, as in France generally, the tariffs on wheat introduced in 1883 shielded cereal farming from international competi-

tion, giving cereal farmers a reprieve not enjoyed by their British counterparts. To examine this, we mapped the pertinent attributes: percentage change in wheat cultivation by canton (comparable to the British
registration district) and the distance from the centers of communes
(comparable to British parishes). In figure 1.6 the gray lines connected
to station nodes represent the closest distance from any given commune
to a station. As for wheat acreage and cattle density, a strict comparison
with Britain at the parish/commune level is not feasible, because the
data needed for the communes of the Côte-d'Or are incomplete. Our
data pertain to the next higher French administrative unit of the canton.

    An examination of the percentage change in cereal production be-
tween 1881 and 1905 across the cantons of the Côte-d'Or shows what one
would expect. Protected by tariffs, wheat production remained fairly
stable from the 1880s to the mid-1890s, even during the great fall in wheat
prices internationally. By 1905, however, the shift from wheat to cattle
raising and to other uses of agricultural land was marked in all thirty-
three cantons of the department except those of Dijon and Beaune,
where the two largest cities of the department are located. Centered on
the cities of Dijon and Beaune, these two cantons saw wheat production
rise in that decade (see figure 1.6). However, beyond the Dijon region
and the major vine-growing districts running from Dijon to Beaune,
an increase in pasture and cattle numbers attests to the expansion and
intensification of livestock farming (see figure 1.7).

    When this information is combined with data on railway accessi-
bility, the results suggest that rail service proximity was one factor that
influenced changes in wheat production not in the 1880s, as was true in
Dorset, but in the 1890s. By 1905 the building of branch lines and the
opening of new stations in underserved areas was well under way, much
as the Freycinet program had envisaged. Consequently, more farmers in
the Côte-d'Or and elsewhere had rail service closer to hand. To describe
the effect of improved accessibility, scatter plots depict the relationships
between proximity to a station and the change in cereal production and
cattle raising.[34]

    The decline of wheat cultivation and the proximity of rail transport
were inversely related: from 1892 to 1905 the percentage decline in wheat

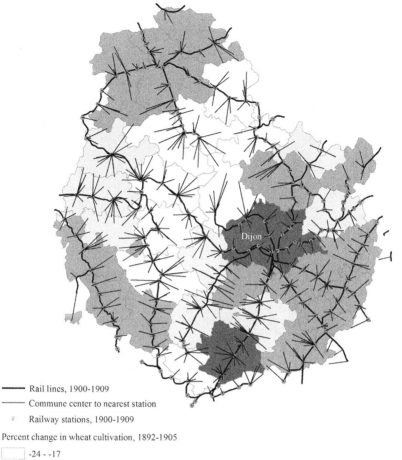

1.6. Percent change in wheat cultivation (in hectares) by canton in the department of Côte-d'Or, 1892–1905, and proximity of communes to the nearest railway station, 1900–1909. *Sources:* 6M 12, IIa31, IIa37, IIa50, Statistique agricole des communes et cantons, 1881, 1892, 1905, Archives Départementales de la Côte-d'Or; *Carte des chemins de fer français,* SNCF, 1944, Ge BB 368, Bibliothèque Nationale de France.

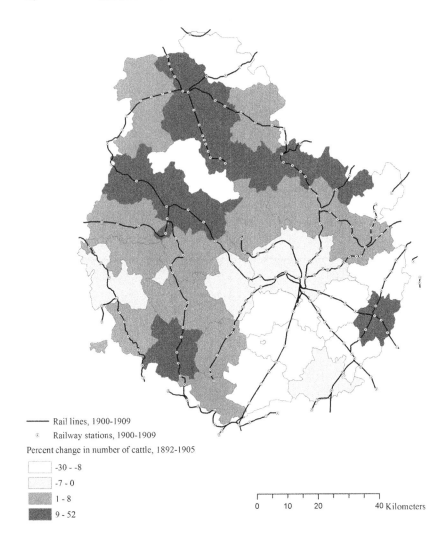

——— Rail lines, 1900-1909

⊚   Railway stations, 1900-1909

Percent change in number of cattle, 1892-1905

☐ -30 - -8

☐ -7 - 0

▨ 1 - 8

■ 9 - 52

0   10   20   40 Kilometers

1.7. Percent change in numbers of cattle by canton in the department of Côte-d'Or, *1892–1905. Sources:* 6M 12, IIa31, IIa37, IIa50, Statistique agricole des communes et cantons, 1881, 1892, 1905, Archives Départementales de la Côte-d'Or; *Carte des chemins de fer français,* SNCF, 1944, Ge BB 368, Bibliothèque Nationale de France.

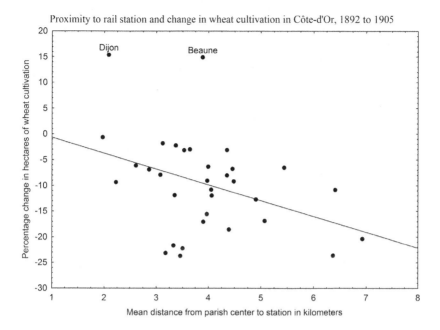

1.8. Railway station proximity and change in wheat cultivation in Côte-d'Or cantons, 1892–1905. *Sources:* 6M 12, IIa31, IIa37, IIa50, Statistique agricole des communes et cantons, 1881, 1892, 1905, Archives Départementales de la Côte-d'Or; *Carte des chemins de fer français,* SNCF, 1944, Ge BB 368, Bibliothèque Nationale de France.

(hectares) was greater as the distance to the nearest rail station increased (see figure 1.8).[35] As in parts of lowland Dorset, farmers closer to a station tended to reduce wheat production to a lesser extent than those who were farther away. Farmers at a greater distance from rail transport more likely put their land and labor to uses more profitable than growing more wheat than was needed for their own consumption. Even when wheat prices were protected, they were low by earlier standards. The additional cost of transporting wheat from remote farms was doubtless a disincentive. On the other hand, farmers close to the cities of Dijon and Beaune enjoyed a competitive advantage in their proximity both to rail service and to the largest regional markets for grain and flour. To meet the local demand for grain and flour, wheat farming in the plains around the two cities expanded.

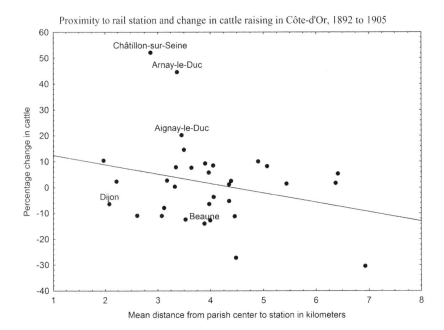

1.9. Proximity to railway station and change in cattle raising in Côte-d'Or, 1892–1905. *Sources:* 6M 12, IIa31, IIa37, IIa50, Statistique agricole des communes et cantons, 1881, 1892, 1905, Archives Départementales de la Côte-d'Or; *Carte des chemins de fer français,* SNCF, 1944, Ge BB 368, Bibliothèque Nationale de France.

In cattle raising, percentage changes from 1892 to 1905 ranged from positive increases to steep declines, and there was an inverse relationship with mean distance from a commune to a station (see figure 1.9). By and large, the greater the accessibility (shorter distance), the greater the increase in livestock numbers; conversely, the lesser accessibility (greater distance), the smaller the density of cattle in 1905 as compared to 1891. This pattern was more pronounced in upland areas than in the plains. In contrast to the plains of Dijon and eastern Beaune, where wheat farming was expanding, in the upland cantons of Châtillon-sur-Seine, Arnay-le-Duc, and Aignay-le-Duc, cattle farming was expanding significantly. In 1905 compared to 1892, upland farmers who were relatively close to a station (one or two miles) were typically raising more stock than those farther away. In so doing, they followed a national trend and depended upon rail transport to adjust to the shifting conditions of markets for milk, beef cattle, and meat. In sum, in the Côte-d'Or at the turn of the century, the proximity to rail transport facilitated, to a varied degree, the shift from wheat cultivation to livestock farming.

The same advantage held more or less true in the French department of the Allier and in the English county of Derbyshire.[36] In Dorset the role of railways in farmers' adjustments to difficult market conditions was significant, if complex, in wheat production. Whether these patterns held true in other French and British regions and in the two countries generally are matters next on our agenda.

CONCLUSION: A REFLECTION ON SPATIAL HISTORY

This chapter tries to illustrate how HGIS, geographic thinking, and spatial statistics, in the good company of traditional forms of historical narrative and analysis, are key ingredients in the making of spatial history. The story presented here of globalizing agricultural markets, intensifying international competition, expanding rail transportation, and increasing agricultural change offers a sketch of a far-reaching historical transformation. Some important features, to be sure, are there, thanks to GIS and spatial analysis. In spatial history, however, HGIS works best as a junior partner. Given the data, it can help identify problems and facilitate their examination. But, like other tools in the historian's kit, it cannot frame problems that are worth investigation. Nor does it generate interpretations and meanings. Its complexities carry a risk. Because the preparation of georeferenced data and the learning of the technology can take a great deal of time, practitioners of HGIS often get caught up in the methods and give too little attention in their papers and publications to substantive results. We practitioners should do a better job interpreting and communicating our discoveries to make clearer why HGIS is worth the effort.

A related imperative is to recognize both the limits of HGIS and the importance of complementary sources and approaches. If GIS technology were to drive the investigation, one might easily overlook records documenting the lived experience of nineteenth-century farmers, their wives, sons, and daughters, the observations and opinions of journalists like Jefferies, or the testimony of farmers before the British and French investigations into agricultural and agrarian crises.[37] That would be a loss. On the positive side, the analysis of census records and agricultural statistics in a GIS can provide the broader patterns needed for situating case studies and rich qualitative evidence in their proper historical context.

Spatial history ought to do more than examine questions about geographic distributions over time, as when we use shaded thematic maps to show percentage change in wheat cultivation in Dorset and the Côte-d'Or. Identifying such spatiotemporal patterns is a good first step. To go further, spatial history should concern the study of spatial relationships and of spatial interconnectivity over time, that is, the degree to which a change in one part of an interrelated system alters other parts in turn. How did the arrival of rail transport in agrarian regions affect production and land use in those districts? How were districts closer to major markets, districts that heretofore enjoyed the advantage of proximity to large and growing numbers of urban consumers, affected by the expansion of rail transport into more remote regions? Or, as so concerned Jefferies, how did the expansion of rail transport in America affect farmers in Britain?

The geographer's concept of "scale" and historian Marc Bloch's conception of comparative history should also be components of spatial history.[38] Incorporating multiple scales of geographic resolution and their interrelationships brings out the interconnectivity of change – or persistence – at different levels of human activity and natural forces. In the case described here, interconnectivity was significant at the global, national, and local levels of activity. American farmers harvesting wheat in Nebraska and the Dakotas were ultimately influential in decisions about agricultural land use in Dorset County and in the Department of the Côte-d'Or, just as bad weather and poor harvests in the American Great Plains could result in higher wheat prices in Liverpool.[39] In the 1890s, as American wheat farmers themselves came to suffer from falling prices, they came to believe that the Liverpool market set the low prices that threatened their livelihoods.[40]

Another task in spatial history is to tease out links between temporal and spatial change.[41] Although only briefly treated here, the expansion of rail transport and its effects on agriculture provide a revealing example of change moving across territory and time. Another imperative is to open the conversation about spatial history to a wider audience than specialists in HGIS. The opening offered here, imperfect as it is, starts by framing the problem through the eyes of a contemporary observer and then continues by incorporating GIS-related findings into an accessible narrative about historical change. Narrative, after all, remains the lingua franca of most historians and readers of history.

Finally, there is the urgent task of interesting historians in spatial relationships and renewing their regard for geographical thinking. This does not require GIS, and to presume that it does may be more hindrance than aid. A salutary reminder in this regard is to recall the insistent belief shared by some geographers and historians in the 1960s and 1970s that quantitative methods were *the* keys to the kingdom.

Concerning the promise of interconnected spatial history, Richard Jefferies, in some sense, showed us a way forward. A keen observer of agricultural change in Britain and abroad, he recognized both the international connection between American and British farmers and the regional and local significance of rapid and convenient transportation in the age of growing globalization. True, as an advocate for British farming interests he was apt to stretch the truth in his characterizations of American and French rivals and of the inadequacies of rural rail service in Britain in order to inspire ingenuity and resolve to restore British agriculture to its proper place in the world. Although he overstated the challenge of moving crops from farm gate to station platform, he anticipated the day when gasoline-powered trucks and automobiles would ply the roads of rural Britain. An ardent observer of Britain's agrarian world in an international perspective, he was a visionary too.

ACKNOWLEDGMENTS

This article is based on research supported by a Collaborative Research Grant from the National Endowment for the Humanities (RA-50577-060). We would like to thank the following for their support in producing the GIS data on British railways from M. H. Cobb's remarkable work *The Railways of Great Britain: A Historical At-* *las,* 2 vols. (Shepperton: Ian Allan, 2005): Meritxell Gallart, Mateu Morillas, and J. Martí-Domínguez. This work was part of a European Science Foundation initiative (Eurocores) and the project within it, "Water, Road and Rail: The Development of European Waterways, Road and Rail Infrastructures: A Geographical Information System for the History of European Integration (1825–2005)," directed by Jordi Martí Henneberg, Inventing Europe grant FP-005. The GIS data on the French rail system have been constructed with the help of Mathilde Pizzuto with funds from the NEH Grant and Loïc Sapet with grant funds from the French National Agency of Research (ANR 07 Corp 019). Much of the data for Britain were taken from the Great Britain Historical GIS (GBHGIS), http://www.gbhgis.org, and the cantonal boundaries were kindly supplied by G. William Skinner of the University of California, Davis. Schwartz thanks students for their assistance: Jacinta Edebeli, and Ayla Ben-

Chaim, Kirsten Hansen, and Morgan Wilson for help in preparing the GIS data on Dorset County agriculture. Special thanks go to our collaborator, Ian Gregory, and for his indispensable help over the years. For this part of our project, Ian provided the standardized parish units and associated population data (1861–1911) and the digital photographs he made of the agricultural census returns for Dorset County at the National Archives, Kew; Thevenin provided the georeferenced communal boundaries and settlement centers and supervised the work of Mathilde Pizzuto and Loïc Sapet, who digitized the rail lines and stations for France.

NOTES

1. Richard Jefferies, "Steam on Country Roads," in *Field and Hedgerow, Being the Last Essays of Richard Jefferies* (London: Longmans, Green and Co., 1889), 238, 231. This was a posthumously published collection of his essays of the 1880s. Jefferies died in 1887. See Eric L. Jones, "The Land That Richard Jefferies Inherited," *Rural History* 16 (2005): 83–93; P. J. Perry, "An Agricultural Journalist on the 'Great Depression': Richard Jefferies," *Journal of British Studies* 9 (1970): 126–40.

2. Jefferies, "Steam on Country Roads," 231.

3. Ibid., 236.

4. Ibid., 239.

5. There are several notable exceptions that specifically apply a comparative approach to the study of agriculture and agricultural policies. See N. Koning, *The Failure of Agrarian Capitalism: Agrarian Politics in the UK, Germany, the Netherlands and the USA, 1846–1919* (London: Routledge, 1994); M. Tracy, *Government and Agriculture in Western Europe, 1880–1988*, 3rd ed. (New York: Harvester Wheatsheaf, 1989); K. H. O'Rourke,

"The European Grain Invasion, 1870–1913," *Journal of Economic History* 57 (1997): 775–801; and J. L. van Zanden, "The Growth of Production and Productivity in European Agriculture, 1870–1914," *Economic History Review* 44 (1991): 215–39.

6. E. J. T. Collins, "The Great Depression, 1875–1896," in *The Agrarian History of England and Wales: Volume VII 1850–1914*, ed. E. J. T. Collins (Cambridge: Cambridge University Press, 2000), 138–207; R. Perren, *Agriculture in Depression, 1870–1940*, New Studies in Economic and Social History (Cambridge: Cambridge University Press, 1995).

7. E. H. Hunt and S. J. Pam, "Prices and Structural Response in English Agriculture, 1873–1896," *Economic History Review* 50 (1997): 477–505; B. Afton, "The Great Agricultural Depression on the English Chalklands: The Hampshire Experience," *Agricultural History Review* 44 (1996): 191–205; M. Turner, "Output and Prices in UK Agriculture, 1867–1914, and the Great Agricultural Depression Reconsidered," *Agricultural History Review* 40 (1992): 38–51; M. E. Turner, "Agricultural

Output, Income, and Productivity," in Collins, *Agrarian History,* 224–320; van Zanden, "The Growth of Production."

8. See, for example, the limited treatment of railways in Collins, *Agrarian History.* Important exceptions include C. Hallas, *The Wensleydale Railway* (Clapham [Bedfordshire]: Dalesman Books, 1984); D. W. Howell, "The Impact of Railways on Agricultural Development in Nineteenth-Century Wales," *Welsh History Review* 7 (1974–75): 40–62; C. Hallas, "The Social and Economic Impact of Rural Railway: The Wensleydale Line," *Agricultural History Review* 34 (1986): 29–44; and D. Turnock, *An Historical Geography of Railways in Great Britain and Ireland* (Aldershot: Ashgate, 1998).

9. C. Bouneau, "Chemins de fer et développement rural en France de 1852 à 1937: La contribution de la Compagnie du Midi," *Histoire, Economie et Société* 1 (1990): 95–112; H. Clout, "The Pays de Bray: A Vale of Dairies in Northern France," *Agricultural History Review* 51 (2003): 190–208.

10. J.-P. Dormois, "La 'vocation agricole de la France': L'agriculture française face à la concurrence britannique avant la guerre de 1914," *Histoire et Mesure* 11 (1996): 329–66; A. Broder, "La longue stagnation française: Panorama général," in *La Longue Stagnation en France: L'autre grande dépression 1873–1897,* ed. Y. Breton, A. Broder, and M. Lutfalla (Paris: Économica, 1997), 9–58; J.-F. Vidal, *Dépression et retour de la prospérité: Les économie-seuropéenes à la fin du XIXᵉ siècle* (Paris: L'Harmattan, 2000); van Zanden, "The Growth of Production."

11. J. Carmona, "Sharecropping and Livestock Specialization in France, 1830–1930," *Continuity and Change* 21 (2006): 235–59; A. Straus and P. Verley, "L'économie française au XIXᵉ siècle: Analyse macro-économique, une oeuvre isolée ou une ouverture vers des recher-

ches novatrices?," *Revue d'Histoire du XIXᵉ Siècle* 23 (2001): 14; Vidal, *Dépression et retour;* Michel. Hau, "La résistance des régions d'agriculture intensive aux crises de la fin du XIXᵉ siècle: Les cas de l'Alsace, du Vaucluse et du Bas-Languedoc," *Economie rurale* 184 (1988): 31–41; G. Schmitt, "Agriculture in Nineteenth Century France and Britain: Another Explanation of International and Intersectoral Productivity Differences," *Journal of European Economic History* 19 (1990): 81–116.

12. J.-C. Toutain, *La production agricole de la France de 1810 à 1990: Départements et Régions. Croissance, productivité, structures,* 3 vols., Histoire quantitative de l'économie française (Grenoble: Cahiers de l'ISMÉA [Économies et sociétés], 1992–93); Toutain, "La croissance inégales des régions françaises: L'agriculture de 1810–1990," *Revue Historique* 590 (1994): 315–59.

13. Dormois, "La 'vocation agricole,'" 358.

14. A good, brief introduction to HGIS is I. N. Gregory, *A Place in History: A Guide to Using GIS in Historical Research* (Oxford: Oxford University Press, 2003). For a fuller account, see I. N. Gregory and P. S. Ell, *Historical GIS: Technology, Methodology and Scholarship* (Cambridge: Cambridge University Press, 2008). The most convenient survey of the GIS field in its variety and techniques is the collection of essays by leading specialists in A. S. Fotheringham and J. P. Wilson, eds., *The Handbook of Geographic Information Science,* Blackwell Companions to Geography (Malden, Mass.: Blackwell, 2008).

15. The following discussion draws on research Schwartz has presented in previous conference papers and several recent articles, including "New Tools for Clio: GIS, Railways, and Change over Time and Space in France and Great Britain, 1840–1914," 2007, a digital publication (University of Nebraska and University of Illinois Press), http://digitalhistory

.unl.edu/essays/schwartzessay.php (9 July 2009); "Rail Transport, Agrarian Crisis, and the Restructuring of Agriculture: France and Great Britain Confront Globalization, 1860–1900," *Social Science History* 34 (2010): 229–55; and "Spatial History: Railways, Uneven Development, and a Crisis of Globalization in France and Great Britain," *Journal of Interdisciplinary History* 62 (2011): 53–88 with coauthors I. N. Gregory and T. Thevenin.

16. A brief introduction to the subject is P. A. Coclanis, "Back to the Future: The Globalization of Agriculture in Historical Context," *SAIS Review* 23 (2003): 71–84. For Britain, see Collins, "The Great Depression." For France, see J. Lhomme, "La crise agricole à la fin du XIXe siècle en France: Essai d'interprétation économique et sociale," *Revue Économique* 21 (1970): 521–53. For a comparative perspective, see Koning, *Failure of Agrarian Capitalism;* Tracy, *Government and Agriculture;* and O'Rourke, "The European Grain Invasion."

17. M. Rothstein, "America in the International Rivalry for the British Wheat Market, 1860–1914," *Mississippi Valley Historical Review* 47 (1960): 401–18; H. J. Carman, "English Views of Middle Western Agriculture, 1850–1870," *Agricultural History* 8 (1934): 3–19.

18. G. E. Fussel, "The Collection of Agricultural Statistics in Great Britain: Its Origin and Evolution," *Agricultural History* 18 (1944): 161–67.

19. Quoted in Carman, "English Views," 4.

20. "Supplementary report by Mr. John Clay, Jun., on American Agriculture, showing its influence on that of Great Britain," 705–18, Royal Commission on Agriculture, Reports of the Assistant Commissioners, Southern District of England, "Report by Mr. Little on Devon, Cornwall, Dorset and Somerset, (with summary of previous reports.)," British Parliamentary Papers, Command Papers: Reports of Commissioners T2 (London, 1882), http://gateway.proquest.com/openurl?url_ver=Z39.88–2004&res_dat=xri:hcpp-us&rft_dat=xri:hcpp:rec:1882–058159, *http://gateway.proquest.com/openurl?url_ver=Z39.88–2004&res_dat=xri:hcpp-us&rft_dat=xri:hcpp:fulltext:1882-*, 058159.

21. Rothstein, "America," 412–16.

22. Ministry of Agriculture, *Exposition universelle, Paris, 1889, Rapports du jury international, Groupe VIII, Agriculture, viticulture et pisciculture* (Paris: Imprimerie nationale, 1892), 99. The figure on American railroads in 1890 seems to be the figure for 1885, according to a later compilation by the US publication. See Association of American Railroads and Bureau of Railway Economics, *Comparative Railway Statistics of the United States, the United Kingdom, France and Germany for 1900 and 1909* (Washington, D.C., 1911).

23. In kilometers, 38,000 and 30,000, respectively. Figures for Britain and France are from J. Simmons, *The Railway in England and Wales, 1830–1914* (Leicester: Leicester University Press, 1978), app. 2; Ministère des Travaux Public, *Statistique centrale des chemins de ferres français au 31 décembre 1932.*

24. F. Caron, *Histoire des chemins de fer en France, 1740–1883* (Paris: Fayard, 1997), 86, 361–70; Y. Gonjo, "Le 'Plan Freycinet,' 1878–1882: Un aspect de la 'Grande Dépression' économique en France," *Revue Historique* 248 (1972): 49–86.

25. The GIS databases we used for this article are described in the acknowledgments for this chapter.

26. Rider Haggard, *Rural England* (London, 1922), 1:511, cited by J. T. Coppock, "Agricultural Changes in the Chilterns 1875–1900," *Agricultural History Review* 10 (1961): 16.

27. The figures should be taken as estimates of orders of magnitude. Worked up for presentation at the International

Institute of Statistics in 1897 by P. G. Craigie, head of the Statistical Service of the British Board of Agriculture, the figures reflect the improvement in estimates made after 1850, which occurred in step with growing global competition, state interest in agricultural policy and what we now call "food security," more accurate and comprehensive statistical collections by individual nation-states, and greater European collaboration in collecting and sharing statistics via the International Institute and other bodies. Craigie's estimates were accepted by the French Ministry of Agriculture as sufficiently accurate to publish them in its report on the state of French agriculture in 1897.

28. P. J. Atkins, "The Growth of London's Railway Milk Trade, c. 1845–1914," *Journal of Transport History* 4 (1978): 208–26; D. Taylor, "London's Milk Supply, 1850–1900: A Reinterpretation," *Agricultural History* 45 (1971): 33–38; O. Fanica, "Du lait pour la capitale: La production laitière autourde Paris (1700–1914)," in *Acteurs et espaces de l'élevage (XVIIᵉ–XXIᵉ siècle): Évolution, structuration, spécialisation,* ed. P. Moriceau and J.-M. Madeline, Bibliothèque d'histoire rurale (Rennes: Presses Universitaires de Rennes, 2006); R. Perren, *The Meat Trade in Britain, 1840–1914,* Studies in Economic History (London: Routledge and Kegan Paul, 1978).

29. R. M. Schwartz, I. Gregory, and J. Márti-Henneburg, "History and GIS: Railways, Population Change, and Agricultural Development in Late Nineteenth Century Wales," in *GeoHumanities,* ed. M. Dear, J. Ketchum, S. Luria, and D. Richardson (London: Routledge, 2010), 251–66.

30. For a fuller discussion, see Schwartz, "Rail Transport," 234–37; R. Perren, "Marketing of Agricultural Products," in Collins, *Agrarian History,* 254–55; Turnock, *Historical Geography,* 254–55.

31. Although examining Wiltshire would take us to Jefferies's backyard, the data needed for that county have not yet been added to our database.

32. GWR is arguably the tool of choice here and in other situations when the relationships under investigation are likely to vary across a study area, as was true of wheat growing in Dorset.

33. For our French GIS, Thevenin has recently created estimates of real travel costs from each commune in France to its nearest station, but they were not available at the time of writing. See Thomas Thevenin and Robert Schwartz, "Mapping the Distortions in Time and Space: The French Railway Network, 1830–1930," *Historical Methods Newsletter* (forthcoming).

34. The limited number of units (thirty-three) that comprise the Côte-d'Or cantonal database makes the application of GWR analysis unfeasible at this point in our research.

35. The average is the mean distance from each commune in a canton to the nearest station. This is a better measure than the distance from the center or seat of a canton alone, because the accessibility of outlying communes would be ignored. It was a state priority to open a station in each cantonal seat (*chef-lieu*).

36. Schwartz, "Rail Transport," 239–45, 247–50.

37. Robert M. Schwartz, "Agricultural Change and Politics in Late Nineteenth Century Britain: The Enquiries of Two Royal Commissions, 1879–1897," in *Agricultural Enquiries in Nineteenth Century Europe,* ed. Nadine Vivier (forthcoming).

38. N. Brenner, "Between Fixity and Motion: Accumulation, Territorial Organization and the Historical Geography of Spatial Scales," *Environment and Planning D: Society and Space* 16 (1998): 459–81; M. Bloch, "A Contribution towards a Comparative History of European Societies," in *Land and Work in Medieval Europe,*

ed. M. Bloch (New York: Harper & Row, 1967), 44–81.

39. M. Finn, "Effects of Local Weather on a Global Market," unpublished seminar paper, Mount Holyoke College, South Hadley, Mass., December 2009, 12–14, demonstrates the likelihood that drought and poor wheat harvests in Nebraska in the early 1870s led to wheat price increases in Liverpool, England.

40. U.S. House of Representatives, *Depression of American Agricultural Staples,* Report 1899, testimony of David Lubin and Alex Wedderburn, presidents of the state Grange associations of California and Virginia, respectively, 2 March 1895, 31–33, 54–55.

41. Geographic information scientists are currently exploring ways to formally incorporate time in GIS. On this, see M. Yuan, "Adding Time into Geographic Information Systems," in Fotheringham and Wilson, *Handbook of Geographic Information Science,* 169–84.

TWO

The Development, Persistence, and Change of Racial Segregation in U.S. Urban Areas, 1880–2010

ANDREW A. BEVERIDGE

DUBBED THE "GREAT MIGRATION," THE MOVEMENT OF THE African American population in the United States from the mostly ag-ricultural areas of the South to the cities and metropolitan areas in the North is one of the major population shifts that shaped the United States in the twentieth century.[1] After the Civil War ended, so-called Jim Crow laws subjected African Americans in the South to second-class citizen-ship. Many of the common rights of U.S. citizens were denied, including the rights to vote, hold property, and marry freely. To escape this seg-regated regime, many blacks began to move to the North. A recent and widely noted chronicle of the Great Migration pegs it as occurring dur-ing the period from 1915 to 1970, when six million African Americans left the South for cities in the Northeast, Midwest, and West. Indeed, though substantial before the World War II, this migration increased again after 1950, when a significant number of African Americans began to be seen in many of the cities in the North.[2] However, instead of finding equal-ity in the North, African Americans were relegated to segregated living areas with inadequate schools and diminished economic opportunities. These patterns were enforced by both law and custom. African Ameri-cans were also denied full equality in other realms, including housing, transportation, and education.[3]

Using relatively newly available data, this essay traces the changing patterns of African American and white residence in U.S. cities both before and after this massive population redistribution. Though African Americans were closer to equal in the North, where they did not suffer the brunt of the "Jim Crow" system of the South, nonetheless they were denied full opportunity. One of the main areas where segregation continued, even without legal force behind it, was in housing. The extent to which blacks in the North were segregated residentially, were relegated to the black quarters of ghettos, and continue to be segregated has major implications for the United States. Putting it simply, the extent to which racial segregation and discrimination was replicated in the North meant that even with some claim to formal equality, African Americans, former slaves, and children of former slaves were still not completely free in the United States.

This essay answers two groups of questions:

1. When did the system of segregation with respect to African Americans develop in U.S. cities and urban areas? Did it develop similarly in many cities? Were there differences in the South from the Northeast and Midwest and later from the West?
2. How persistent is segregation in various urban areas? What factors may have served to mitigate it to some extent?

Using other research, some comparisons are also made regarding ethnic and immigrant groups (both the early European immigrants and more recent immigrants from Latin America and Asia). However, the core of this work is to follow change in patterns of segregation of African Americans from whites over a long time period and for all available urban areas using data that have not heretofore been organized and analyzed in this manner. Studies of the development of cities and urban agglomerations and the population distribution within them in the United States usually rely upon data from one or a few locations or make comparisons based upon impressionistic evidence. Many such studies in U.S. sociology and demography have used decennial materials created by the Bureau of the Census to compare and contrast urban patterns. However, since comparable georeferenced information about different cities or urban regions was difficult to compile for earlier periods, it had not previously been possible to rigorously track change at the small-area level in a number of cities and assess how comparable their patterns of change were. With the advent of the National Historical Geographical Information System (NHGIS), data and maps depicting relatively small areas of a few thousand people for about fifty urban areas now exist for the decennial censuses from 1940 to 2010, some nineteen of these from 1930, some ten from 1920, and some limited information back to 1910 for eight of these cities.[4] Using new materials recently developed from both the NHGIS and data from the 1880 census, it is now possible to see emerging patterns well before the Great Migration began.[5]

This essay makes use of these data to begin to look at the actual pattern of residential segregation of African Americans in the United States. Using these materials, it is possible to begin to address the patterns of change in a more rigorous manner. Maps will be used to visualize patterns of segregation and how it changed in Chicago, the city that for many reasons is the most used to typify the urban United States. Using conventional measures of segregation, this analysis will examine how typical the patterns found in Chicago were compared to those found in cities in the rest of the United States.

Making this project possible was the development of census tracts in the United States, a process that began in 1910, and compilation of the early census tract data from a variety of cities for the early twentieth century. Census tracts make it possible to report data from relatively small areas; these areas were developed by the Census Bureau in consultation with local officials. Currently, each tract averages roughly four thousand in population. Until 1990 the tracts were delineated with hand-drawn maps. It was only the advent of NHGIS that made it possible to actually map urban areas using tracts over time. Tracts were expressly designed to report on small areas in urban settings and thus provide more detail for highly populated places. Indeed, the Census Bureau introduced tracts for the purpose of making New York City more comprehensible. The census tract movement began in New York in 1906 when urban planner Walter Laidlaw suggested that the city be divided into units according to population for the 1910 census. For the most populous neighborhoods, such as most of Manhattan and portions of Brooklyn and the Bronx, a measure of approximately forty acres was used, with each tract averaging about eight city blocks. The rest of the city was divided into larger areas. Laidlaw also convinced the Census Bureau to create and draw census tracts and to tabulate data for other cities that had more than 500,000 inhabitants in 1910. These cities included Boston, Philadelphia, Baltimore, Pittsburgh, Cleveland, Chicago, and St. Louis. Tract-level data from Washington, D.C., as well as the original eight cities, became available in 1920. By 1930 the number of cities for which tracts were defined had increased to fifteen, and by 1940 that number reached nearly sixty. In addition, Works Progress Administration projects created census tracts retrospectively back to 1920 in several other cities, including Detroit, Nashville, New Orleans, and Milwaukee. More areas were tracted in 1950, 1960, 1970, and 1980. By 1990 the Census Bureau had divided the entire United States into tracts.[6]

The data for 1880 also come from the Census Bureau, but here the data were digitized by the Church of Jesus Christ of Latter-Day Saints (Mormons). The 100 percent sample from the 1880 census was then processed by the Minnesota Population Center, and other information was added. For major cities, these data recorded the enumeration district for each person counted. The enumeration district was developed by the Census Bureau to keep track of who was counted and generally where they were counted. A project at Brown University mapped those districts, and they were aggregated to enumeration districts.[7] Thus, data very similar to those from census tracts in the later period are available for 1880.

Though this effort is largely a "first impression," since these data have never been arrayed in this manner before, a conventional approach to the analysis of segregation that developed in the 1950s and 1960s in the United States will be applied to 130 years of urban change. By using a longer historical period, the development and persistence of the patterns of segregation will be highlighted and put into context. Furthermore, even with the existence of the NHGIS data and the recently aggregated 1880 census, many questions remain regarding data comparability and measurement from decade to decade. Beyond this, the data in use include only population and a simple race classification, albeit from a large array of urban agglomerations. Information on land-use patterns beyond residence and more information on geographic features would be useful. At this time, we only consider the overall patterns seen in the population regarding whites and African Americans, not how these may be affected by the rise of other ethnic groups (e.g., Hispanics) or by the impact of changing economic and social status. Nonetheless, the use of the NHGIS and other materials makes it possible to address in a reasonably comparative framework how long-term patterns of segregation, separation, and exclusion developed between the African American community and the rest of the population of the United States. Even with the relatively simple data used here, it is possible to address questions about the emergence and persistence of racial segregation with respect to African Americans. In short, this essay should be seen as a starting point to put the discussion of the trajectory of segregation in cities and metropolitan areas in the United States and elsewhere on a more empirical footing.

THE IMPORTANCE OF SEGREGATION AND ITS STUDY IN THE UNITED STATES

Segregation in housing, schools, and workplaces has plagued the United States since slavery was abolished after the Civil War. Though formally free, African Americans faced numerous legal restrictions in the South. Many traded their slave status for that of sharecropper. In other words, newly freed slaves worked the land of their former owners and received only a portion of the crops that they produced after putting in long hours planting and harvesting the crops and paying for the seed. The landowners' portion was seen as rent, but in many instances the former slaves were even worse off economically than they had been before.[8] Because of the slave system, African Americans and whites in the South, including in the cities, initially lived in closer proximity to one another than they did in the North. However, once African Americans moved to the northern cities in large numbers, it became plain that though perhaps not explicitly discriminated against with respect to seating in restaurants, using public transportation, and other public realms, both the job and housing markets were not open to them in the same way they were open to others, including many members of immigrant groups. The persistence of residential racial segregation and its impact has been a central focus of American social science since the mid-twentieth century.

The study of residential segregation in the United States grew hand in hand with the development of the census tract system, which became institutionalized in the census of 1940. The tract system allowed the compilation and dissemination of statistics from so-called small areas within U.S. urban areas. Before tracts, the Census Bureau only published data from large wards, which could be well over 100,000 in population and encompassed big areas that could be quite diverse. Once tracts were defined, the enhanced view of the population made it relatively easy to compute the extent to which segregation existed. This was done by developing various measures of the degree to which different groups, in the mid-twentieth century African Americans (also called Negroes and then later blacks by the Census Bureau), were separated from whites. Segregation is conceptualized and measured as the degree of separation between two groups. Thus, the mere presence of African Americans and whites in a city does not mean that that city is integrated; rather, segregation measures report the degree to which the groups live separately, as defined technically.

In the United States, urban studies, urban sociology, and certain types of demography have been dominated by the so-called Chicago School, which favored an underlying conception or model of urban society that drew on a biological analogy.[9] Developed after the founding of the University of Chicago sociology department in the 1920s, it featured one of the earliest models designed to explain the spatial organization of urban areas, and it is associated with Professors Robert Park and Ernest Burgess. The Chicago School's classic model was Burgess's "concentric ring" theory of how various sectors of the city evolved. Figure 2.1 presents a diagram that displays these rings. At the center of this model was the central business district, which was also where the homeless of those days lived. This zone was surrounded by a zone in transition, into which business, light manufacturing, and new immigrants were moving and where the city's "slums" and vice were concentrated. The next zone out was inhabited by workers, often second-generation immigrants, who wanted to live within easy access of work and could afford modest homes. The inhabitants of this zone looked to move farther out to the "promised land" of the next two zones. Thus, the next zone out was high-class apartment buildings or somewhat exclusive areas of single-family housing for the middle class. The zone farthest out contained the commuter suburbs.[10] The dynamic terms of the model were "invasion," "succession," and "segregation," which, encapsulating the belief that moving

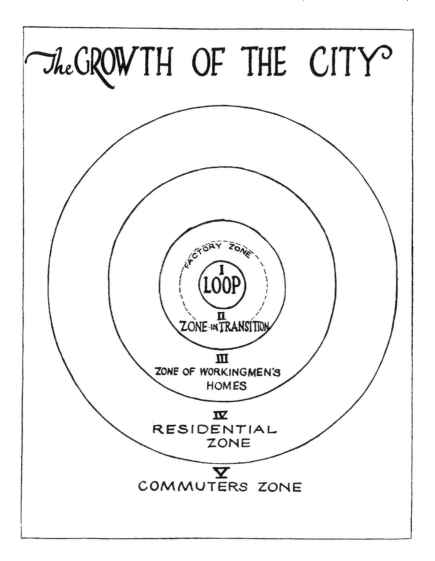

2.1. Concentric diagram of city growth. *Source:* E. W. Burgess, "Residential Segregation in American Cities," *Annals of the American Academy of Political and Social Science* 140 (November 1928): 105–15. Used by permission.

outward was the preferred goal, indicated the struggles social groups encountered as they attempted to move from inner to outer rings.

The substantial movement of African Americans to Chicago and their living conditions in the city led to a spate of scholarly work on their transition.[11] It was a simple thing to incorporate African Americans into the Park and Burgess concentric model. When African Americans began to migrate from the southern United States, they "invaded" the area called the "zone in transition." The original theoretical formulation of the Chicago School, which saw the city as a series of natural concentric rings, fit easily with the migration of African Americans to Chicago and other cities. Burgess wrote: "The concentration and scatter of Negroes and like the Poles, Lithuanians and Italians seems in general the same."[12]

The influence of the Chicago School, with its emphasis on ecology, led researchers working with the Census Bureau to define seventy-five community areas for Chicago in the late 1920s, which helped capture the concentric model. The Census Bureau collected and released data for these areas; each one roughly encompassed a large neighborhood. The typical map produced during this time by those in the Chicago School was a dot or chloropleth map showing the rate or incidence of certain social characteristics throughout the city, and researchers used these maps to identify gradients between areas that might indicate zone boundaries.[13] These areas, however, were quite large in both population and physical size and as such did not clearly depict the population and racial shifts occurring in Chicago. It is interesting that even though data existed at the census tract level for Chicago from 1910, the researchers in Chicago did not explicitly define segregation until years later. They did, of course, notice the concentration of African Americans in certain areas, but they drew the analogy between African Americans and immigrant groups from eastern and central Europe. Nor did they incorporate into their models the levels of discrimination that existed toward African Americans.

Once the census tract system was firmly put into place with the censuses of 1940 and 1950, researchers began to measure segregation explicitly.[14] The classic work on this topic is Karl E. Taeuber and Alma F. Taeuber's *Negroes in Cities: Residential Segregation and Neighborhood*

Change, a book cited over a thousand times, according to a citation analysis.[15] Originally published in 1965, the book summarized the patterns of segregation using the dissimilarity index, which is still one of the fundamental indexes for measuring segregation and will be discussed below. In short, the line of scholarly work on segregation was driven by the Great Migration, the effects of which had become quite noticeable in Chicago and elsewhere by 1950. Using data that did not exist when Taeuber and Taeuber wrote, this essay examines the emergence of segregation in major northern cities and charts its course from 1880 to the end of the twentieth century.

Once begun, the analysis of segregation became a solid tradition in sociological and demographic research. As each census was released, the classic and other measures of segregation were computed by more and more researchers. Starting when the Census Bureau began producing tracts for many cities in the United States, the more precise measurement and analysis of segregation became an important area of research. Other researchers examined the segregation patterns of immigrant groups in the cities. Despite some similarities with the patterns of segregation with respect to African Americans as expressed by Burgess and others, the levels of segregation for non-Hispanic white immigrants groups were much lower than those for African Americans. Furthermore, the level of segregation among those groups faded over time, while segregation between African Americans and whites remained high.[16] The source and the consequences of current levels of segregation with respect to African Americans are controversial. In their work entitled *American Apartheid,* Douglas Massey and Nancy Denton argue that residential segregation substantially altered a whole range of life chances for African Americans.[17] Until the advent of U.S. civil rights laws in the 1960s with the passage of the Civil Rights Act, it was perfectly legal to deny housing or jobs to anyone based merely on their membership or affiliation, racial, ethnic, or otherwise. Furthermore, throughout much of the North, so-called restrictive covenants were added to deeds that prohibited the sale of property to African Americans. For all of these reasons it is particularly important to understand the emergence and persistence of segregation with respect to African Americans. How persistent is it? Has it abated in recent decades? Is it different in different locales, and for what reasons?

ANALYZING SEGREGATION

To look at patterns of persistence and change in segregation ideally requires data with spatial characteristics from all of the areas under study
for the entire time period. Since 1910 the United States has had a limited
set of urban small-area census data, growing to include some sixty cities in forty-nine areas by 1940. For 1990 small-area data were available
for every part of the United States. This pattern of data availability has
several consequences:

1. Data are not provided for comparative areas for each decade.
2. Data are not provided for all areas for all decades.
3. Some of the variables may not be available or completely
   comparable from decade to decade.
4. The boundaries from decade to decade for those areas where
   small-area data exist were changed from decade to decade.

The NHGIS has developed tract boundaries for all areas of the United
States for which they existed and has also experimented with using other
methods of adding spatial data. With these advancements in data availability, this essay is able to study segregation over a larger period of time
than ever before. For each year of tracted data, the NHGIS has created
boundary files that match those reported by the Census Bureau. Because residential and population patterns shift, this means that there is
no guarantee that the tract boundaries for one year will match those in
a succeeding year. For the analysis of segregation, however, the boundaries current in each decade were used. For 1880 enumeration district
boundaries were used, which are the same order of magnitude in population as are census tracts.

In this essay two partially overlapping sets of time series segregation
analyses were used. One set included all cities for which data existed
at the small-area level from 1880 through 1960 and included data on
race by tract or enumeration district (for 1880). These data used the city
boundaries that existed for each decade. Since segregation measures are
not very sensitive to changing boundaries, this does not inject much bias
into the results.[18] The second set included data on metropolitan areas for
the seven decades from 1950 through 2010 as defined in the 2000 census

release. Once again, whatever part of the area that had census tracts defined was used.

The original analysis of segregation relied upon the dissimilarity index. Technically, this index is the proportion of a minority (or majority) group that would need to move to make the distribution of that group the same over all geographic units. It can vary from 0.0, representing no segregation at all, to 1.0, representing total segregation. A second measure of segregation is the isolation index, which is also a useful standard measure. It describes the average proportion of a group (e.g., African American or white) living in the neighborhood (e.g., census tract) that is inhabited by that group. A related measure is the exposure index, which gives the average proportion of another group (e.g., African American or white) that lives in the neighborhood (e.g., census tract) that is inhabited by a member of one or more other groups.[19]

Thus, the two sets of measures describe different dimensions of segregation. Dissimilarity looks at how evenly spread a group is within a particular areal unit. It is not at all dependent upon the size or actual proportion of the group. The isolation and exposure measures are related to the actual proportion of a group in a set of neighborhoods. Thus, one would well expect that the actual experience of either isolation or exposure would be highly dependent upon how concentrated the various groups were in a given city or metropolitan area as well as how many members of each group lived in the city or metropolitan area.

GROWTH AND SEGREGATION IN CHICAGO AND FIFTEEN OTHER U.S. CITIES, 1880–1960

Population growth in Chicago during this period – both overall and in the African American community – is well known. In 1880 Chicago had a total population of about 503,000, of which 6,395 were African American, or about 1.3 percent. This number of African Americans represents what the 1880 census classified as Negro and mulatto, the latter term meaning "of mixed blood." Through most of the twentieth century until 2000, the census used a single race classification that combined mulatto with Negro. In short, just a tiny fraction of Chicago residents were African American. Figure 2.2 presents a chloropleth map (now sometimes called

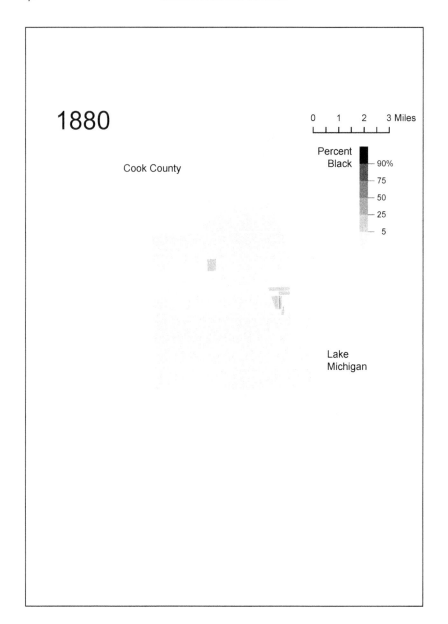

2.2. Percent of blacks in Chicago in 1880 by enumeration districts.
Source: By author from data and map boundary files available from
the National Historical Geographical Information System.

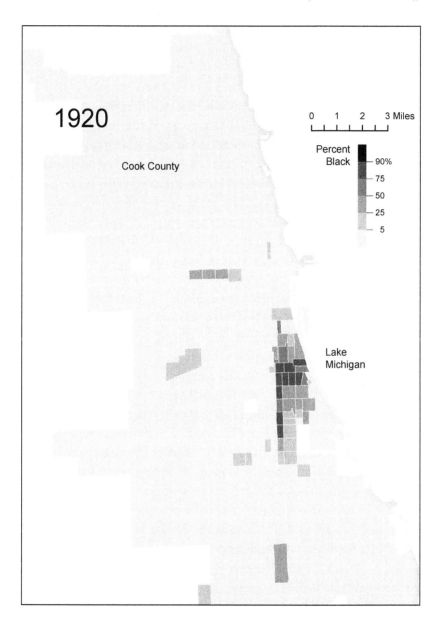

2.3. Percent black Chicago, 1920, by census tracts. *Source:* By author from data and map boundary files available from the National Historical Geographical Information System.

a "heat map") of the distribution of the African American population by enumeration district. Even with only about 6,400 African Americans in Chicago, it is plain that areas in the south near the lake already had a larger proportion of African Americans than most of the rest of the city. Indeed, the dissimilarity index for blacks with respect to whites in Chicago in 1880 was 0.69, meaning that over two-thirds of blacks would need to relocate to even out the distribution across the enumeration districts.[20] Incidentally, compared to the other cities for which we have data for 1880 and 1930, Chicago was the most segregated with respect to dissimilarity in 1880. By contrast, African Americans were not particularly isolated. Indeed, their isolation index was only 0.15, while the isolation index for the white population was 0.99. However, these figures are not surprising, since even though African Americans were concentrated in certain parts of Chicago, there still were not many of them. However, the cities south of the Mason-Dixon Line (Nashville, Baltimore, and Washington, D.C.) had higher levels of black isolation but lower levels of white isolation. All of this is due, of course, to the much higher proportion of African Americans in the southern cities.

Though there were few African Americans in Chicago in 1880, figure 2.3 makes it plain that the areas that had been identified to be African American in 1880 became much more racially concentrated by 1920. At the beginning of that decade, Chicago had grown by more than 400 percent to about 2.7 million, and the African American population had grown 1,500 percent to about 109,000, or about 4 percent. Chicago also expanded to include much more territory in 1920 than it had in 1880. With all of this growth came increased segregation. The dissimilarity index grew to 0.86, while black isolation jumped to 0.52.

The consolidation of African American segregation is made very plain by figure 2.4, which is a map of Chicago in 1960. The identifiable African American area had grown massively. Chicago grew by about half a million, and almost 400,000 of those new residents were African Americans, although they were still in the minority. The dissimilarity index had reached 0.91, black isolation was 0.84, and white isolation was 0.97. In short, for Chicago there was a very substantial increase in segregation between African Americans and whites over this period. In 1880 a few African Americans were living in Chicago, and even then they were

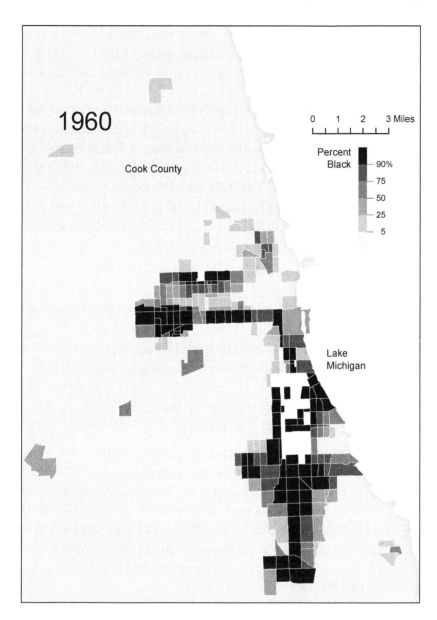

2.4. Percent black Chicago, 1960, by census tracts. *Source:* By author from data and map boundary files available from the National Historical Geographical Information System.

quite residentially concentrated. By 1960 it was plain that the growing African American population had formed into a highly concentrated area. This is clear from examining figures 2.2, 2.3, and 2.4 and the various segregation indexes.

To what extent does Chicago's growth pattern reflect those of other cities in the United States? Chicago's development, while typical, is more segregated than other cities with available data, including Baltimore, Boston, Buffalo, Chicago, Cincinnati, Cleveland, Columbus, Indianapolis, Los Angeles, Nashville, New York City, Pittsburgh, St. Louis, Syracuse, Washington, D.C., and Yonkers. Figure 2.5 is a chart that compares trends in six indicators of change and segregation in these cities from 1880 to 1960.[21] The figure shows the following patterns:

1. a gradual increase in the proportion of African Americans in the population;
2. a very modest increase in the exposure of whites to members of other groups;
3. a very large increase in the isolation of blacks from whites;
4. a very large decrease in the exposure of blacks to members of other groups;
5. a steep increase in the dissimilarity index; and
6. a minimal decline in white isolation.

In short, these changes indicate that on average in these U.S. cities there was a marked increase in the segregation of blacks and whites. This increase accompanied the increase in African American population growth in these cities. When the cities are considered separately, only one, Yonkers, has a dissimilarity index below 0.60; and only one other, Washington, D.C., has an index between 0.60 and 0.70.[22] At the same time, only Chicago is above 0.90, with an index of 0.91 (the next highest is Cleveland, with 0.86).

CONCLUSIONS FROM THIS ANALYSIS

1. There is a general pattern of increased segregation in these U.S. cities from 1880 to 1960. African Americans experienced a substantial increase in number and proportion while also becoming more isolated from whites.

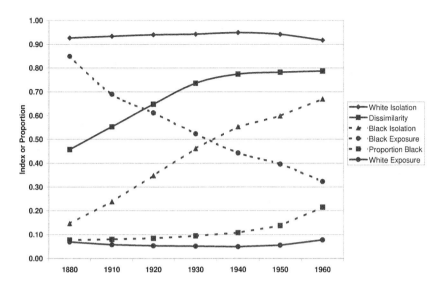

2.5. Average proportion black and average measures of segregation for sixteen U.S. cities (where data are available), 1880–1960. *Source:* Computed by author from data available from the National Historical Geographical Information System.

2. At the same time, there was some variation in the segregation patterns. Chicago, which has been studied extensively and is considered the prototypical city, in fact exhibits the most extreme manifestation of the common pattern. Cleveland, also a northern industrial city, is the second most segregated of these selected cities.

In short, the cities were becoming highly segregated municipalities, and by the mid-twentieth century blacks were extremely segregated and isolated in most of them. It should also be noted that as segregation developed, the areas that had attracted the first black settlers in the most northern cities became the most concentrated with these newcomers. Then, the growth of the black population centered there and then spread outward but in a way that preserved and increased segregation. Indeed, sometimes this is referred to as the movement of the "color line," the line that delineates the area of African American settlement from white areas. Unlike the white immigrants in the Burgess model, few blacks moved beyond the zones where African Americans were initially concentrated.

THE PERSISTENCE AND DECLINE OF THE PATTERN

For Chicago, heralded as the iconic and ideal area for study, figure 2.6 from 2010 makes plain that the concentration and segregation of the African American population has persisted into the twenty-first century. Furthermore, the segregation patterns also followed the population into the suburbs and permeated the entire metropolitan area. By 1960 the Chicago metropolitan area included cities in Indiana, including Gary, and cities in Wisconsin, including Kenosha, as well as Illinois suburbs well to the north and west of the city. In that year the Chicago metro had a population of about 6.8 million, of which almost 1 million were African American, or about 14.7 percent. The dissimilarity index was 0.91, African American isolation stood at 0.83, and white isolation stood at 0.97. Not only was Chicago highly segregated, but its metropolitan area was too. Indeed, one could say that, developing from the small urban core of 1880, when there were only a few thousand African Americans, Chicago and its metro area grew into one of the most segregated cities and metros in the United States eighty years later. Furthermore, when one looks at the metropolitan area in 2010, high levels of segregation remain. The metropolitan area included 9.5 million people, of whom 1.6 million were identified as black, or about 17.5 percent. The dissimilarity index had declined to 0.73, black isolation was then 0.69, and white isolation was 0.92. So as the black population almost doubled, some decreases in segregation in Chicago occurred. However, the basic pattern of relatively high levels of segregation of blacks and whites continued. Also, one must acknowledge that by the year 2010 substantial numbers of Hispanics, including many Mexicans, now lived in the Chicago area, and the segregation indexes ignore these groups. In general, if one looked at non-Hispanic black segregation with reference to non-Hispanic whites, the segregation indexes would be even higher.[23] So, if these groups were taken into account, segregation in Chicago would appear even starker. The common pattern of highly segregated African Americans in Chicago that had developed by 1960 (exactly the pattern that the Taeubers were writing about) continues and intensifies into the twenty-first century.

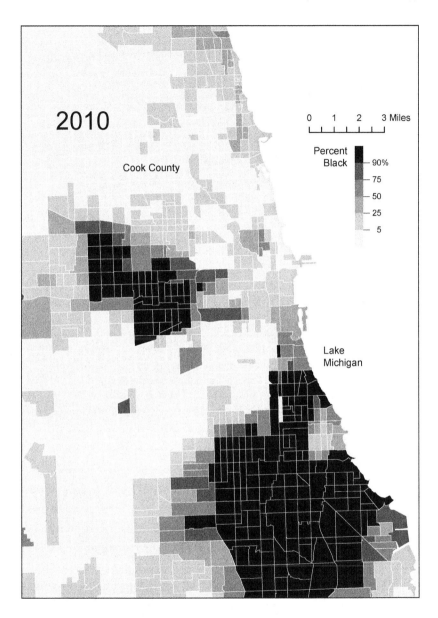

2.6. Percent black Chicago, 2010, by census tracts. *Source:* By author from data and map boundary files from the 2010 census.

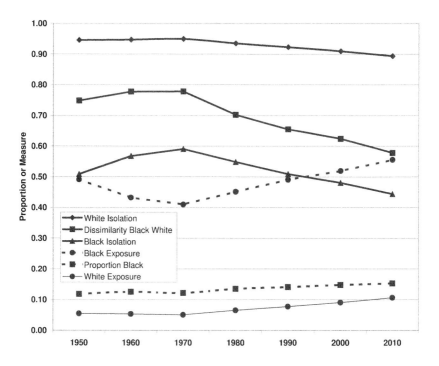

2.7. Average proportion black and average segregation measures for fifty-eight major U.S. metropolitan areas, 1950–2010. *Source:* Computed by author from data available from the National Historical Geographical Information System and the 2010 census.

The analysis is performed for cities for 1880 to 1960 was conducted for fifty-eight metropolitan areas (where tracts existed) for the period 1950 through 2010. Consolidated metropolitan areas for 2000 were used when available. Some of these included several other metropolitan areas within them, so this analysis uses most of the metropolitan United States.[24]

The results from that analysis are presented in figure 2.7. From this, it is obvious that white isolation continued to be very high, slightly below 0.90 on average. Dissimilarity peaked in 1960 and 1970 at nearly 0.80 and then gradually declined to a little below 0.60. Black isolation also declined, while the proportion increased slightly. In short, there were gradual declines in segregation from 1970 to 2010 as the black population continued to grow.

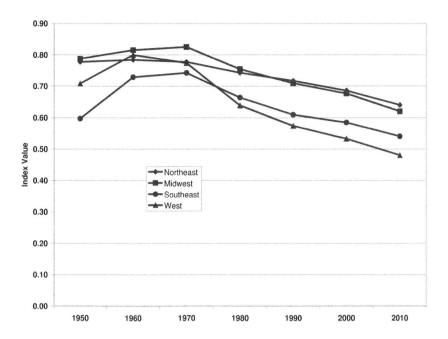

2.8. Average dissimilarity index black from white for selected metropolitan areas by region, 1950–2010. *Source:* Computed by author from data available from the National Historical Geographical Information System and the 2010 census.

The changing patterns of dissimilarity vary by region of the United States. These patterns are shown in figure 2.8. The Midwest and Northeast start with relatively high levels of segregation, with almost 0.80 in 1950. In 1960 and 1970 the segregation levels in the Midwest exceed 0.80, while those in the Northeast do not change significantly. However, by 2010 the levels in both regions had declined, to 0.64 in the Northeast and 0.62 in the Midwest. The segregation levels in the Southeast and West follow a somewhat different pattern. In 1950 they started at 0.60 in the Southeast and 0.71 in the West, and then by 1960 they increased greatly in the West to 0.80 and somewhat in the Southeast to 0.74, before both declined through 2010. Indeed, the 2010 levels were about 0.48 in the West and 0.54 in the Southeast, which are low though significant levels of segregation.

There are several explanations for the forces that affect these levels of segregation, making them hard to untangle. Thomas Schelling developed a model that requires only modest preferences for living with one's own group to influence settling patterns and lead to very high levels of segregation.[25] Studies of housing preferences among blacks and whites indicate that while blacks and whites both prefer integrated neighborhoods, whites prefer a much lower proportion of African Americans in the population than do blacks. This means that as more blacks move into an all-white neighborhood, it becomes more preferable for blacks but less so for whites. Reynolds Farley's work supports this but also shows that the strict racial preferences have been easing in recent decades.[26] He also credits the Civil Rights Act of the 1960s for making it less likely that newer suburbs will be segregated, since it is now illegal for developers and real estate firms to discriminate based on race. However, since change to settlement patterns only occurs when some residents move in and others move out, it would take a long time to overcome historical segregation. Nonetheless, ebbing of segregation is to be expected as the population is replaced.

Somewhat complementary to this analysis is the research by Douglas Massey and Andrew Gross, which shows the relationship between dissimilarity, isolation, and exposure.[27] They demonstrate that where there are only a small proportion of African Americans in a given community, to achieve the same level of isolation, much lower levels of dissimilarity are required. Given the low levels of African American presence in large cities during the post-slavery era, it is not surprising that the dissimilarity levels were quite low in the beginning of this analysis. Maintaining a comparably high level of white isolation found in the early periods required that as African Americans moved to the cities, they lived in areas of high racial concentration, which led directly to the high levels of dissimilarity found. Given the Jim Crow legal framework in the United States in the late nineteenth to the mid-twentieth century, which allowed blatant discrimination against African Americans in all realms of life, it is not surprising that segregation developed. By the same token, given the laws against discrimination that are the legacy of the civil rights movement and the low levels of segregation in some of the "newer" cities, it is not surprising that recent development has led to less extreme levels of racial segregation.

Following on established social science research, it is not surprising that segregation developed the way it did in virtually every northern city with a significant presence of African Americans. Nor is it surprising that in areas where it has taken root, it persists, though it has been mitigated to some extent. Once areas are designated in certain ways, only people who have a preference for living in such areas and who can afford to move freely will move in. Furthermore, many of the realities of urban renewal and public housing meant that those who did not have the choice to move where they pleased were relegated to segregated conditions. Additionally, restrictive covenants to deeds that prevented African Americans from buying certain homes or moving to specific areas may no longer be legally enforceable, but they did set a pattern.

CONCLUSION

This first-ever analysis of the patterns of racial (black-white) segregation in the United States that examines a very long time horizon using relatively comparable geographic units resulted in a number of interesting results. Residential segregation in northern cities developed quickly in the United States as African Americans made the journey from the former slave South to the urban North. There is a general pattern of increased segregation in the U.S. cities examined in this study from 1880 to 1960, and Chicago is the most highly segregated of them all. African Americans experienced a substantial increase in number and proportion while also becoming more isolated from whites. In short, the cities were becoming highly segregated municipalities, and by the mid-twentieth century blacks were extremely segregated and isolated in most of them. The areas that had attracted the first black settlers in the most northern cities became the most concentrated with these newcomers, and the growth of the black population centered there and then spread outward, but in a way that preserved and increased segregation.

When one tracks the segregation patterns in the metropolitan regions examined from 1950 through 2010, it is obvious that white isolation remained very high, at nearly 0.90 on average. Dissimilarity peaked in 1960 and 1970 at nearly 0.80 and then gradually declined to slightly below

0.60. Black isolation also declined as the proportion of blacks increased slightly. In short, there were gradual declines in segregation from 1970 to 2010 as the black population continued to grow. There are definite differences in the changing regional patterns of dissimilarity in the United States. While the Northeast and Midwest continued to experience quite high levels of segregation, the initially high levels in the South and West declined further.

The explanation for the different patterns and the prospects for change are quite controversial. Most recently, the African American population in many large cities has declined, and the white population has increased. New immigrant groups, including many who are not conventionally white (such as Asians and Hispanics), have moved to the cities. Often, the initial segregation of such groups is high. However, the degree to which they remain segregated is an open question. Nonetheless, we can expect that the segregation of African Americans in the United States will continue to be quite high in most places. Whether other groups will follow that pattern is still an open question that requires further research.

The use of newly developed large-scale datasets using GIS has made this work possible. It shows the promise of shedding new light on historical questions using GIS techniques. Here four points need to be highlighted:

1. Segregation developed very rapidly in the United States with respect to African Americans and whites. Even with a small proportion of African Americans in the United States by 1940, the index of dissimilarity was nearly 0.80. Black exposure to other groups was minimal, and black isolation had risen greatly.

2. After reaching their peak in 1970, dissimilarity and black isolation trended down somewhat during the rest of the twentieth century and into the twenty-first century, though they remained much higher in the Northeast and Midwest than in the South and West.

3. The advent of the Civil Rights Act of the 1960s and the ban on formal discrimination against African Americans in real estate and other realms may have begun to dismantle the

highly segregated patterns of residential settlement that were customary in the United States.

4. Finally, this analysis makes plain that, rather than being the exemplar of urban society and change in the United States, Chicago was an extreme case with respect to black-white segregation. This is a further argument for looking at many cities before one declares what is typical or what is a trend.

In short, segregation for African Americans in the United States developed very early. Although it has been quite persistent for decades, it may not last forever.

NOTES

1. Throughout this chapter I use the terms "African American" and "black" interchangeably. Currently, the Bureau of the Census has as one answer to its question about race the options "Black, African American or Negro." For purposes of this essay all three terms are equivalent.

2. See Isabel Wilkerson, *The Warmth of Other Suns: The Epic Story of America's Great Migration* (New York: Random House, 2010).

3. See Nicholas Lemann, *The Promised Land: The Great Black Migration and How It Changed America* (New York: Knopf, 1991).

4. Minnesota Population Center, *National Historical Geographic Information System: Pre-release Version 0.1* (Minneapolis: University of Minnesota, 2004), http://www.nhgis.org.

5. See John Logan, *Urban Transition Historical GIS Project, 2010,* Spatial Structures in the Social Sciences (S4) (Providence, R.I.: Brown University, 2010), http://www.s4.brown.edu/utp/index.htm.

6. Howard Whipple Green and Leon E. Truesdell, Census Tracts in American Cities (Census Tract Manual): A Brief History of the Census Tract Movement with an Outline of Procedure and Suggested Modification (Washington, D.C.: U.S. Bureau of the Census, 1937).

7. See Logan, Urban Transition Historical GIS Project.

8. Robert L. Ransom and Richard Sutch, *One Kind of Freedom: The Economic Consequences of Emancipation,* 2nd ed. (Cambridge: Cambridge University Press, 2001).

9. D. W. Miller, "The New Urban Studies," *Chronicle of Higher Education,* 18 August 2000, A15.

10. The model was most well developed in Robert E. Park, "The City: Suggestions for the Investigations of Human Behavior in the Urban Environment," in *The City,* ed. Robert E. Park, Ernest W. Burgess, and Roderick D. McKenzie (Chicago: University of Chicago Press, 1925), 12. Figure 2.1, however, is from Burgess's "Residential Segregation in American Cities: The American Negro," *Annals of the American Academy of Political and Social Science* 140 (November 1928): 105–15.

11. Drake St. Clair and Horace R. Clayton, *Black Metropolis: A Study of Negro Life in a Northern City* (New York: Harcourt, Brace, 1945). This is a volu-

minous work documenting many of the features of life for African Americans in Chicago.

12. Burgess, "Residential Segregation," 108.

13. Martin Bulmer, The Chicago School of Sociology: Institutionalization, Diversity, and the Rise of Sociological Research (Chicago: University of Chicago Press, 1984).

14. Green and Truesdell, Census Tracts in American Cities.

15. Karl E. Taeuber and Alma F. Taeuber, *Negroes in Cities: Residential Segregation and Neighborhood Change* (Chicago: Aldine Publishing Company, 1965).

16. Otis Dudley Duncan and Stanley Lieberson, "Ethnic Segregation and Assimilation," American Journal of Sociology 64 (January 1959): 364–74; Nathan Kantrowitz, *Ethnic and Racial Segregation in the New York Metropolis: Residential Patterns among White Ethnic Groups, Blacks, and Puerto Ricans,* Praeger Special Studies in U.S. Economic, Social and Political Issues (New York: Praeger, 1973). There are many other such studies, all reaching the same basic results.

17. Douglas Massey and Nancy Denton, *American Apartheid: Segregation and the Making of the Underclass* (Cambridge, Mass.: Harvard University Press, 1993).

18. The reason for this is simple. Much of segregation is related to the situation in the most developed portion of the city or metropolitan area. Exactly where the city or metropolitan limits are usually has little effect on segregation, since the population in such areas is relatively small and usually has very low concentrations of African Americans.

19. The various dimensions of segregation are discussed in Douglas Massey and Nancy Denton, "The Dimensions of Residential Segregation," *Social Forces*

67 (1988): 281–315. Following Massey and Denton, the formula for dissimilarity is:

$$D = \sum_{i=1}^{n} \left[t_i \left| p_i - P \right| / 2TP(1-P) \right]$$

where t_i and p_i are the total population and the minority proportion in the areal unit, and T and P are the population size and minority proportion in the whole area.

The formula for exposure is:

$$_xP^*_y = \sum_{i=1}^{n} \left[x_i / X \right] \times \left[y_i / t_i \right]$$

where $x_i, y_i,$ and t_i are the numbers of X members, Y members, and total population of unit i, respectively, and X represents the number of X members area-wide. Thus, the exposure index is computed as the minority weighted average of each spatial unit's majority proportion.

The formula for isolation is:

$$_xP^*_x = \sum_{i=1}^{n} \left[x_i / X \right] \times \left[x_i / t_i \right]$$

where x_i and t_i are the numbers of X members and total population of unit i, respectively, and X represents the number of X members area-wide.

Thus, the isolation index is computed as the minority weighted average of each spatial unit's minority proportion. These three indexes remain the primary measures of segregation.

20. Table 2.1, which is only available in digital form, presents data for all of cities analyzed (sixteen) for 1880 through 1960, where the data are available. Digital copy is available on request from Andrew A. Beveridge (andy@socialexplorer.com).

21. Table 2.1 (see footnote 20) presents information on population, percent African American, and segregation for each city for the decades for which the information is available. Digital copy is available on request from Andrew A. Beveridge

22. The digital data tables, tables 2.1 and 2.2, present detailed results for each city or region. Digital copies are available

on request from Andrew A. Beveridge (andy@socialexplorer.com).

23. Much work has been done on the patterns of segregation in the United States with regard to other groups, including Hispanics and Asians, as well as African Americans. Furthermore, the segregation of immigrants (especially white immigrants such as Mexicans) complicates the patterns still further. John Iceland, *Where We Live Now: Immigration and Race in the United States* (Berkeley: University of California Press, 2009).

24. The detailed results are presented in digital table 2.2. The metropolitan areas covered include the following: Atlanta, GA, Metropolitan Statistical Area (MSA); Augusta, GA/Aiken, SC, MSA; Austin/San Marcos, TX, MSA; Birmingham, AL, MSA; Boston/Worcester/Lawrence/Lowell/Brockton, MA, MSA; Buffalo/Niagara Falls, NY, MSA; Chattanooga, TN/GA, MSA; Chicago/Gary/Kenosha, IL/IN/WI, Consolidated Metropolitan Statistical Area (CMSA); Cincinnati/Hamilton, OH/KY/IN, CMSA; Cleveland/Akron, OH, CMSA; Columbus, OH, MSA; Dallas/Fort Worth, TX, CMSA; Dayton/Springfield, OH, MSA; Denver/Boulder/Greeley, CO, CMSA; Des Moines, IA, MSA; Detroit/Ann Arbor/Flint, MI, CMSA; Duluth/Superior, MN/WI, MSA; Greensboro/Winston-Salem/High Point, NC, MSA; Hartford, CT, New England Consolidated Metropolitan Area (NECMA); Houston/Galveston/Brazoria, TX, CMSA; Indianapolis, IN, MSA; Kalamazoo/Battle Creek, MI, MSA; Kansas City, MO/KS, MSA; Los Angeles/Riverside/Orange County, CA, CMSA; Louisville, KY/IN, MSA; Macon, GA, MSA; Memphis, TN/AR/MS, MSA; Miami/Fort Lauderdale, FL, CMSA; Milwaukee/Racine, WI, CMSA; Minneapolis/St. Paul, MN/WI, MSA; Nashville, TN, MSA; New Orleans, LA, MSA; New York/northern New Jersey/Long Island, NY/NJ, MSA; Norfolk/Virginia Beach/Newport News, VA/NC, MSA; Oklahoma City, OK, MSA; Omaha, NE/IA, MSA; Philadelphia/Wilmington/Atlantic City, PA/NJ, MSA; Pittsburgh, PA, MSA; Portland/Salem, OR/WA, CMSA; Providence/Warwick/Pawtucket, RI, NECMA; Raleigh/Durham/Chapel Hill, NC, MSA; Richmond/Petersburg, VA, MSA; Rochester, NY, MSA; Sacramento/Yolo, CA, CMSA; Saginaw/Bay City/Midland, MI, MSA; San Diego, CA, MSA; San Francisco/Oakland/San Jose, CA, CMSA; Savannah, GA, MSA; Seattle/Tacoma/Bremerton, WA, CMSA; Spokane, WA, MSA; Springfield, MA, NECMA; St. Louis, MO/IL, MSA; Stockton/Lodi, CA, MSA; Syracuse, NY, MSA; Toledo, OH, MSA; Utica/Rome, NY, MSA; Washington, D.C./Baltimore, MD/VA/WV, CMSA; and Wichita, KS, MSA.

25. Thomas Schelling, "Models of Segregation," *American Economic Review* 59, no. 2 (1969): 488–93.

26. Reynolds Farley, Howard Schuman, S. Bianchi, Diane Colasanto, and S. Hatchett, "Chocolate City, Vanilla Suburbs: Will the Trend toward Racially Separate Communities Continue?," Social Science Research 7, no. 4 (1978): 319–44; and Reynolds Farley, Charlotte Steeh, Tara Jackson, Maria Krysan, and Keith Reeves, "Racial Residential Segregation in Detroit: 'Chocolate City, Vanilla Suburb' Revisited," *Journal of Housing Research* 4, no. 1 (1993): 1–38.

27. Douglas Massey and Andrew Gross, "Explaining Trends in Racial Segregation, 1970–1980," *Urban Affairs Quarterly* 27, no. 1 (1991): 13–35.

THREE

Troubled Geographies: A Historical GIS of Religion, Society, and Conflict in Ireland since the Great Famine

NIALL CUNNINGHAM

THROUGHOUT THE DEVELOPMENT OF MODERN IRELAND RELIGION has played a central role in the persistence of complex communal identities.[1] Notwithstanding what has been considered to be the substantive resolution of "the Troubles" in Northern Ireland, religious identity has continued to significantly influence attitudes and behavior.[2] However, this is not to be reductive: the divisions between Catholics and Protestants have not been representative of substantive theological conflict; instead, they have reflected the political chasm between nationalists, the overwhelming majority of whom are Catholic, and Protestants, who have always made up the vast majority of the unionist political bloc that seeks to maintain the constitutional link with the rest of the United Kingdom. Many scholars have set out to appraise these complexities and their outcomes, but few have explored them through an overtly geographical framing to understand how the conflict that has so dogged Northern Ireland in contemporary decades relates to longer-term (re)configurations of identities right across the island. In that context, this chapter will provide some insights into "Troubled Geographies: Two Centuries of Religious Division in Ireland," a major project funded by the UK's Arts and Humanities Research Council (AHRC) that has gone some way in addressing this lacuna.

BACKGROUND

For historical reasons, primarily the legacy of the partial and inconsistent nature of successive attempts to systematically colonize Ireland during the sixteenth and seventeenth centuries, the island has been left with a religious landscape that has proved both highly distinctive and in certain regards remarkably persistent over time.[3] The close identification of Catholicism with nationalist aspirations and the emergence of a unionist ideology in response among the Protestant population in the late nineteenth century have meant that there still exists an extremely powerful coalescence between religious affiliation and political belief unparalleled in the Western world.[4] The corollary of this is that political disagreements surrounding identities, rights, and loyalties have usually reflected broader religious or ethnic antagonisms and that conflicts accruing from these have had distinctive spatial characteristics.[5] A desire to disentangle some of these interwoven strands and to provide a better understanding of change in Ireland's contested religious geographies since the mid-nineteenth century therefore provided a compelling basis for this work.

"Spatial analysis" encompasses a growing class of techniques for studying phenomena using their geographical characteristics and distributions. A major spatial analysis of change in Ireland's religious geographies was made possible in particular by the availability of census data at detailed territorial levels. Unlike Britain, religion has continuously formed part of the Irish census since the mid-nineteenth century. The availability of census data on the subject from 1861 onward is testament to the differing role of religion within the political cultures of Ireland and Britain historically, with Irish enthusiasm for enumerating Catholic and Protestant groups being based on a desire to establish the levels of support for the broader competing ideologies of nationalism and unionism.[6] The availability of detailed data from successive Irish censuses not only on religion but on a range of other demographic and social variables as well made it possible to propose a collaborative project between Lancaster University and Queen's University Belfast (QUB). A key objective of this collaboration was to integrate a Geographical Information System (GIS) with the preexisting Database of Irish Historical Statistics (DIHS) and to use the resultant data to analyze the relationships between religious identity, place, and other characteristics. A second objective, to extend the analysis of these relations to another database of Troubles-related fatalities, is described later in the chapter.

Starting with 1821 and running up to the last census in the predigital era in 1971, the Irish censuses, usually conducted on a decennial basis, form one of the principal elements in the DIHS. The DIHS program was initiated by the Department of Social and Economic History at QUB in 1990 to draw together the main sources of census and survey data in Irish history and provide a repository for a wide range of other related material, including annual emigration estimates and poverty assessments derived from Poor Law Union statistics.[7] Funded by the Economic and Social Research Council (ESRC) and by QUB itself, the initial phase of the DIHS project was focused on bringing together these data from the period up to 1911. Subsequent funding made possible the inclusion of additional data for the later period since the partition of Ireland in 1921 up to 1971.[8] In the earlier phase, manual inputting of statistics from the source papers was required, but thereafter the availability of high-quality Optical Character Recognition (OCR) considerably hastened the process of data capture.[9] Since 1971 decennial census data have been published in digital format by both the Northern Ireland Statistics and Research Agency (NISRA) and its counterpart in the Republic of Ireland, the Central Statistics Office (CSO). The inclusion of these data in the DIHS made it possible to construct a time series extending from the mid-nineteenth century up to the most recent censuses for both Northern Ireland and the Republic. Furthermore, after the "Troubled Geographies" project commenced, it was discovered that data coverage could be extended farther back in time by utilizing the survey on religious demography available from the 1834 First Report of Commissioners of Public Instruction, Ireland. The 1834 report differed from later censuses in that it was a poll of church service attendance on a given Sunday in that year, thus giving a measure of practice, rather than being a census of nominal religious affiliation, as would later become the norm.[10] However, the report has been judged to be a reliable indicator of the populations of the major denominations at that time. Use of these 1834 data in conjunction with data for later years facilitated an analysis of the impact of the Great Famine on the different religious groupings, although that is not the main focus here.[11]

The "Troubled Geographies" project can be viewed as contributing to a trend being established by some leading scholars toward using geographically referenced statistics in the study of modern Ireland.[12] As elaborated below, the integration of GIS with the DIHS has facilitated analysis using the exploratory spatial statistical techniques that are increasingly included as standard in GIS software packages. To a degree these techniques can be used to explore temporal changes as well as geographic patterns and differences for the years for which data are available. However, the lack of boundary stability for the territorial divisions used in organizing and referencing data is a significant issue. Various boundary adjustments made at different dates make it challenging to distinguish between actual change, identifiable from data, and changes in the definition of spatial units.[13] These boundary changes include myriad alterations that were relatively minor but also wholesale changes, notably with the creation of entirely new jurisdictions after the partition of Ireland in 1921.

APPROACHES AND CHALLENGES IN THE CONSTRUCTION OF THE IRISH HISTORICAL GIS

The GIS development referred to above has been named the Irish Historical GIS (HGIS). An initial data-inventorying exercise confirmed the availability and compatibility of data on religious denomination across the time frame under study. This is not the case with all key social variables, with some, such as the categories used for recording occupation, having been much more changeable.

While "the Troubles" most commonly refers to the conflict emerging in the late 1960s, it is sometimes also used to refer to the trauma of the years 1918 to 1923 surrounding the partition of Ireland, which broke the continuum of decennial censuses established earlier. At that time both what was then the Irish Free State and Northern Ireland held censuses in the mid-1920s in order to gain perspective on the demographic and broader socioeconomic ramifications of partition. The Second World War caused a further hiatus in obtaining data, but after the war decadal census taking resumed. Census data that had already been digitized prior to the "Troubled Geographies" project are held on the Histpop website, which is hosted by the Online Historical Population Reports Project, a development of the Arts and Humanities Data

Service History operating within the UK Data Archive at the University of Essex.[14]

The approach taken with the GIS may be regarded as a repeated cross-sectional approach; that is, it is based on analyzing successive sets of data for different points in time and comparing the results. Support for more integrated space-time representation and analyses remains a research topic for HGIS and GIS more generally.[15] However, the afore-mentioned changes to territorial boundaries complicated even this cross-sectional approach. In most national contexts, boundary changes for statistical and administrative units are at some point inevitable if those units are to continue to reflect changes in population size and distribution. Ireland is of course no exception to those trends, but while it did see rapid population growth up until the 1840s, from that point onward its demographic experience differed markedly from every other developed nation, being the only one with a population to *decrease* com-pared to the level in the mid-nineteenth century.[16] This may mean that the boundary adjustments occurring over Ireland, although substantial in their own right, are, comparatively speaking, less in total than the corresponding level of changes experienced in other modern states. Nonetheless, these boundary alterations posed challenges in terms of the ability to determine key changes in the island's demography and religious geographies over time. The extreme version of this is when an entire set of administrative divisions becomes redundant and is re-placed by another. Both of these scenarios have been recurrent themes in the construction of analyses possible using the Irish HGIS.

Figure 3.1 presents the core geographies for which data in the Irish HGIS are available. The earliest material from the 1834 First Report men-tioned earlier is on attendance at religious services on the chosen census day and was published at the very aggregate level of the contemporary Church of Ireland diocese (there were thirty-two dioceses at this time). The next available data came from the first inclusion of a religion inquiry in the decennial census in 1861. These data were available at the bar-ony level (there were 334 baronies across Ireland in that year). A major change occurred after 1901, with the medieval baronies replaced by the urban and rural district (URD) structure, the latter lasting through to the second half of the twentieth century, with 220 districts in the then Re-

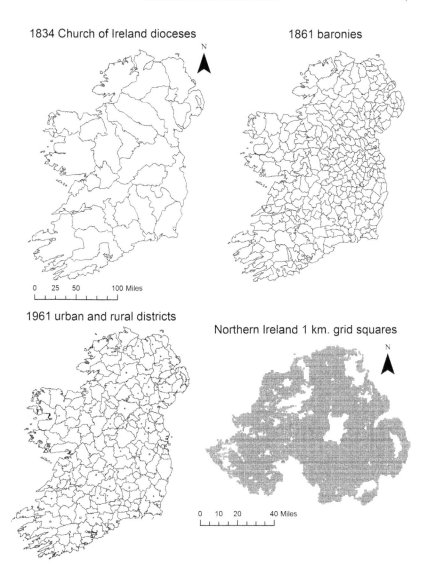

1834 Church of Ireland dioceses

1861 baronies

0 25 50   100 Miles

1961 urban and rural districts

Northern Ireland 1 km. grid squares

0 10 20   40 Miles

3.1. Core spatial units for the Troubled Geographies project.

public of Ireland and 67 in Northern Ireland in 1961. However, during the course of the twentieth century, the number of units changed with each census, as new urban areas tended to be incorporated and rural districts merged, reflecting broader population shifts from the countryside to the towns. From 1971 another major change occurred, as NISRA adopted a novel approach to the problem of dealing with inconsistent boundaries over time with the introduction of the grid square package. This has led to publication of census data at 1-kilometer squares across all of Northern Ireland and for smaller 100-meter squares for all urban areas.

The two major changes in territorial organization just noted subsequently marked a divide between two different data-handling strategies. In the project the data available for baronies from the censuses between 1861 and 1901 were analyzed without any attempt to relate baronies to the structure of districts that succeeded them. The earlier data for 1834 were handled in a similar way. However, for the district-level material from 1911 forward, it was possible to take a different course and use spatial interpolation to produce estimates of all data values in the period referenced to a single standardized version of districts as they existed at the time of the 1961 census, irrespective of the particular prior version of district boundaries for which the data were originally produced.[17] By recourse to this strategy, it has become possible to appreciate temporal changes in Ireland's contested religious geographies.

RELIGIOUS CHANGE IN IRELAND
SINCE THE GREAT FAMINE

An initial impression of the dynamics in Ireland's religious geographies is apparent from figure 3.2. The series of maps in this figure shows Catholics as a percentage of the entire population at URD level at four census dates between 1911 and the start of the current millennium. In the remainder, non-Catholic population, the two largest Protestant denominations have been the Episcopalian Church of Ireland and the Presbyterian Church in Ireland.[18] The maps in figure 3.2 highlight the historical dominance of the Catholic population in the south and west of the island and the impact of the Ulster plantations of the seventeenth century in establishing an enduring Protestant influence in the north, particularly in the extreme northeast. Also shown on the maps is the border of Northern Ireland, established after the 1920 Government of Ireland Act took effect in 1921. The somewhat lower percentages of Catholics in the southern districts along the eastern seaboard and in the counties around Dublin (known as "the Pale"), the Midlands, and West Cork indicate areas

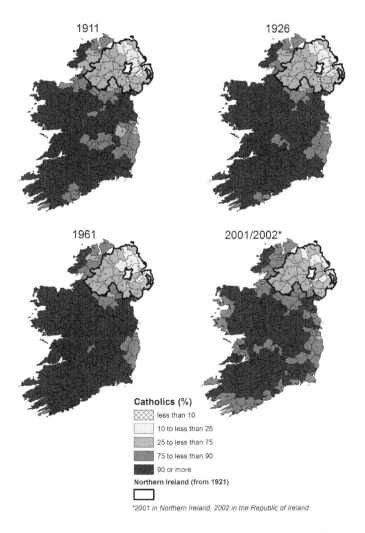

3.2. Series of maps showing changes in district-level percentages of Catholics over four snapshots between and including 1911 and 2001/2002. For the district maps here and in subsequent figures, the percentages are derived from census data interpolated to districts as they existed in 1961, affording direct comparison over time.

of modest Protestant population. These patterns are not especially novel to anyone with a reasonable knowledge of modern Irish history, but the maps organize the data into an unprecedented view that highlights the changes occurring over time. Between 1911 and 1926 there was a marked contraction in the Protestant population of the Irish Free State from the aforementioned districts and also in districts immediately south of the border. As a whole the proportion of Protestant population in the south went from about 25 percent in 1911 to less than 8 percent by 1926.[19] This process continued through 1961 as the south became even more Catholic dominated. However, by 2001–2002 the trend appears to have changed again, in fact reversing, as a new pattern of non-Catholic settlement began to become apparent, very much associated with the coastal regions of the east and west as well as the southern border districts. With the Republic's "tiger economy" of the mid-1990s and also as a result of European Union membership, the country went from being a net exporter to an importer of people.[20] The coastal character of much of this change in some of the island's most scenic areas perhaps results from countercultural in-migration into these districts, particularly from the more traditionally Protestant countries of northern Europe.[21] Conversely, the maps also indicate a consistent pattern of relative growth in the Catholic population in the Greater Belfast area throughout the twentieth century, such that Catholics and Protestants are living in greater numbers closer together than before. The population of the Greater Belfast area has grown significantly, even if the City of Belfast's population has itself declined since its 1911 peak owing to suburbanization, industrial collapse, and the dangers, real and perceived, of the Troubles. However, further analysis confirms that the formation of enclaves based on religious and political identities rather than on widespread residential integration has remained a feature in this trend.

The last census for which data are available at URD level across all of Ireland for the three largest religions (Catholic, Church of Ireland, and Presbyterian) is 1961. The maps in figure 3.3 begin to compare changes in the distributions of Catholic and Church of Ireland populations from 1911 up to that date. These maps were created using a so-called local indicator technique, namely, a local Moran's I test for assessing whether the district-level percentages for either religion are spatially autocorrelated. "Autocorrelation" is the formal term for patterning in values; that is, values do not simply vary randomly over space. The Moran's I test can be used to assess both positive and negative spatial autocorrelation (as well as zero autocorrelation). Positive local Moran's I values indicate clustering of similar values, whether high or low, while negative values indi-

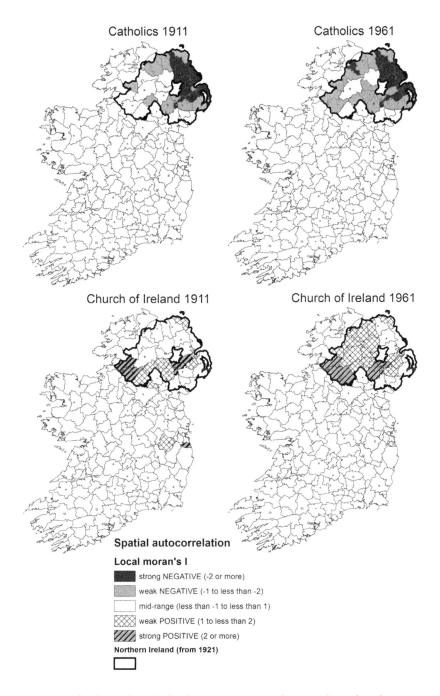

3.3. District-level maps from the local Moran's *I* autocorrelation analysis, identifying particular clusters of districts in 1911 and again in 1961. The maps are based on their percentage Catholic (*top*) and percentage Church of Ireland (*bottom*) populations.

cate locations surrounded by widely differing values. The "raw" I values mapped in figure 3.3 alone do not indicate if such clustering is statistically significant. However, application of this exploratory technique serves to convey the distinct picture in Northern Ireland, where clusters of districts having lower percentages of Catholics can be seen in the northeast area in and near Belfast. Comparing the two maps for Catholics in figure 3.3 also suggests that the extent of clusters of neighboring Northern Ireland districts having low Catholic percentages changed between 1911 and 1961. The maps on the bottom tier of the figure are based on the percentages of district populations who were members of the Church of Ireland. In all but a few districts south of the border, the proportion of population in the Church of Ireland was too small to identify spatial clusters, although, as shown on the 1911 map, a few eastern districts in the counties of Kildare and Wicklow and along the border itself stand out as having somewhat higher percentages. These were a throwback to patterns of colonial settlement in the Pale. By 1961, however, there were barely any signs of significant clusters in the south. Conversely, north of the border, clusters of districts with high proportions of population that identified as Church of Ireland had increased in size. These changes reflected an ongoing process of religio-spatial realignment perhaps linked to but certainly continuing beyond the partition of the island in 1921.[22]

Figures 3.4a and 3.4b present another view on these trends, showing changes in the district-level percentages of *non*-Catholics over the fifteen years between 1911 and 1926, before and after partition. As with the maps in figure 3.3, these percentages are based on estimates interpolated for the 1961 version of the U R D framework. Each circle on these scatter plots represents a separate district. Generally speaking, non-Catholic percentages are higher in districts in Northern Ireland than in the Irish Free State/Republic of Ireland at both dates. In the Northern Ireland area it appears that a few districts saw a slight decrease in the percentage of non-Catholics by 1926. Otherwise, for other districts north of the border, there is a high degree of consistency in the percentages at both dates. This correspondence is indicated by the clustering of the circles around the upward-sloping regression line and the high R2 value (close to 1). Clear outliers are also labeled on the chart, including Ballycastle Urban, Downpatrick, and Portstewart. These districts did not exist in

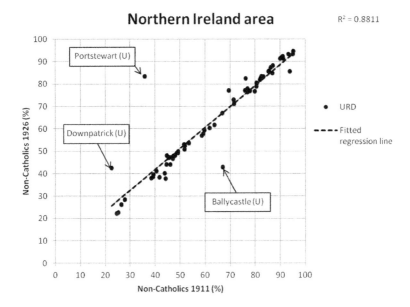

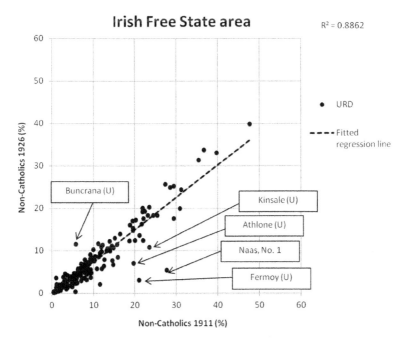

3.4. a and b. Scatter graphs plotting district-level percentages of non-Catholics in 1926 against the corresponding percentages in 1911 in (*a*) districts in Northern Ireland, and (*b*) districts in the Irish Free State.

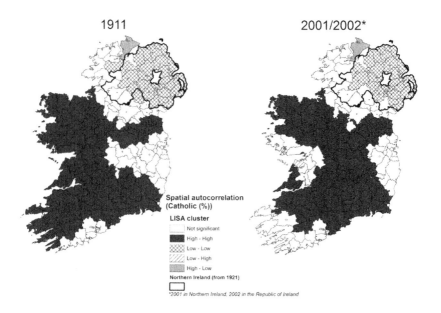

3.5. Maps from the LISA autocorrelation analysis of district-level percentages showing the type of spatial autocorrelation present between neighboring districts based on the percentage of their populations recorded as Catholic.

1911 but were formed by 1926, and the clear disparity in the 1911 and 1926 percentages for these districts is an extreme example of the error that can arise as a consequence of using spatial interpolation to estimate values for the standardized districts. For the other districts, which were created before partition and for which boundary changes have been less dramatic, the interpolation errors are likely to be much less extreme.[23]

The second chart for the districts in the Irish Free State/Republic of Ireland area highlights the much smaller fraction of districts there in which percentages of non-Catholics approached the levels in Northern Ireland. Moreover, the distribution of circles suggests a general decrease in these percentages in 1926. Some of the greatest changes were in districts with large British military garrisons, and the evacuation of Crown forces en masse *after* 1922 is the primary reason for the much lower percentages in 1926 in towns such as Athlone and Fermoy as well as the rural district of Naas, No. 1, which was home to the Curragh Camp, the British Army's main infantry base in Ireland.[24] Conversely, Buncrana Urban was the only district in the south to have a noticeably higher percentage of non-Catholics in 1926 compared to the percentage in the district in 1911. Buncrana was one of the "Treaty Ports," which were to be retained for the use of Britain's Royal Navy under the Anglo-Irish accord of December 1921.[25] However, these are exceptional cases. More generally, the decreased percentages in 1926 for many districts in the south indicate a rapid reduction of the Protestant population from an already low base.

The message from the preceding figures is that the contours of Irish religion were changing with the 1921 partition but that this trend continued into later decades as well. The polarization between Catholic-dominated districts in the south and Protestant districts in the north was becoming clearer and was a reflection of deeper political differences. A final illustration of this is provided by the maps in figure 3.5, which again were produced using a local indicator technique for identifying spatial clustering.[26] Anselin's LISA method has a specific advantage over the local Moran's I, as it can identify clusters of both low and high values simultaneously. The local Moran's I technique used in figure 3.3 cannot identify significant clusters where populations are universally high or low across wider geographical areas. In figure 3.5 the results show more clearly changes in prominent (statistically significant) clusters. These clusters are labeled by type, "high-high" and "low-low" indicating significant clusters of districts having similarly high or low percentages, respectively. The two other types, "low-high" and "high-low," conversely indicate districts with percentages that are significantly different from their neighbors. In 1911 the Catholic population was highest over vast swathes of the south and west of the island, covering almost all of the provinces of Connacht and Munster and signified by the "high-high" designation covering many districts in those locations. Conversely, they were lowest in the extreme northeast in the districts included in the "low-low" cluster, which covers almost all of what was soon to become Northern Ireland. By 2001–2002, however, there had been a change in this pattern. The significant cluster identified at this date is smaller than that shown on the 1911 map (excluding districts along the Atlantic seaboard), pointing to a growth in the non-Catholic share of the populations of these areas. Indeed, a lone "low-high" district has emerged on the shores of Galway Bay, indicating an area of lower Catholic population surrounded by districts with much higher proportions of Catholics. This is likely to be the result of the process of countercultural migration noted earlier, matched by a movement of young Catholics away from these rural areas toward the major urban centers both within and beyond Ireland. In addition, the "high-high" cluster of districts for 2001–2002 includes districts farther to the east of Ireland than in 1911, where the Catholic proportion of the Pale has increased over the course of the twentieth century. In Northern Ireland a significant cluster of districts with similarly low percentages of Catholics is present, but it includes fewer districts than the cluster identified on the 1911 map, reflecting in turn the growth of the Catholic population within Northern Ireland during the second half of the twentieth century. Taken together, the maps in this section of the chapter underscore the dynamism as well as the continuity that has defined the religious geographies of twentieth-century Ireland.

THE GEOGRAPHY OF THE TROUBLES

The conflict in and over Northern Ireland that erupted in 1969 and was to last for most of the remainder of the century was the starkest manifestation of the cleavages in political and religious identities to have beset the island. The cycle of conflict hardened territorial differences as parts of Belfast, Derry/Londonderry, and other locations became "safe" or "no go" areas for different groups. Now, as Ireland pulls away from that darker period, more can be learned about the varied dimensions of violence and terror and how these touched people's lives. While the conflict itself has received a great deal of academic and media attention, comparatively less time has been spent on the spatial aspects of the crisis.[27] This is all the more remarkable when we consider how integral geography was to the Troubles. According to the historian A. T. Q. Stewart, "topography is the key to the Ulster conflict. Unless you know exactly who lives where, and why, much of it does not make sense. . . . Ulster's troubles arise from the fact that people who live there know this information to the square inch, while strangers know nothing of it."[28]

The "Troubled Geographies" project was the first to georeference records of the more than 3,500 fatalities that occurred in Northern Ireland as a result of the conflict between 1969 and 2001. The starting point for

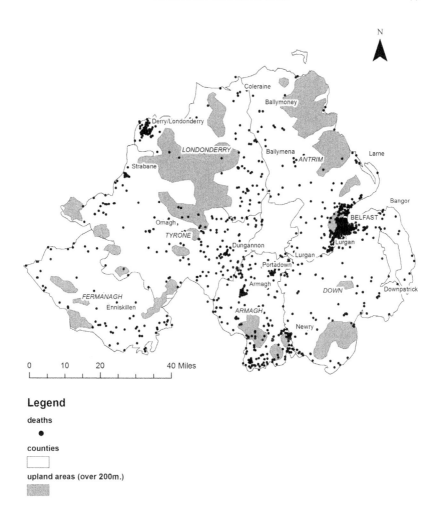

3.6. Mapped locations of all Troubles fatalities in Northern Ireland between 1969 and 2001.

this was a database compiled previously by Malcolm Sutton to commemorate all individuals who lost their lives, irrespective of creed or role in the conflict.[29] This database is also hosted on the University of Ulster's Conflict Archive on the Internet (CAIN) website.[30] The Sutton database provides a wide range of information about the victims and the circumstances in which they died. Importantly, this information includes the locations where fatal incidents occurred, and locational information is

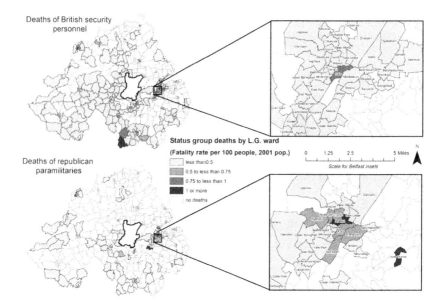

3.7. Northern Ireland map of fatalities by British security personnel (*top*) and by republican paramilitary groups (*bottom*). Deaths standardized by ward population size, with the Belfast area shown in more detail (*inset map*).

available for the majority of records. Where this is not the case or where the information is vague, other sources were used in the "Troubled Geographies" project to try and identify locations for recorded fatalities.[31]

Figure 3.6 uses points to map the georeferenced records of fatalities sourced from the Sutton index. Unsurprisingly, clear signs of clustering are apparent. Many fatalities were concentrated in the major urban centers of Belfast and Derry, and beyond these centers fatalities occurred in large numbers in an arc stretching southwest from Belfast and south of Lough Neagh and encompassing the towns and hinterlands of Lurgan, Portadown, Armagh, and Dungannon. Another cluster is evident in the South Armagh salient, south and west of Newry, close to the border with the Republic. Similarly, fatalities are also evident at other frontier locations farther to the west.

Once these records were georeferenced, the additional detail contained in the Sutton database enabled further analysis of fatalities occurring within different groups. This is illustrated in figure 3.7, which shows how fatalities for the British security services and for all republican para-militaries were distributed.[32] These distributions are standardized to ward-level populations using 2001 census data, giving a crude indication of rates. For members of the security services, deaths occurred at a low rate across a broad sweep covering most wards in the western counties of Fermanagh and Tyrone. Higher rates are most evident in the bor-der area in the south of County Armagh. The South Armagh brigade of the Provisional Irish Republican Army (PIRA) waged a particularly successful campaign against the security services, earning the region a fearsome reputation among troops deployed there, so much so that from the mid-1970s it was deemed too dangerous for soldiers to use ground transportation to access the many mountaintop observation posts along the border, with all deployments and supplies moved by air instead.[33] In the inset map in figure 3.7, covering the Belfast area, it can be seen that the rate of fatalities among members of security services was higher in the Catholic Falls ward of West Belfast than in other city wards.

For republican paramilitaries the distribution of rates is quite differ-ent. Deaths tended to be spatially focused in the areas of South Down and South Armagh, where there was significant paramilitary activity. In addition, the map of rates shows that some paramilitary fatalities also oc-curred in parts of East Tyrone, perhaps reflecting more effective deploy-ment of specialist military units there than in South Armagh in terms of their ability to infiltrate the PIRA.[34] The isolated ward southwest of Belfast for which a high rate is evident in fact locates the Maze prison, in which the deaths of thirteen PIRA and Irish National Liberation Army (INLA) volunteers occurred during the hunger strikes of the early 1980s.[35] In Belfast itself the inset map shows the highest rates of republican para-military fatalities in the Protestant wards of Shankill, Woodvale, and Highfield. In addition, the mixed Shaftesbury ward, covering most of the city center, stands out as the location of many republican bomb attacks, particularly in the early phases of the conflict.[36]

The Sutton index also includes information on the perpetrators of fatalities, and in the "Troubled Geographies" project this meant that locations of fatalities cross-referenced by known perpetrators could be subject to further analysis using GIS analytical techniques. The maps of Belfast in figure 3.8 were produced using a technique known as kernel

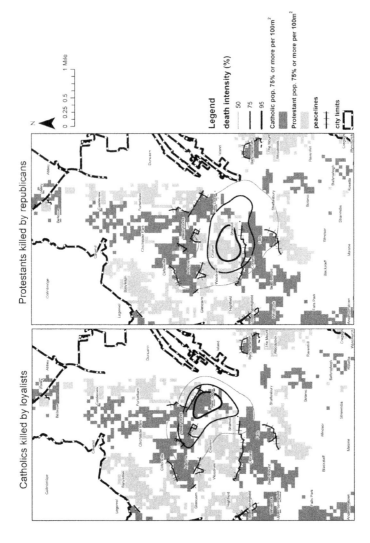

3.8. Smoothed map of fatalities in Belfast (*left*) for Catholics killed by loyalist paramilitaries (*right*) and Protestants killed by republican paramilitaries. Both are overlaid onto chloropleth map of religious geographies generated using 2001 census data for 100-by-100-meter grid squares.

density smoothing, applied to locations of Catholic fatalities at the hands of loyalist paramilitaries and vice versa to Protestant killings by republican paramilitaries. As its name implies, the technique works to generate a smooth surface-based representation from a set of point-based records, where the surface can be represented as values for a grid of cells or, as here, using isopleth contour lines.[37] The amount of smoothing applied can be varied, but the point is to use the approach to aid more clear identification of "hot spots."[38] The smoothed surfaces are represented in the maps in figure 3.8 using the black contour lines. The more "blocky" patterns also shown on these maps portray the 100-by-100-meter grid cells now used by NISRA in publishing key census variables. The squares having Catholics as 75 percent or more of their total enumerated population according to the 2001 census are shaded in the darker gray, while light gray is for squares in which Protestants made up 75 percent or more of the population. Locations of so-called peace lines – barriers erected by the security services between Catholic and Protestant neighborhoods – are also shown.

Comparing the two maps in figure 3.8 shows that Catholic fatalities were greatest in Catholic areas, notably in the New Lodge neighborhood; similarly, Protestant deaths were focused in the almost exclusively Protestant Shankill area. However, there are also distinctions between the two distributions, since Protestants appeared to be killed more often in an area where the boundaries between the two communities were relatively well defined and where their numbers might have afforded them greater protection. For the Catholic population, loyalist paramilitaries tended not to target the Falls heartland as often as the New Lodge, and this may have been because the interfaces between the Catholic and Protestant areas of this part of inner-city North Belfast have historically been less well defined and more contested. On the other hand, the long peace line in the west of the city between the Falls and the Shankill districts constricted access to the former from the early 1970s, perhaps affording the Catholics of the Falls a modest protection that those in the New Lodge did not enjoy. In contrast, in the New Lodge area it would have been easier for loyalist paramilitaries to launch attacks and then escape back to the surrounding Protestant districts.[39]

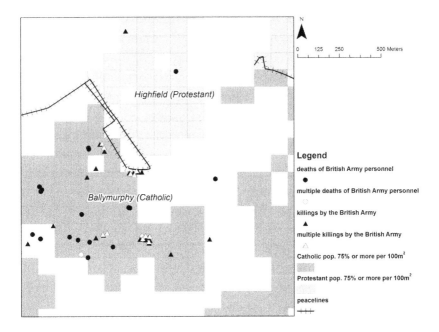

3.9. Large-scale map showing an interface area of West Belfast overlaid with locations of fatalities of and by British Army personnel during the Troubles.

A final map display serves to show that religious geographies influenced the occurrence of other fatalities and the shape of the Troubles more generally. The map in figure 3.9 focuses in on a highly contested interface area of West Belfast between the Protestant Highfield and Catholic Ballymurphy areas. The same shading has been applied to 100-by-100-meter grid cells as in figure 3.8. Here, however, the goal is not to smooth a general surface; instead, point symbols representing locations of individual killings are retained in the display. These locations are for fatalities among and committed by the British Army, which was heavily deployed in Catholic areas as the threat from the PIRA and other republican splinter factions intensified from the start of the 1970s. Yet it must be remembered that the arrival of soldiers in those areas was initially seen by both the military and the resident Catholic population as necessary and defensive.[40] However, just a year later the battle for "hearts and minds" was already being lost, and the Catholic perception of the army had already swung from friend to foe.[41] The concentration of fatalities on the Catholic Ballymurphy side of the peace line provides a stark view of this change, as both the soldiers and the communities they were sent in to protect became targets in a protracted and bitter conflict.

CONCLUSIONS

This chapter has given an overview of the "Troubled Geographies" project and the light it has been shedding on Ireland's religious geographies at a variety of scales. Elsewhere, conflict in modern Ireland has sometimes been portrayed simplistically as a religious war between Catholics and Protestants. In contrast, the project has shown that changing spatial relationships have also been a key part of this difference, contributing to and manifest in the crisis in Northern Ireland in the latter part of the twentieth century.[42]

This chapter has focused on the spatial dimensions of religious difference over two centuries. Yet, looking ahead, we should not lose sight of the common experience that has been forged by these differences. While the island of Ireland is still characterized by a historic religio-spatial polarity between a nominally Catholic south and a supposed Protestant north, we need to acknowledge that the social meaning of such descriptors has completely changed over the past 150 years and that now more emblematic of both jurisdictions is a growing unwillingness among citizens to be categorized in religious terms. Furthermore, the ancient north–south divide is increasingly being supplanted by a wider dichotomy between an undeveloped western hinterland and a bloated metropolitan east, the product of transnational forces of industrialization and urbanization and, latterly, deindustrialization and suburbanization that have transformed the island utterly, transcending any parochial border.

ACKNOWLEDGMENTS

Work on this essay was funded by the AHRC/ESRC's "Religion and Society" program under Large Grant AH/F008929, "Troubled Geographies: Two Centuries of Religious Division in Ireland" (principal investigator, Professor Ian Gregory, Lancaster University). The project collaborators are also grateful to Dr. Martin Melaugh (University of Ulster) for making the Sutton database available to us. Thanks are also due to the CSO and NISRA for the modern census data that made much of this analysis possible.

NOTES

1. D. H. Akenson, *Small Differences: Irish Catholics and Irish Protestants 1815–1922* (Kingston, Ontario/Dublin: McGill-Queen's University Press/Gill & Macmillan, 1991), 4; M. Elliott, *When God Took Sides: Religion and Identity in Ireland: Unfinished History* (Oxford: Oxford University Press, 2009), 6–9; A. T. Q. Stewart, *The Narrow Ground: Aspects of Ulster 1609–1969* (Belfast: Blackstaff Press, 1977), 21; J. Coakley, "Religion, National Identity and Political Change in Modern Ireland," *Irish Political Studies* 17 (2002): 4–28, see 6; R. V. Comerford, "Ireland 1870–1921," in *A New History of Ireland VI: Ireland under the Union II 1870–1921*, ed. W. E. Vaughan (Oxford: Oxford University Press, 1989), xliii–lvii, see xliv; F. S. L. Lyons, *Culture and Anarchy in Ireland* (Oxford: Clarendon Press, 1980), 192.

2. J. H. Whyte, *Interpreting Northern Ireland* (Dublin: Gill & Macmillan, 1991), 103; S. Bruce, *God Save Ulster! The Religion and Politics of Paisleyism* (Oxford: Oxford University Press, 1986), 263; and R. English, "Sectarianism and Politics in Modern Ireland," in *Nothing but Trouble? Religion and the Irish Problem*, ed. D. Kennedy (Belfast: Irish Association for Cultural, Economic and Social Relations, 2004), 45–49, see 45.

3. R. F. Foster, *Modern Ireland 1900–1972* (Harmondsworth: Penguin, 1989), 59; and A. Clarke with R. D. Edwards, "Pacification, Plantation and the Catholic Question, 1603–23," in *A New History of Ireland III: Early Modern Ireland 1534–1691*, ed. T. W. Moody, F. X. Martin, and F. J. Byrne (Oxford: Clarendon Press, 1976), 187–232, see 188; B. Graham, "Ireland and Irishness: Place, Culture and Identity," in *In Search of Ireland: A Cultural Geography*, ed. B. Graham (London: Routledge, 1997), 1–16, see 1; W. J. Smyth, "The Cultural Geography of Rural Ireland in the Twentieth Century," in *The Shaping of Ireland: The Geographical Perspective*, ed. W. Nolan, Thomas Davis Lecture Series (Cork/Dublin: RTÉ/Mercier Press, 1986), 165–75, see 175.

4. J. McGarry and B. O'Leary, *Explaining Northern Ireland* (Oxford: Blackwell, 1995), 174; C. Mitchell, *Religion, Identity and Politics in Northern Ireland: Boundaries of Belonging and Belief* (Aldershot: Ashgate Publishing, 2006), 13; and C. Coulter, *Contemporary Northern Irish Society: An Introduction* (London: Pluto Press, 1999), 55–58.

5. This will become evident in the analysis of patterns of violence during the Troubles from 1969, but the power of territory in the wider context also helps explain why the dropping of the recidivist articles 2 and 3 from the constitution of the Irish Republic was seen as a critical step in the peace process. See A. Guelke, "Northern Ireland: International and North/South Issues," in *Ireland and the Politics of Change*, ed. W. Crotty and D. E. Schmitt (Harlow: Addison Wesley Longman Ltd., 1998), 195–209, see 198.

6. M. P. A. Macourt, "The Religious Inquiry in the Irish Census of 1861," *Irish Historical Studies* 21, no. 82 (1978): 168–87, see 176.

7. L. Kennedy, P. S. Ell, E. M. Crawford, and L. A. Clarkson, *Mapping the Great Irish Famine* (Dublin: Four Courts Press, 1999), 13.

8. L. A. Clarkson, L. Kennedy, E. M. Crawford, and M. W. Dowling, "Religion, 1861–1911," in *Database of Irish Historical Statistics* (computer file), UK Data Archive (distributor), Colchester, Essex, November 1997, SN: 3579; and M. W. Dowling, L. A. Clarkson, L. Kennedy, and E. M. Crawford, "Census Material, 1901–1971," in *Database of Irish Historical Statistics* (computer file), UK Data Archive (distributor), Colchester, Essex, May 1998, SN: 3542.

9. Queen's University of Belfast, *Centre for Data Digitisation and Analysis,* http://www.qub.ac.uk/cdda/CDDA _2011/Welcome.

10. D. W. Miller, "Irish Catholicism and the Great Famine," *Journal of Social History* 9 (1975): 81–100, see 83–84.

11. Ibid., 95.

12. See, for example, Akenson, *Small Differences;* D. Fitzpatrick, "The Geography of Irish Nationalism," *Past and Present* 78 (1978): 113–44; P. Hart, *The I.R.A. at War 1916–1923* (Oxford: Oxford University Press, 2005); D. W. Miller, "Mass Attendance in Ireland in 1834," in *Piety and Power in Ireland, 1760–1960: Essays in Honour of Emmet Larkin,* ed. S. J. Brown and D. W. Miller (Belfast/South Bend, Ind.: Institute of Irish Studies/Notre Dame University Press, 2000), 158–79; D. W. Miller and L. J. Hochberg, "Modernisation and Inequality in Pre-Famine Ireland: An Exploratory Spatial Analysis," *Social Science History* 31 (2007): 35–60; C. Ó Gráda, *Ireland: A New Economic History 1780–1939* (Oxford: Clarendon Press, 1994).

13. I. N. Gregory, C. Bennett, V. L. Gilham, and H. R. Southall, "The Great Britain Historical GIS Project: From Maps to Changing Human Geography," *Cartographic Journal* 39 (2002): 37–49, see 37.

14. Online Historical Population Reports, *Histpop – Home* (2007), http://www.histpop.org/ohpr/servlet/.

15. I. N. Gregory and P. S. Ell, *Historical GIS: Technologies, Methodologies and Scholarship* (Cambridge: Cambridge University Press, 2007), 143.

16. In pre-Famine Ireland, population growth was a largely rural, as opposed to an urban, phenomenon, a product of farm subdivision on the western seaboard. In Britain and other places, towns and cities saw enormous growth as a result of the Industrial Revolution. Second, while most nations only saw their populations begin to level off during the middle of the twentieth century, in Ireland the Great Famine of 1845–52 brought that process to an abrupt and tragic end. See M. E. Daly, *The Slow Failure: Population Decline in Independent Ireland, 1922–1973* (Madison: University of Wisconsin Press, 2006), 3.

17. I. N. Gregory, "Different Places, Different Stories: Infant Mortality Decline in England and Wales, 1851–1911," *Annals of the American Association of Geographers* 98 (2008): 773–94, see 784–86.

18. In 2001–2002 Christians or those of a Christian upbringing accounted for 97 percent of the population of Northern Ireland and 92 percent of the Republic of Ireland. See Northern Ireland Statistics and Research Agency, *2001 Key Statistics to Output Area Level* (2001 census key statistics report, 22) (2003), http://www.nisra .gov.uk/archive/census/2001/key%20 statistics/Key%20Statistics%20Report Tables.pdf; Central Statistics Office, *Census 2002 Volume 12 – Religion – Entire Volume* (2002 census religion report, 9) (2004), http://www.cso.ie/en/media/csoie /census/documents/vol12_entire.pdf.

19. T. Brown, *Ireland, A Social and Cultural History 1922–1985* (London: Fontana Press, 1985), 107.

20. M. L. Ferreira and P. Vanhoudt, "Catching the Celtic Tiger by Its Tail," *European Journal of Education* 39 (2004): 209–35, see 209; J. D. House and K. McGrath, "Innovative Governance and Development in the New Ireland: Social Partnership and the Integrated Approach," *Governance: An International Journal of Policy, Administration and Institutions* 17 (2004): 29–58, see 29–33; D. Ferriter, *The Transformation of Ireland 1900–2000* (London: Profile Books, 2004), 663–64. The situation has, of course, been transformed disastrously since the start of the new century, but it is too soon to gauge the demographic impacts of the global financial crisis on the republic.

21. U. Kockel, "Countercultural Migrants in the West of Ireland," in *Contemporary Irish Migration,* ed. R. King (Dublin: Geographical Society of Ireland, 1991), 70–82, see 70–71.

22. A microscale example comes from the Military Archives of Ireland (MAI). The area around the town of Pettigo was ceded back to Free State control in early 1923 from Northern Ireland. The prospect for many local Protestants was clearly too much to bear. A Free State officer advised headquarters, "No incident marked the handing over, but we were informed that six Unionist and Protestant families had left Pettigo the day previous. The Unionist Postmaster left for Canada some months ago." See "Border situation – Pettigo and General (Dispatch to GHQ – 9th January 1923)," DoD A/04311, Military Archives of Ireland, Dublin.

23. I. N. Gregory, "The Accuracy of Areal Interpolation Techniques: Standardising 19th and 20th Century Census Data to Allow Long-Term Comparisons," *Computers, Environment and Urban Systems* 26 (2002): 293–314, see 311.

24. C. Costello, *A Most Delightful Station: The British Army on the Curragh of Kildare* (Cork: Collins Press, 1996), 327–31; and P. M. Kerrigan, *Castle and Fortifications in Ireland 1485–1945* (Cork: Collins Press, 1995), 156, 232.

25. F. Pakenham, *Peace by Ordeal: The Negotiation of the Anglo-Irish Treaty, 1921* (London: Pimlico, 1992), 289.

26. L. Anselin, "Local Indicators of Spatial Association – LISA," *Geographical Analysis* 27 (1995): 93–115.

27. See J. A. Schellenberg, "Area Variations of Violence in Northern Ireland," *Sociological Focus* 10 (1977): 69–78; M. A. Poole, "The Spatial Distribution of Political Violence in Northern Ireland: An Update to 1993," in *Terrorism's Laboratory: The Case of Northern Ireland,* ed. A. O'Day (Aldershot: Dartmouth Publishing Group,

1995), 27–45; M. T. Fay, M. Morrissey, M. Smyth, and the Cost of the Troubles Study, *Mapping Troubles-Related Deaths in Northern Ireland 1969–1998,* 2nd ed. (Londonderry: INCORE [University of Ulster & the United Nations University], 1998); V. Mesev, J. Downs, A. Binns, R. S. Courtney, and P. Shirlow, "Measuring and Mapping Conflict-Related Deaths and Segregation: Lessons from the Belfast 'Troubles,'" in *Geospatial Technologies and Homeland Security,* ed. D. Z. Sui (Berlin: Springer Science and Business Media, 2008), 83–101; V. Mesev, P. Shirlow, and J. Downs, "The Geography of Conflict and Death in Belfast, Northern Ireland," *Annals of the American Association of Geographers* 99 (2009): 893–903.

28. Stewart, *Narrow Ground,* 56.

29. M. Sutton, *Bear in Mind These Dead . . . an Index of Deaths from the Conflict in Ireland 1969–2001,* 2nd ed. (Belfast: Beyond the Pale Publications, 2001).

30. University of Ulster's Conflict Archive on the Internet, *"Remembering": Victims, Survivors and Commemoration – Sutton Index of Deaths* (CAIN Sutton database of Troubles deaths) (1999), http://cain.ulst.ac.uk/victims/archive/sutton.html. The project team members are very grateful to Dr. Martin Melaugh for access to the Sutton database, which made this work possible.

31. Additional information on the circumstances and locations of deaths of individual victims of the Troubles came from contemporary newspapers and the book *Lost Lives.* See D. McKittrick, S. Kelters, B. Feeney, C. Thornton, and D. McVea, *Lost Lives: The Stories of the Men, Women and Children Who Died as a Result of the Northern Ireland Troubles,* 2nd ed. (Edinburgh: Mainstream Publishing, 2007).

32. The figure for British security comprises all Crown forces operating

in Northern Ireland during the conflict, namely, all units of the British Army, the Royal Ulster Constabulary (RUC), the RUC Reserve, the Ulster Defence Regiment (UDR), and the UDR Reserve. The figure for republican paramilitaries consists of the Provisional Irish Republican Army (PIRA) and Official IRA, the Irish National Liberation Army (INLA), and the Irish People's Liberation Organisation (IPLO). It also includes deaths of republican paramilitaries operating under associated cover names.

33. T. Harnden, *Bandit Country: The IRA & South Armagh* (London: Hodder & Stoughton, 1999), 14–19.

34. M. Urban, *Big Boys' Rules: The SAS and the Secret Struggle against the IRA* (London: Faber and Faber, 1992), 224–29; and E. Moloney, *A Secret History of the IRA* (London: Penguin, 2003), 304–9.

35. P. Bew and G. Gillespie, *Northern Ireland: A Chronology of the Troubles, 1968–1999* (Dublin: Gill & Macmillan, 1999), 143–59.

36. D. McKittrick and D. McVea, *Making Sense of the Troubles* (London: Penguin, 2000), 85–87.

37. Mesev, Shirlow, and Downs, "The Geography of Conflict," 896.

38. D. O'Sullivan and D. Unwin, *Geographic Information Analysis* (Hoboken, N.J.: John Wiley & Sons, 2003), 85–88; and Gregory and Ell, *Historical GIS*, 177–80.

39. M. Dillon, *The Shankill Butchers: A Case Study of Mass Murder* (London: Arrow Books, 1990), 11–12, 107; I. S. Wood, *Crimes of Loyalty: A History of the UDA* (Edinburgh: Edinburgh University Press, 2006), 172.

40. Public Records Office of Northern Ireland (PRONI), CAB/9/G/49/9, Cabinet Subject Files (2nd Series), Military and Police "G" Files, Military Assistance to the Civil Power (letter from the General Officer Commanding [Northern Ireland] Sir Harry Tuzo to N.I. Prime Minister Brian Faulkner, 27 September 1971).

41. PRONI, HA/32/3/2, N.I. Ministry of Home Affairs, Secret Series Files, Minutes of the Joint Security Committee (JSC), 16 August 1969–18 December 1969 (minutes of meeting of the JSC, 20 August 1969).

42. L. Curtis, *Nothing but the Same Old Story: The Roots of Anti-Irish Racism* (London: Information on Ireland, 1984), 82; and R. Douglas, L. Harte, and J. O'Hara, *Drawing Conclusions: A Cartoon History of Anglo-Irish Relations 1798–1998* (Belfast: Blackstaff Press, 1998), 273, 294.

Broadening Technology: Applying GIS to New Sources and Disciplines

THE PREVIOUS THREE CHAPTERS TAKE WHAT MIGHT BE TERMED "traditional GIS data" and apply them to historical research. By "traditional GIS data" we mean that they are based on quantitative attribute data that can be well represented spatially using points, lines, or polygons. The major sources used by all three chapters are censuses – statistical information about clearly defined administrative units that can be represented by polygons – with additional information on railway lines and stations in the case of Schwartz and Thevenin and locations of killings during the Troubles in the case of Cunningham. Representing these in a GIS is relatively straightforward, and the methodological challenges – exploring change over time in the face of changing administrative boundaries and analyzing data in ways that allow relationships to vary spatially – have been resolved previously and are not the main subject under discussion. As a consequence, the essays are able to focus on learning new knowledge about the topic under study, although what they can teach us about what GIS can, and cannot, offer to the study of the past is also of interest.

The three chapters that follow face a different set of challenges. In each case the major issue that confronts the study is that conventional GIS technology does not easily do what the authors require. They face two sets of challenges. First, how can the technology be developed and enhanced in such a way that it is able to handle the sources that they are using? Second, how can the technology be used to reach new audiences, including academics who would not traditionally be interested in history, and people from beyond the academy in fields such as the commercial and heritage sectors?

The three chapters are based on projects that have contrasts as well as similarities. The biggest contrasts perhaps lie in the size of the projects and the stages they are at. Humphrey Southall has been working on the system that is at the center of his essay for nearly two decades, and it has received extensive funding from a large number of sources for many different purposes. Julia Hallam and Les Roberts lie at the opposite extreme, with much of their work being based on a single focused two-year project. Elijah Meeks and Ruth Mostern lie between these two.

Four areas of similarity can be identified from the essays: the challenge of incorporating historical sources that are not easily represented into a GIS using the quantitative attribute data linked to points, lines, or polygons; using GIS to conduct academic studies in areas beyond traditional social science history; going further than this to use the technology to present results to users beyond the academy; and the problems of sustaining and enhancing major infrastructural resources.

The first of these issues suggests the wide range of potential sources that researchers increasingly want to incorporate into a GIS framework that the original GIS data model is not well suited to handling. In the cases of both Southall and Meeks and Mostern the most important of these is place-names and the coordinates of the locations that the names refer to. While these can easily be represented as points or polygons, difficulties arise once additional information such as which higher-level administrations or jurisdictions the place-names belonged to at different dates also need to be added. Changes over time add further complications. In both cases the authors have had to develop complex relational database structures to cope with these challenges. Southall additionally points out that environmental historical data tend to be in raster form, and he explores how these types of sources can be integrated with more traditional HGIS sources. Hallam and Roberts have a somewhat different challenge in that their material consists of historical amateur movies. Their challenge is to use such a qualitative and unconventional source of attribute data within a technology that was designed to represent and analyze quantitative material.

Taking these sources and analyzing them is complex, but it also opens new opportunities. The authors of all three essays point to the potential of studies that lie well beyond traditional social science history, including modern medical research (Southall), environmental change (Southall and Meeks and Mostern), and film studies (Hallam and Roberts). Beyond finding these new academic audiences, two of the essays also explore the potential with engaging with nonacademic groups, including the commercial sector, environment managers (Southall), and the heritage sector in the form of museums (Hallam and Roberts).

The final issue returns us to the introduction to the first set of chapters, where we noted that HGIS projects start with a database construction phase that is expensive in terms of time and money and for which there is little if any direct academic credit. This being the case, it is incumbent on researchers, and perhaps the wider academic community, to make best use of this investment, in part to prevent the resource from being lost and in part to enhance it in new ways that enable as much benefit as possible to be derived from it. All three essays explore this use in different ways. Southall also points to the need to develop revenue streams to simply keep complex resources such as websites with complex functionality operating. This is a valid point as any database or website will rapidly become obsolete. Even keeping files in open-source formats that are likely to be stable in the long term (and it is debatable whether any of these exist for GIS data) will not preserve them, as hardware will go out of date, and complex functionality simply cannot be preserved through choice of file format. Often the only preservation option is for researchers themselves to bear the effort and costs of looking after the data.

The emphasis of these essays is thus not on developing the historiography but instead on broadening the technology by applying it in new and innovative ways to develop more general humanities GIS approaches. These essays also attempt to make HGIS relevant both to subjects that are not centered on the study of the past and beyond the academy.

FOUR

Applying Historical GIS beyond the Academy: Four Use Cases for the Great Britain HGIS

HUMPHREY R. SOUTHALL

MANY HISTORICAL GIS PROJECTS ARE THE WORK OF INDIVIDUAL scholars, carried out in their own research time without external funding. Most of the projects that do receive external funding are relatively small scale, employing a single research assistant to work alongside the principal investigator. However, a small minority of HGIS research projects are among the most expensive projects of any kind in the arts and humanities. They are also more expensive than most nonhistorical academic projects using GIS technology. This is because the latter can use the vast bodies of georeferenced data describing the modern world that are available from national mapping agencies and through remote sensing. Conversely, even where historical maps are available, the historical researcher needs to scan, georeference, and probably vectorize them; and often spatial data need to be constructed from textual information containing geographical names, not coordinates.

As a result, it is hard if not impossible to fund a major national HGIS, one that identifies every town and village and covers a century or more of change, with the kind of funding available for academic historical research. Total funding for the Great Britain HGIS now totals over $3.5 million, but obtaining this funding required us to demonstrate that the results would benefit an audience beyond academic history. This chapter describes how we have worked with four other groups to meet their needs: health researchers, archivists, government environmental agencies, and companies selling advice to the property sector.

Four caveats are needed. First, the main focus is on the reasons for the collaboration, with details of the actual research provided mainly via references. Second, be very clear that our main source of funding remains grants, not commercial contracts, but the kind of evidence presented here, showing we were delivering wider economic and social benefits, has been crucial to obtaining grants. The other benefits of this kind of activity are further discussed in the conclusion. Third, the case studies presented here are of course all drawn from the experience of one project, but that experience is quite diverse, and each case study ends with some more general lessons.

The fourth and possibly the largest caveat is that the case studies here do not include the largest audience for our work, the users of our website, A Vision of Britain through Time, as originally funded by the UK National Lottery. Courtesy of Google Analytics, we can supply impressive statistics of raw volume, such as that the site was used by 1,811,265 different people ("unique users") in the year from June 2012 to May 2013. However, because the site is completely open access, we know relatively little about who these people are and can only infer their motives. The available usage data are further analyzed in the third of three papers on our rebuilding of the Great Britain HGIS,[1] but the focus here is on professional audiences we have worked closely with.

DEMOGRAPHY AND HEALTH

Most national HGIS projects at least started with the goal of providing a framework for the analysis of historical census and vital registration data. This is certainly true of both the Great Britain HGIS and the U.S. National Historical GIS. Both projects not only created computerized boundaries for the main demographic reporting units but also assembled large bodies of historical statistics. However, my aim here is not to review the very clear contribution of HGIS to historical demography but to explore what more needs to be done to make it useful to nonhistorical demographers, especially to contemporary medical researchers, and, more importantly, to explain why HGIS can make a large contribution to modern medical research.

Twenty years or so ago, the growing number of retired people, especially those aged over eighty, produced near panic among policy makers in advanced societies because they were seen as an inevitable large burden on health systems as well as pension funds. It is now recognized that many people have a healthy old age, requiring constant care only in the final months of life, but this has led to a new emphasis on re-search into the factors deciding who will experience healthy old age and how the proportion of such people can be increased. This has become linked to medical research that has demonstrated a strong relationship between what happens to people before they are born and in infancy and their health much later in life. This research began with a classic study by David Barker into the relationship between a baby's nourishment, as recorded by weight at birth and subsequently, and the risk of death from coronary heart disease.[2] More recent research into the "Barker hypothesis" has explored the wider impact of deprivation in infancy.[3] Such research forms the background to major government programs such as Head Start in the United States and Australia and Sure Start in the UK.[4]

Given that such research is an urgent public priority, starting to gather data on babies now and reporting the results in sixty to eighty years will not do. The research has to be based on recent data on health in old age for individuals whose experience as babies has already been recorded: it has to be based on historical data. Three different approaches have been taken in UK research.

First, George Davey Smith and his collaborators located data on 4,999 babies studied by Sir John Boyd-Orr in 1937–39, which included, as well as measurements of height and weight, names and addresses. The same individuals were then in 1988 located in the modern National Health Service Central Register and asked if they were willing to take part in a follow-up study.[5] Note that all the research described in this section is substantially limited by rules governing access to confidential data on living people and their health, although space also does not allow a detailed account.

Second, David Strachan used data from the Office of National Statistics Longitudinal Study (LS), which links together data for 1 percent of the population of England and Wales from the 1971, 1981, 1991, and 2001 censuses plus information on events such as births, deaths, and cancer registrations; it covers just over half a million people at each census.[6] That clearly tells us nothing about conditions in childhood, but Strachan discovered that the members of the LS were identified by their

National Health Service identity numbers and that, if they were alive on 30 September 1939 and did not subsequently join the armed forces, their NHS number was the National Registration number they were issued on that date. That number identified the local authority area they were then living in. Strachan showed that LS members who were in the north of England in 1939 had worse health today, even if they were now living in a healthier region.[7]

This is where the Great Britain HGIS first became involved, as Strachan's work was based on some broad assumptions about certain regions being deprived, not on historical data about actual localities. We assembled a range of data on unemployment, social class, and overcrowded housing from the 1931 census and contemporary infant mortality data from the 1931 census and supplied it to the LS support team, who made our data a permanent part of the LS. The LS already contained two variables measuring individual health: whether or not the individual died between 1981 and 1991, and whether or not individuals reported in 1991 that their lives were limited by long-term illness. We then ran new analyses that related these two outcome variables to both individual-level data on LS members' recent experience and the locality-level data from the 1930s we had contributed.

Two factors greatly complicated this work. First, we had no direct access to the LS, instead supplying data to the LS support unit and specifying analyses for them to run. Second, although the basic architecture of local government remained constant between 1931 and 1939, consisting of county boroughs, municipal boroughs, urban districts (all urban units), rural districts, and London boroughs, the detailed geography of local government was greatly changed through a rolling program of county reviews: the 1931 census, which provided most of our explanatory variables, reported on 1,800 local government districts, but this had been reduced to 1,472 by 1939. Further, many of the districts that were not abolished were altered through boundary changes: 289 (19.6 percent) of the 1939 districts were new creations or had been affected by boundary changes. To solve this problem, we constructed a geography conversion table from the 1931 and 1939 reports plus the 1,805 boundary changes listed for the intervening period using 1931 populations rather than geographical areas.[8] By linking this table to 1931 census data, we cut the data for the 1,800 1931 districts up into 2,916 fragments and then reassembled them into the 1,472 1939 units. The table was very carefully cross-checked by comparing the 1931 populations of 1939 units computed by applying the boundary change information to the 1931 census figures with the 1931 populations listed in the 1939 report. The results showed that people brought up in Britain's depressed areas in the 1930s have significantly worse health today, even if they later moved to other localities.[9]

The third approach works with samples of people, inevitably small, who have been surveyed repeatedly starting at birth. The first such British project, the National Survey of Health and Development (NSHD), covers 5,362 people born in March 1946.[10] Similar "birth cohorts" were started in 1958, 1970, and 2000, but the NSHD is the most relevant to aging research, as its members are now in their midsixties. Our work on the NSHD has two distinct elements. One task was assisting in converting postal addresses for cohort members into geographical coordinates. The 3,354 addresses from 1999 all include postal codes, and locations were easily found for all members. All but 50 of the 3,519 addresses from the 1972 survey were automatically matched against a modern address list. However, of the 4,856 addresses from 1950, 2,658 (54.7 percent) could not be matched automatically. Although the number of residential addresses today is vastly greater than in 1950, the majority of houses and flats that existed in 1950 still exist, so many of the nonmatches were due to detailed variations in spelling and punctuation. However, our particular focus was the relatively small fraction of 1950 addresses that simply no longer exist, because these were concentrated in areas in which the street pattern has been completely replaced by "comprehensive redevelopment." These are inner-city areas with very poor housing conditions, whose consequences the project is especially interested in. Locating these addresses involved working with georeferenced scans of mid-twentieth century mapping at 1:10,560 scale.

The other focus of our work is including additional area-based data in the study. There are two distinct reasons for doing this. One is that when the NSHD was started it was more narrowly medical than today, so while we know a lot about the babies' physiology, we know little, for example, about the houses they lived in. Aggregate data from the 1951 census about, for example, the percentage of homes lacking their own toilet can serve as a proxy for data on whether or not the cohort member's home had a toilet. The other reason is that some factors, such as pollution, are inherently area based. For example, in an analysis of the determinants of individual-level infant mortality as recorded by the special fertility survey within the 1911 census, Eilidh Garrett and colleagues found that children in certain types of occupationally specialized communities had higher mortality rates, even when fully controlling for parental occupations: the children of teachers in mining communities were more likely to die in infancy than the children of teachers elsewhere.[11] Our analysis of the NSHD has shown that growing up in areas with a high percentage of the population in a low social class significantly impacts physical capacity in later life.[12]

Our work with the NSHD is continuing and means we are working closely with geneticists and historians of nutrition. Directly parallel research may not be possible in all countries, as it depends on the existence of these major individual-level longitudinal studies. However, a general precondition for HGIS to contribute to medical or demographic research, as distinct from the history of medicine or historical demography, is that it must construct a continuous narrative of geographical change coming up to the present. Most British historical demographers, including those using GIS-based techniques, stop in 1911, when demographic reporting stopped using the relatively simple system of registration districts.[13] Conversely, much of our work has focused on the subsequent system of local government districts used up to 1974, and our data holdings come right up to the present. Our work on the Longitudinal Study was possible only because we had reconstructed the very complex history of changes to local government districts during the 1930s.

ARCHIVES AND "NAME AUTHORITIES"

It is unlikely that any academic seeking to develop lucrative lines of contract research would choose the archives sector, and few archivists would claim much knowledge of GIS. However, the largest single grant for the development of the Great Britain HGIS, from the UK National Lottery, was possible only through support from the archives sector. Our first steps toward building a multinational HGIS were funded by the European Union's Framework Program 6, but here again it was essential that our partners in the QVIZ project included the National Archives of Estonia and of Sweden; the name is a shortening of "query visualization."[14]

With the obvious exception of archives with map collections, archives have very limited interest in coordinate data, but they have a large interest in geographical names, especially the names of administrative units. One consequence is that archivists are one of only two professions within the cultural heritage sector to systematically catalog by geography. Archaeologists systematically catalog finds by location but are well served by mainstream GIS software and will not be further discussed here. In a systematic survey in 2009 of British archives by the Name Authorities and Indexing Working Group, part of the UK Archives Discovery Network (ADN), out of eighty-four archives replying, 77 percent said they maintained some form of place-name index, and most maintained one covering individual files or documents, not just broad collections.[15]

Unlike libraries, archives hold unpublished documents, generally created by organizations rather than identifiable individuals. The single most important catalog information for an archival document is therefore the identity of the organization that created it. National archives are primarily concerned with the records of national governments and their interactions with other nations. In the UK at least, the best-organized system of archives is the network of local record offices. Local government bodies are required by law to maintain an archive containing, as a minimum, their own most important records, and one of the functions of the UK's National Archives is to inspect these local record offices, which, generally speaking, exist for counties and for the largest cities, other districts depositing their records with the relevant county office.[16]

In other words, archives catalog their records by the organizations, or "corporate bodies," that created them; but the most important corporate bodies they are concerned with are national and local governments, which are defined by and usually named after the geographical areas they govern. Further, in most countries and certainly in Estonia and Sweden as well as the UK, much the largest group of archive users are not academic historians or government officials but ordinary people researching the history of their families. As well as being the most numerous group of users, family historians are economically important to archives because they are willing to pay significant sums for facsimiles of archival documents concerning their families, such as birth certificates and wills. These documents were generally created by historical administrative units such as parishes and registration districts, and amateur researchers may have large problems identifying which administrative area contained their ancestor's place of residence; in other words, they need to identify the polygon containing a known point. One key recent development is that an increasing proportion of archival documents, especially those of interest to family historians, have been digitized and are available for purchase online, so researchers do not need to visit the places their ancestors lived in, but they still need to find documents organized geographically.

Traditional archive catalogs, like traditional library catalogs, are held on filing cards arranged alphabetically. Computerizing these catalogs has usually meant transferring the text from each card to a database record. In this context, creating a "geographical catalog" means associating one geographical name with each record. One problem is deciding which name to use, for example, the name of a house, the name of the street it was in, or the name of the settlement. English local record offices have tried to standardize these records by using the name of the parish. The second problem is deciding the exact form of the name, which may have large consequences for arranging the cards in alphabetical order, for example, "Great Barford," "Barford, Great," or "Barford Magna"? Should the saint's dedication of the parish be included and, if so, where: "Barford St. Margaret" or "St. Margaret Barford"? "Great Barford" is fairly clearly a different parish from "Little Barford," but is it the same as "Barford St. Margaret"?

"Name authorities" are lists that define which form of a name should appear in a catalog. Where the catalog is computerized, name authorities define a "controlled vocabulary," meaning the set of character strings that can appear in a given database column. Although a name authority can be a simple list, a better name authority will include "alternate names" and identify for each which "preferred name" should be used instead. In Wales or Estonia we also need to identify the languages names are in. A name authority of the parishes of England will also need to deal with the many parish names that correctly refer to more than one parish, names such as "Newton" and "Aston." The usual way to disambiguate such cases is to identify higher-level units – most obviously counties – that contain the parish. A reference work that includes preferred and alternate versions of terms and places them in a hierarchy is a thesaurus.

By now, anyone with a GIS background will be wondering what the difference is between a name authority and a gazetteer, and anyway, why not use coordinates rather than names, removing all problems of locational ambiguity? Only three out of sixty-two archives in the ADN survey included a coordinate in their indexing of places. There are three problems with coordinates. First, archival documents rarely contain them, so even if we are going to store coordinates in the catalog, we still need a reference resource that translates the names in the documents to coordinates. Second, no human being could search a card catalog containing coordinates, and the off-the-shelf records management packages used by most archives, like Calm and Adlib, are modeled on card catalogs and completely lack spatial functionality. No GIS software in existence provides the broader document management capabilities that archives require. Third, while one aim clearly has to be to raise awareness of spatial functionality among archivists and their software suppliers, there are real performance problems with adding spatial functionality to heavily used online systems, while name-based searching is computationally very efficient. Conversely, it is impossible to build a digital name authority on top of packaged GIS software, as there is no mechanism for holding multiple names or labels for each entity. While card indexes may be going out of fashion, most people looking for place-specific information type place-names into Google, and basing our website A Vision of Britain through Time around an ontology-based architecture rather than a conventional GIS has consequently led to much higher usage.[17]

Obviously, a gazetteer can be a name authority, especially if it includes variant forms as cross-references to a main entry; several British local record offices use *Bartholomew's Gazetteer of the British Isles* as their main name authority for place-names. However, when the UK National Council on Archives (NCA) published its *Rules for the Construction of Personal, Place and Corporate Names* in 1997, it prioritized a set of books listing administrative areas: Frederick Youngs's *Guide to the Local Administrative Units of England* (1979 and 1991), Melville Richards's *Welsh Administrative and Territorial Units* (1969), and the General Register Office's *Index of Scottish Place Names from 1971 Census* (1975).[18] One oddity revealed by the ADN survey is that of the fifty-two archives that responded to the relevant question, thirty-two said they were following the NCA rules on place-name indexing rather than an in-house standard, but the two commonest authorities cited were *Bartholomew's Gazetteer of the British Isles* and the Getty Information Institute's *Thesaurus of Geographical Names,* both of which cover "places" rather than the administrative units emphasized by the NCA rules.

Although our National Lottery funding required us to create a public website with wider popular appeal, a central deliverable was a computerized replacement for the authorities identified by the NCA. This clearly could not be achieved by modifying our existing ArcGIS system. First, ArcGIS could not hold a mass of variant names for each entity plus additional attributes for each name. Second and more fundamentally, much the largest of the authorities identified by the NCA was Youngs's *Local Administrative Units,* and this contains no maps or coordinates. We clearly lacked the time to research boundaries for all the units Youngs lists. Conversely, Youngs provides a mass of textual information on relationships, especially on hierarchical relationships: district A is in county B and contains parishes C, D, and so on. We had therefore to develop an architecture in which hierarchical relationships were required but boundary polygons were a highly desirable extra and in which entities could have any number of names.[19]

Figure 4.1 uses the parish of Carisbrooke on the Isle of Wight to illustrate the resulting architecture, in particular, the organization of the system around hierarchical relationships. While this structure could be implemented in any relational database, we actually implemented it in an *object*-relational database, originally Oracle and now Postgres. We could then use the object extensions to hold the boundary polygons from the original system as unit attributes. Because the core of this system is a set of entities rather than a set of terms, and because it holds more than one kind of relationship, it is not just a thesaurus but an ontology. Our current production system defines 79,266 units, 129,695 names for those

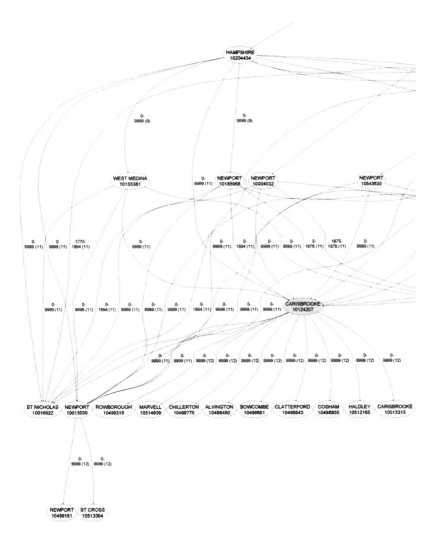

4.1. The parish of Carisbrooke, Isle of Wight, and its "IsPartOf" relationships. The units below Carisbrooke are mostly manors, added from the UK National Archives' Manorial Documents Register, but they include the chapelries of St. Nicholas in the Castle and Newport. By the nineteenth century the market town of Newport was more important than the fortified village of Carisbrooke, so Carisbrooke came under the Urban Sanitary District of Newport, the Municipal Borough of Newport, and so on. All these units were within the Ancient County of Hampshire, but not the later Administrative County of Hampshire as the Isle of Wight was a separate Administrative County. Visualization created by Vojtech Kupca of the University of Umeå.

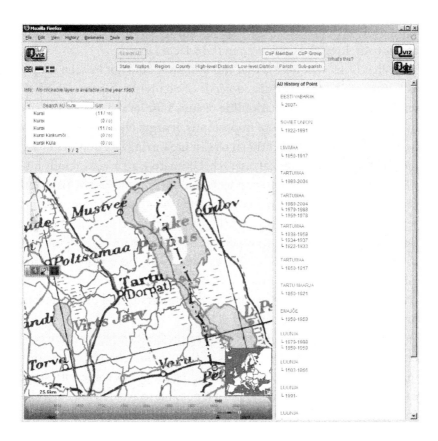

4.2. The QVIZ User Interface presenting information about the city of Tartu, the home of the Estonian National Archives, and the administrative units that covered it at different dates. Just as with Carisbrooke in figure 4.1, there has been a complex sequence of historical units. The earliest unit listed here, Luunja, covered Tartu from 1503 to 1866. This interface was created by teams at AS Regio (Estonia) and the University of Umeå, accessing a data structure created by the GBH GIS team.

units, and 251,260 relationships between these units. It includes 83,706 boundary polygons, but only 40,626 units have associated polygons: units have multiple polygons because of boundary changes.

While figure 4.1 shows something very different from a traditional GIS, the system can do far more for units that have associated polygons. Figure 4.2 shows the interface developed for our data structure by the QVIZ project, which allows nonexpert users to identify historical units of interest via a point-in-polygon query. The QVIZ system then provides access to archival documents from the selected unit.

What is relevant here is that this system should not be seen simply as a response to the specialized needs of archivists. It provides a better foundation for a popular online resource for local history than any mainstream GIS. Even more importantly, it arguably provides a better way forward than a conventional GIS in organizing large bodies of demographic data for historical research. Ultimately, archivists, family historians, and historical demographers share a strong interest in historical censuses and vital registration data and the geographical units used for reporting them. In England that primarily means parishes and registration districts, and it is not a coincidence that the main units of interest to the National Council on Archives had already been mapped by the Great Britain HGIS with funding from research bodies. Similarly, the QVIZ project was led by Sweden's Umeå University and drew on work by its Demographic Database.

However, working with archivists or the heritage sector more generally does mean basing your work around genuinely open standards for data and metadata. Digitization funding programs come with strict rules on standards compliance, and it is possible to avoid following widespread standards that provide inadequate support for geography, such as Dublin Core and Encoded Archival Context, only by knowing about and implementing more appropriate alternatives, notably the work of the Open Geospatial Consortium.[20] Claiming that ArcGIS Shapefiles are a "de facto industry standard" will not do.

Lastly, while this section has discussed working with archivists, with family historians sometimes the ultimate beneficiaries, the underlying aim of this work is to make the world's archives searchable by geography. This would be of immense benefit to academic historians and especially historical geographers.

ENVIRONMENTAL MANAGEMENT

One regrettable oddity is that although many environmental historians now make significant use of GIS technology, this work has developed separately from HGIS. One reason is that environmental historians have focused on raster data, while HGIS, so defined, has focused mainly on vector data and on tools like ArcGIS and MapInfo. However, some of the largest technical challenges in HGIS concern the adaptation of image-processing technology developed for the analysis of aerial and satellite photographs to the automated analysis of historical maps.

We became involved in this area through work on historical land utilization survey maps, developed in collaboration with and partly funded by the UK's Department of the Environment, Farming and Rural Affairs (DEFRA) and two of its executive agencies, the Environment Agency and Natural England. One interesting aspect of this work is the differences in goals and perspectives between even these very closely related bodies.

First, DEFRA's Agricultural Change and Environment Observatory was established to monitor and, where possible, anticipate changes in agriculture, particularly those changes arising from the 2003 Common Agricultural Policy reforms, and to assess the environmental implications of these reforms. DEFRA's main focus is on strategic trends rather than managing particular local environments. One issue is how changes in the structure of farm businesses affect farming practices and so alter the landscape.

Second, the Environment Agency is concerned primarily with rivers, flooding, and pollution and is consequently focused on the management of river basins. It has primary responsibility for implementing the European Union's Water Quality Directive. One aspect of this is reducing the amounts of nitrates in "nitrate-vulnerable zones," which currently cover 20 percent of England. Given that reducing fertilizer use may make arable farming nonviable, identifying which areas and additional farms were traditionally pastoral and converted to arable during or after World War II is one way of targeting action.

Third, Natural England exists "to ensure sustainable stewardship of the land and sea so that people and nature can thrive. It is our responsibility to see that England's rich natural environment can adapt and survive intact for future generations to enjoy."[21] One aspect of this is the Environmental Stewardship scheme, funded by the European Union as part of the Common Agricultural Policy, Pillar 2. UK funding under this policy for 2007–2013 was £4.5 billion. "Place based evidence of long term change will greatly aid in our interpretation of the evidence arising from landscape monitoring programmes such as Countryside Quality Counts."[22] One way this can happen is through better understanding of the landscapes associated with "low input farming," which we are maybe moving back toward.

All of these agencies therefore have an interest in past land use, especially agricultural land use. To some extent, any conventional topographic map provides information on the uses people make of the land they live on: maps usually identify buildings and transport routes. However, large areas of topographic maps are simply empty or identified only as fields. In recent years, we know considerably more from satellite imagery, especially "false color" images showing nonvisible wavelengths. Some information for historical periods can be derived from sources such as tithe maps, but these were not created for all areas, and not all survive. For Britain, the first systematic national survey of land use was the Land Utilisation Survey of Great Britain (LUSGB), directed in the 1930s by Professor Sir L. Dudley Stamp of the London School of Economics (LSE), working in collaboration with the Geographical Association and county education committees and through them with the country's schools.

Participating schools were supplied with instructions and with six-inches-to-one-mile maps of their locality. Pupils, supervised by their teachers, went out into the countryside and recorded land use by marking each plot on the maps with a code letter, as shown in figure 4.3. These field survey maps were returned to Stamp's team and used to prepare one-inch-to-one-mile maps for publication. Stamp paid the Ordnance Survey for the use of the printing plates for the black layer of the then-current Popular Edition maps – effectively a GIS coverage – and then overprinted land-use information as a series of different colors, including brown for arable, green for pasture, yellow for rough grazing, and red for "agriculturally unproductive," which covers both dense urban areas and industrial sites. Although the bulk of the survey was carried out quite quickly between 1931 and 1934, funding publication of the maps proved much harder, even with government support once Stamp became chief advisor to the Ministry of Agriculture in 1942. A total of

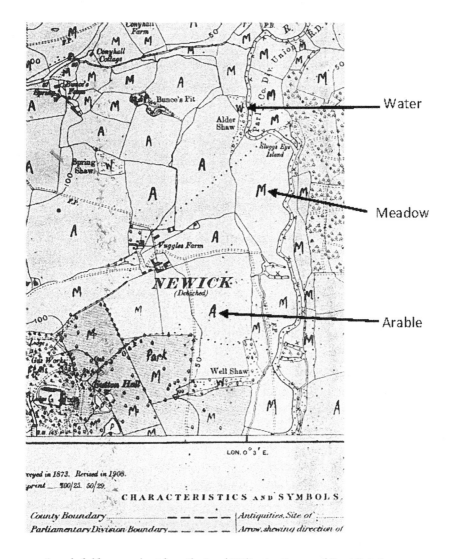

4.3. Sample field survey sheet from the Land Utilisation Survey of Great Britain, showing part of Newick, Sussex. These six-inches-to-one-mile (1:10,560) Ordnance Survey maps were issued by the Land Utilisation Survey to schools and then by the schools to individual pupils, who hand-annotated them to record land use: a very simple set of polygons and attributes. They were then returned to the Survey and although some have been lost, the London School of Economics Archives hold a large collection. Reproduced by kind permission of Audrey N. Clark and Giles Clark.

167 maps were published between 1933 and 1949 using nine different printers, with consequent variations in the inks used. A further 56 maps showing upland Scotland were very carefully colored using watercolor paints and deposited with the Royal Geographical Society (RGS) library in London.

Our first problem was establishing who owned copyright in the maps. The Ordnance Survey base maps had clearly been in Crown Copyright, but this lasts for only fifty years. An initial assumption was that the LSE owned some rights, but in 1936 it made Stamp sign an agreement taking full personal responsibility for the LUSGB. He was a very successful author of geography textbooks, so his personal resources were significant, and he established and owned a company, Geographical Publications Ltd., that published the maps. It is absolutely clear that Stamp was the principal author of the maps, and copyright therefore runs for seventy years from his death in 1966. He left the company to a member of his team, with whom we have established contact. She and her son have been enormously supportive of our work.

A second problem was assembling and scanning a complete set of good quality copies of the maps: our university had some, the Environment Agency bought a significant number from a dealer, and the LSE was able to sell us some mint-condition maps from unsold stock. However, the most important sources were other university map libraries, which freely lent us maps from their collections for scanning. Similarly, we were eventually able to include the unpublished maps of upland Scotland at minimal cost: a commercial republisher of historical maps was scanning a large number of other maps at the Royal Geographical Society and did the LUSGB maps for us, while the RGS also imposed no charge.

Once all the maps had been scanned by ourselves or our partners, georeferencing and the construction of a seamless mosaic were time-consuming but straightforward. The only real complication was that the georeferencing had to be done without using modern Ordnance Survey (OS) copyright data, as otherwise the OS would have been able to claim rights in the final product. However, our collection already included a digital version of the late 1940s New Popular Edition of one-inch maps, which was the first edition to include the modern National Grid, making it trivially easy to georeference. We georeferenced the L U S G B map scans by overlaying them on the relevant New Popular scans.

The large remaining problem is the systematic extraction of vector features from the georeferenced images, and this work is continuing. One way of doing this would be to manually construct polygons by tracing around each color zone on each map, but this would be very time-consuming and expensive, costing upward of £200,000. The alternative approach is to use image-processing software, in our case Erdas Imagine, to automatically identify areas of similar colors. However, a number of problems with the maps complicate this: their complicated publishing history means that the original inks used to indicate a particular land use vary between map sheets, which means each sheet must be manually calibrated separately; the place-names and other information from the black base layer confuse the software; and a large problem especially in upland areas is that the reddish brown used for contour lines is indistinguishable from the red used for "agriculturally unproductive." Although solutions have been found for these problems, all require additional manual input, and, to date, three separate technical studies have been funded by the Environment Agency to try to find the best way forward.[23]

However, our archival research has identified another way forward, although it does not meet the specific needs of the Environment Agency. We located the original color separations used to prepare printing plates for the southern national summary sheet, as shown in figure 4.4, and covering most of England and Wales and about twenty of the one-inch sheets published by the Stamp survey. As each separation defines just one of the color layers, they are far more easily and accurately vectorized. Our current research, following our own agenda with funding from the Frederick Soddy Trust, is constructing vector versions of this national summary sheet plus the detailed surveys of Birmingham and Dartmoor, enabling detailed studies of change on the urban and moorland fringes. "Modern" land use is recorded via the Land Cover 2000 digital mapping created from satellite data by the Centre for Environment and Hydrology. One challenge is distinguishing differences due to historical change from differences due to the very different survey methods, but we also have access to a detailed survey of the Brighton area made in 1996–97

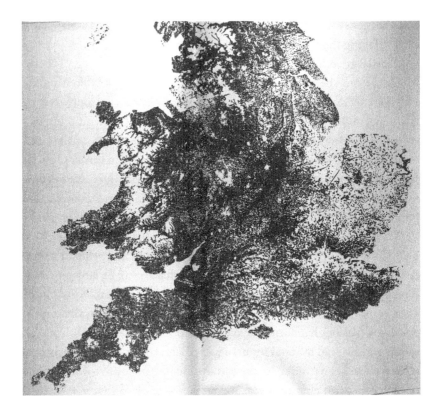

4.4. Land Utilisation Survey of Great Britain National Summary Sheet (South): color separation for the green (pasture) layer. The survey team in London collated the information from the field survey sheets to create a set of maps at a scale of one inch to one mile (1:63,360). They then further condensed the information to create two national summary sheets at a scale of ten miles to one inch (1:625,000). The published maps are difficult to process due to the mix of colors and overprinted names and topographical features. Color separations such as this were created as a stage in the printing process and contain just one of the color layers, making image processing much simpler. Most separations were destroyed, but about 10 percent of the separations were preserved by a member of the Survey's staff and passed to the London School of Economics Archives by a relative. Reproduced by kind permission of Audrey N. Clark and Giles Clark.

by the Land Use UK project using the same methods as the LUSGB but at a very similar date to the Land Cover data.[24]

    If one conclusion is the need for HGIS to explore the potential of raster-based GIS techniques, another is the need to balance contract research with our own agenda. Our work on long-run land-use change,

which also includes analysis of farm census data, would have been impossible without the support of DEFRA and its agencies; but it would also
have been impossible without the goodwill of numerous map librarians,
of the LUSGB copyright holder, and of the Frederick Soddy Trust, all
gained through our commitment to creating a public resource.

PROPERTY SERVICES

"Old maps" are of course essential to defining property boundaries and
to understanding the past history of properties, and academic historical
geographers have sometimes acted as consultants in legal disputes.[25]
However, individual disputes are unlikely to justify construction of a
GIS, and the two examples discussed here use specialized HGIS to drive
websites that serve mass markets – not lawyers involved in disputes, but
lawyers handling routine property transactions. Anyone purchasing a
property, whether a large industrial site or an ordinary house, needs
information on associated liabilities. Some information needs will be
obvious, such as council or property taxes. Others will relate to the site's
past history and be far less obvious.

First, the Landmark Information Group is a commercial partner
of the Ordnance Survey and has created what is essentially a very large
GIS built primarily from nearly a million historical maps at six inches to
one mile (1:10,560) and more detailed scales for Britain between ca. 1848
and ca. 1995.[26] By contrast, the largest noncommercial historical maps
database is that constructed by the US Geological Survey's Historical
Quadrangle Scanning Project, covering approximately 200,000 maps.[27]
Landmark's database forms the basis for a number of distinct products
sold online. These include the old-maps.co.uk website, which straightfor-
wardly sells reproductions of historic maps to the general public. However, this is a sideline compared to Envirocheck:

> The Envirocheck Historical Data Report identifies historical land use, such as:
> potentially contaminative industrial uses; potentially infilled land; historical
> tanks and energy facilities; data captured from Landmark's unique set of
> historical building plans such as potentially contaminative features from
> historical building plans, which includes asbestos and areas cleared due to
> enemy action (bomb damage); list of the historical building plans analyzed for

your selected area. This report comprises of an A4 datasheet, an A3 map sheet at 1:10,000 scale and up to 16 map sheets at 1:2,500 scale. A separate report is produced for each site slice.[28]

The second example directly involves the Great Britain HGIS and has been a significant source of income to cover the running costs of our website, A Vision of Britain through Time. Under a series of laws, starting with the Tithe Commutation Act of 1836, owners of "rectorial land" in England and Wales are liable for the cost of repairs to the chancels of parish churches.[29] In recent years, a small number of property owners have found themselves suddenly liable for very substantial sums, the largest ever claim being £186,969. Establishing exactly which properties are liable is very time-consuming, but only properties located within certain "tithe districts," as defined in 1836, are potentially liable, amounting to about 35 percent of all parishes.[30] Those property owners form a fairly lucrative market for specialized insurance.

Curiously, the Great Britain HGIS project has been involved in the supply of two quite different maps of nineteenth-century parishes to two different companies, both serving this market. First, research by Roger Kain and Richard Oliver of Exeter University was based mainly on local surveys from late eighteenth- and early nineteenth-century enclosure and tithe maps – these maps are from the right period but unavoidably leave some parts of the country uncovered. The Exeter project created a "digital map" that in fact consisted of a series of separate Adobe Acrobat files, one for each New Popular Edition one-inch map, consisting of vector boundary lines drawn on top of scans of the one-inch maps. The Great Britain HGIS created a true GIS from these by converting the vector data to ArcGIS, constructing a true polygon topology, georeferencing the data, and assembling the data from all the maps into a single national coverage.[31] These data have been licensed to Conveyancing Liability Solutions Ltd.[32]

Our own research used a different methodology, starting by digitizing the civil parish system as it existed in the late 1900s using comprehensive and unproblematic Ordnance Survey maps. We then assembled all the textual descriptions of parish boundary changes in published census reports, including the very extensive changes resulting from the Divided Parishes Acts of 1876 and 1882, as listed by the 1891 census.

Unraveling these changes to map the pre-1876 parish geography then involved a project member spending two years in the National Archives using a range of cartographic sources.[33] The resulting vector boundaries, with some further enhancements, have been licensed to Pinpoint Chancel Search Ltd.[34] Creating a commercial product involved our linking the boundaries to a digitized version of another source in the National Archives, the Record of Ascertainments (class IR 104), which identifies the actual liabilities. This linkage involved extensive use of our historical gazetteers.

Chancel repair liability is financially important to the Great Britain HGIS but is obviously a somewhat special case, especially as after 2013 the liability exists only if it forms part of the registered title. The market for liability searches is presumably disappearing; fortunately, advertising income from our website is now sufficient to cover its running costs. However, the system built by Landmark Information clearly dwarfs anything built by an academic HGIS project. The challenge is to unlock the analytic potential such systems clearly contain. While the government agencies discussed in the previous section actively supported our publishing the raster LUSGB data, licensing data to commercial companies obviously stops it being made available to everyone and has arguably inhibited academic use. Issues of "commercial confidence" have certainly inhibited the account given here, so, for example, nothing has been said about the two occasions when we needed to formally respond to hints of possible legal action against us.

CONCLUSIONS

This chapter has shown both how GIS techniques can be applied to a range of broadly historical challenges outside the accepted realm of HGIS and how our approach has had to adapt to meet the needs of workers in other fields. One general comment is that although many of our collaborators have had limited actual knowledge of the practicalities of GIS, there is a high level of general awareness of GIS and enthusiasm for its potential.

One final large question needs to be answered: Why bother with the kinds of activities described here? One obvious answer is to make money, and this is of course why commercial companies such as Landmark Information have become involved in HGIS. However, this has clearly not been the main justification for the Great Britain HGIS: our main source of funding remains, by far, grants, not contract work or other commercial earnings.

First, the construction of a national HGIS is one of the most expensive possible pieces of academic infrastructure construction in the humanities and social sciences. It is almost impossible to justify the cost, even to grant-giving bodies, if the only benefit will be to academic historians. Note that the other beneficiaries may still be academic researchers, as with the Great Britain HGIS's collaborations with medical researchers. However, this need to demonstrate a wider public benefit is particularly strong when the funding source is a digitization program. That said, we would always emphasize that while the Vision of Britain web interface is of limited use to GIS researchers, it clearly serves a large audience of academic historians researching particular localities.

Second, although our nongrant income is a small percentage of the total, it can be spent more flexibly and for purposes for which grants are not available. Expenditure from grants is always carefully monitored. Many grant-giving bodies pay only in arrears, based on evidence of actual expenditure. It is therefore impossible to build up any reserves and consequently to retain staff during the almost inevitable periods when grant applications go badly. Conversely, a major reason why the Great Britain HGIS has been able to keep staff over long periods despite lacking any core funding is reserves built up from contract work, although universities of course vary in how far such money is available to the researchers who brought it in. Another factor in sustaining staff has been developing relationships with small charitable trusts, whose grants have also been a small percentage of the total but very important in hard times. "Commercial" earnings are also necessary to sustain the Vision of Britain website, as there are *no* sources of grant funding for this kind of ongoing cost.

Third, an increasing factor in the UK is the research assessment framework managed by the higher education funding councils. Up to now, this has been based almost entirely on academic peer review and consequently has emphasized traditional publications, especially in peer-reviewed journals. However, under the new Research Excellence Frame-work, which has replaced the Research Assessment Exercise, 20 percent of funding will be allocated based on "economic and social impact"; the work of the Great Britain HGIS described here very clearly does provide just such a wider economic and social benefit.[35]

However, writing more personally, I would argue that the strongest reason for an HGIS researcher becoming involved in these wider areas is simply that it is more interesting and fulfilling to work with many distinct communities, learning about their different perspectives and finding common ground. As it happens, these particular words are be-ing written on a train to Scotland for a HALCyon meeting at the Royal College of Physicians in Edinburgh, two days after a day spent with envi-ronmental officials and commercial GIS consultants focused on land-use change; but our contribution is always about working with historical sources using GIS tools. This is vastly more fun than trying to convince cultural historians and cultural geographers of the "academic value" of our work, even if one does not care about delivering "economic and social benefits" to the wider society we live in. I do care, a great deal.

NOTES

1. H. Southall, "Rebuilding the Great Britain Historical GIS, Part 1: Building an Indefinitely Scalable Statistical Database," *Historical Methods* 44 (2011): 149–59; Southall, "Rebuilding the Great Britain Historical GIS, Part 2: A Geo-spatial On-tology of Administrative Units," *Historical Methods* 45 (2012): 119–34; Southall, "Re-building the Great Britain Historical GIS, Part 3: Integrating Qualitative Content for a Sense of Place," *Historical Methods* 47 (2014), in press.

2. D. Barker, *Foetal and Infant Origins of Adult Disease* (London: British Medical Journal Publishing Group, 1992); L. Berney, D. Blane, G. Davey-Smith, and P. Holland, "Life Course Influences on Health in Early Old Age," in *Understanding Health Inequali-ties,* ed. H. Graham (Milton Keynes: Open University Press, 2001), 79–95.

3. Y. Ben-Shlomo and G. Davey Smith, "Deprivation in Infancy or in Adult Life: Which Is More Important for Mor-tality Risk?," *Lancet* 337 (1991): 530–34.

4. Department for Education and Skills, *Towards Understanding Sure Start Local Programmes: Summary of Findings of the National Evaluation* (Nottingham: De-partment for Education and Skills, 2004), http://publications.education.gov.uk /eOrderingDownload/NESS-SF-2004 -007.pdf.

5. R. M. Martin, D. Gunnell, J. Pem-berton, S. Frankel, and G. Davey Smith, "Cohort Profile: The Boyd Orr Cohort – an Historical Cohort Study Based on the 65 Year Follow-up of the Carnegie Survey of Diet and Health (1937–39)," *Interna-tional Journal of Epidemiology* 34 (2005): 742–49.

6. For an introduction to the L S, see L. Hattersley and R. Creeser, *Longitudinal Study 1971–1991: History, Organization and Quality of Data,* Longitudinal Study Series no. 7 (London: H M S O, 1995).

7. D. P. Strachan, D. A. Leon, and B. Dodgeon, "Mortality from Cardiovascular Disease among Interregional Migrants in England and Wales," *British Medical Journal* 310 (1995): 423–27.

8. L. Simpson, "Geography Conversion Tables: A Framework for Conversion of Data between Geographical Units," *International Journal of Population Geography* 8 (2002): 69–82.

9. S. Curtis, H. R. Southall, P. Congdon, and B. Dodgeon, "Area Effects on Health Variation over the Life-Course: Analysis of the Longitudinal Study Sample in England Using New Data on Area of Residence in Childhood," *Social Science and Medicine* 58 (2004): 57–74.

10. M. Wadsworth, D. Kuh, M. Richards, and R. Hardy, "Cohort Profile: The 1946 National Birth Cohort (M R C National Survey of Health and Development)," *International Journal of Epidemiology* 35 (2006): 49–54.

11. E. Garrett, A. Reid, K. Schürer, and S. Szreter, *Changing Family Size in England and Wales: Place, Class and Demography, 1891–1911* (New York: Cambridge University Press, 2001).

12. E. T. Murray, H. R. Southall, P. Aucott, K. Tilling, D. Kuh, R. Hardy, and Y. Ben-Shlomo, "Challenges in Examining Area Effects across the Life Course on Physical Capability in Mid-life: Findings from the 1946 British Birth Cohort," *Health and Place* 18 (2012): 366–74; E. T. Murray, Y. Ben-Shlomo, K. Tilling, H. R. Southall, P. Aucott, D. Kuh, and R. Hardy, "Area Deprivation across the Life Course and Physical Capability in Midlife: Findings from the 1946 British Birth Cohort," *American Journal of Epidemiology* 177 (2013): 441–50.

13. For example, S. Szreter, "The Importance of Social Intervention in Britain's Mortality Decline c.1850–1914," *Social History of Medicine* 1 (1988): 1–38; M. R. Haines, "Socio-economic Differentials in Infant and Child Mortality during Mortality Decline: England and Wales, 1890–1911," *Population Studies* 49 (1995): 297–315; I. N. Gregory, "Different Places, Different Stories: Infant Mortality Decline in England and Wales, 1851–1911," *Annals of the Association of American Geographers* 98 (2008): 773–94.

14. P. J. Aucott, A. von Lünen, and H. R. Southall, "Exposing the History of Europe: The Creation of a Structure to Enable Time-Spatial Searching of Historical Resources within a European Framework," O C L C *Systems and Services* 25 (2009): 270–86.

15. The author is a member of this working group. Further details of the survey can be obtained from Patricia Mcguire of King's College, Cambridge (archivist @kings.cam.ac.uk).

16. Until 2002 this inspection function was carried out by the National Register of Archives, which then merged with the Public Record Office to form the National Archives. It was the NRA whose support was crucial to obtaining UK National Lottery funding.

17. J. Stevenson, "Place Names: We Would Be Lost without Them," *Archives Hub Blog,* 7 December 2009, http:// archiveshub.ac.uk/blog/2009/12/place -names-we-would-be-lost-without-them (22 July 2012); H. R. Southall, "Alternative Ways of Indexing by Geography," A R C *Magazine* 254 (2010): 17–19.

18. http://www.nationalarchives.gov .uk/documents/information-manage ment/naming-rules.pdf. For Scotland we used the S C A N gazetteer of Scottish places, which had been created since the N C A report, but this was anyway partly based on the 1971 census listing.

19. A more extensive account of this architecture is provided by Southall, "Rebuilding the Great Britain Historical GIS, Part 2."

20. http://dublincore.org; http://eac.staatsbibliothek-berlin.de; http://www.opengeospatial.org.

21. http://www.naturalengland.org.uk/about_us/whatwedo.

22. Andrew Baker, personal communication, November 2009.

23. B. Baily, M. Riley, P. Aucott, and H. Southall, "Extracting Digital Data from the First Land Utilisation Survey of Great Britain: Methods, Issues and Potential," *Applied Geography* 31 (2011): 959–68. One published study making some use of these data for the Peak District is M. Dallimer, D. Tinch, S. Acs, N. Hanley, H. R. Southall, K. J. Gaston, and P. R. Armsworth, "100 Years of Change: Examining Agricultural Trends, Habitat Change and Stakeholder Perceptions through the 20th Century," *Journal of Applied Ecology* 46 (2009): 334–43.

24. R. Walford, ed., *Land Use – UK: A Survey for the 21st Century* (Sheffield: Geographical Association, 1997).

25. For some examples, see R. Janiskee, "Socially and Ecologically Responsible Historical Geography," *Environmental Review* 4 (1980): 35–40.

26. http://www.landmark.co.uk/page/historic-data.

27. G. J. Allord and W. J. Carswell, "Scanning and Georeferencing Historical USGS Quadrangles," U.S. Geological Survey, Madison, Wis., 2011, http://pubs.usgs.gov/fs/2011/3009/fs20113009_sept2011.pdf.

28. http://www.envirocheck.co.uk/envirocheck/historical_land_use_report.jsp.

29. For much more about chancel liability and the relevant historical records, see National Archives, "Chancel Repair Liabilities in England and Wales," Legal Records Information Leaflet 33, http://www.nationalarchives.gov.uk/records/research-guides/chancel-repairs.htm.

30. http://www.clsl.co.uk/content management/Page.aspx?PageID=254&b2cmode=False.

31. The original Kain and Oliver data are held by the UK Data Archive as SN 4348: "Historic Parishes of England and Wales: An Electronic Map of Boundaries before 1850 with a Gazetteer and Metadata." The GIS constructed by the Great Britain HGIS is similarly held as SN 4828: "GIS of the Ancient Parishes of England and Wales, 1500–1850."

32. Conveyancing Liability Solutions Ltd., http://www.clsl.co.uk.

33. I. N. Gregory, C. Bennett, V. L. Gilham, and H. R. Southall, "The Great Britain Historical GIS: From Maps to Changing Human Geography," *Cartographic Journal* 39 (2002): 37–49.

34. PinPoint Chancel, http://www.pinpointchancel.co.uk.

35. REF2014: Research Excellence Framework, http://www.ref.ac.uk.

FIVE

The Politics of Territory in Song Dynasty China, 960–1276 CE

ELIJAH MEEKS AND RUTH MOSTERN

STATE POWER IS INHERENTLY AND FUNDAMENTALLY GEO-graphical. The existence of states is marked by whether or not they hold sway over some territory on the earth's surface, and their persistence depends upon how the machinery of dominion is spatially distributed throughout their territory. However, territorial logic varies from one regime to another, and it may be significantly transformed over time under the pressure of politics and policies, events and ideologies. Therefore, by mapping and reading a regime's evolving spatial organization, historians can gain insights about the spatial distribution of political authority and changes in sovereign dominion. The advent of historical GIS makes it possible to manage all of the data about a historical empire in a coherent system and to track its transformations through time and space.

HGIS and temporally and spatially referenced gazetteers enable historians to study the spatial history of state power empirically.[1] Analysis of historical gazetteer data reveals shifting geographies of cores and peripheries, divergent regional patterns of state investment, spatial impacts of catastrophes and policies, and other phenomena that have been long theorized but difficult to demonstrate. This essay introduces the Digital Gazetteer of the Song Dynasty (DGSD, http://songgis.ucmerced library.info), an innovative and fully implemented digital gazetteer for frequently changing places.

Now that the DGSD and many other historical gazetteer systems are completed and functional, it is possible to move beyond discussions of methodology and to demonstrate that HGIS reveals new insights about spatial political history. This essay introduces two cases concerning the evolving political landscape of China's Song dynasty (960–1276 CE), research findings based upon the DGSD. Historians have long typified the Song dynasty as an era of high state ambition and demographic and commercial revolution paradoxically coexisting with military weakness and conflict. The combination of factors makes for a fluid and complex spatial history that HGIS analysis helps to reveal and explain.

The first case demonstrates that several Song phenomena – the empowerment of a civil bureaucracy that also controlled the military, the expansion of population and state power in south China, the quest for commercial revenues, and the defense of the northern frontier – transformed Song spatial organization. Spatial analysis reveals that Song rulers split and merged existing tax- and personnel-bearing jurisdictions – counties and prefectures – throughout the empire in order to adjust the density of the state presence. Collectively and over the course of almost two centuries, the court recalibrated military power along international borders and aligned administration with economic and demographic reality in old and new imperial cores as well as the settlement periphery. During the Song, almost 20 percent of the jurisdictions that constituted the realm were founded, abolished, or moved from one parent unit to another. However, while the population of the empire tripled, the total number of jurisdictions remained almost constant.[2]

The second case integrates administrative unit gazetteer data from the DGSD with environmental information on the changing course of the Yellow River. It explains that both sudden catastrophe and long-term environmental degradation shaped the political landscape, not only the natural and agrarian ones. In distinction with the first case, this regional study reveals that even within a single province, environmental factors and settlement distribution created distinctive regional patterns in the organization of political space.

For a century, the historiography of the Song era has had a vaguely spatial cast. Scholars have charted a momentous turn toward imperial centralization and diminishing local and provincial political power.[3] However, the conversation has, ironically, unfolded without much reference to actual imperial geography. In fact, as HGIS analysis reveals, even though court jurisdiction did expand, policies were transacted in and through hundreds of fiscally autonomous and militarily independent prefectures and over a thousand counties, which were repeatedly split and merged as circumstances dictated. Developing a historical gazetteer and performing historical spatial analysis is the way to model and visualize the geography and temporality of sovereignty.

DIGITAL GAZETTEER DEVELOPMENT AND THE DIGITAL GAZETTEER AS A SOURCE FOR HISTORY

An empirical approach to the spatial history of Song state power requires a way to manage information about thousands of individual place-making events that occurred over hundreds of years. In order to accomplish that, we organized the DGSD around named places and their attributes. The DGSD records information about all of the provincial circuits, prefectures, counties, and towns that existed at any time during the Song dynasty and all of the occasions when they were promoted, demoted, split, merged, or renamed or when they changed jurisdictions. It also includes information about population, markets, garrisons, and other attributes that Song authors associated with administrative units. Organized around the histories of named places, the DGSD is optimized for discovering and visualizing both spatial and temporal patterns.

In 1958 Sinologist Hope Wright completed a work entitled *An Alphabetical List of Geographical Names in Sung China.* Originally published in Paris by the Centre de Recherches Historiques of the École Pratique des Hautes Études and reprinted as a second-generation photocopy in 1992 by the *Journal of Song-Yuan Studies,* the *Alphabetical List* is now out of print. Wright's compilation is the most comprehensive print source for Song geography in any language. The *Alphabetical List* is an index to every jurisdiction in the Song spatial administrative hierarchy named in one or more of the following three Song texts: the *Song History* (宋史 *Song shi*) geography monograph, the 980 *Records of the Universal Realm in the Taiping Era* (太平寰宇紀 *Taiping huanyu ji*), and the 1085 *Treatise on the Nine Territories in the Yuanfeng Reign* (元豐九域志 *Yuanfeng jiuyu zhi*).[4]

The DGSD is a MySQL database derived primarily from the *Alphabetical List.* We used a Chinese data entry service to digitize the print *Alphabetical List* into an MS Word document. Next we converted that document into an Excel spreadsheet and processed the content of the spreadsheet into MySQL tables. We cross-checked them using a range of queries to find missing headwords and spatial relationships along with other inconsistencies inherited from the *Alphabetical List*. Although the DGSD content derives from the *Alphabetical List,* most point locations for DGSD entities come from the China HGIS (CHGIS), the Chinese Civilization in Time and Space Project (CCTS), and the Robert Hartwell China Historical Studies GIS.[5] Determining entity matches between the DGSD and the other sources also allowed for another series of error-checking iterations. Hosted by the University of California, Merced library, the DGSD is freely available under a Creative Commons license.[6]

The centralized and effective Song bureaucracy maintained excellent spatial and demographic records for two hundred years, and, following the major sources compiled during the Song, the *Alphabetical List* consists of 3,828 headwords, including all Rank One circuits (路 *lu*), Rank Two prefectures (府 *fu,* 州 *zhou,* 軍 *jun,* and 監 *jian*), Rank Three counties (縣 *xian*) and county-rank *jun* and *jian,* and Rank Four towns (鎮 *zhen*), markets (場 *chang*), and stockades (寨 *zhai*) that existed at any time during the Song dynasty, along with centers of state industry (mines, foundries, and commodity markets) located in prefectures, information about the number of cantons (鄉 *xiang*) in each county, the resident (住 *zhu*) and guest (客 *ke*) population of each prefecture in 980 and 1085, the civil rank of each prefecture and county, the designation of counties that served as prefecture seats, the military-ceremonial designation, if any, of each prefecture, the latitude-longitude coordinate of each prefecture, and the distance of each county from the seat of its parent prefecture. While the *Alphabetical List* is an important and comprehensive source, it suffers from the inherent limitations of a print reference work. It can be searched only by headword, and there is no way to cross-reference information, query its rich content, or use it as the basis for maps and information systems. The DGSD is a rerelease of the *Alphabetical List* in a more technologically current format, and it is optimized for our own research on the spatial history of state power. Our objective has also been to produce a work of spatial history, a growing field that concerns the organization of human geography as it has changed over time.[7]

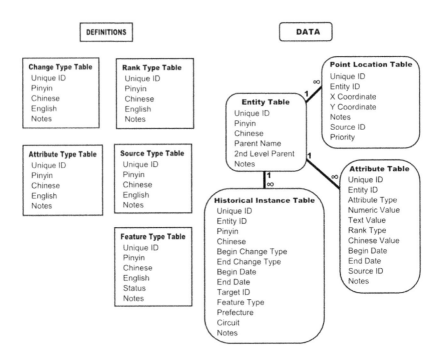

5.1. The DGSD data model.

As shown in figure 5.1, the DGSD tracks administrative entities using an event-based entity-instance model and associated attributes.[8] As Vitit Kantabutra, J. B. "Jack" Owens, and their coauthors have recently explained, a linked entity model is the most efficient structure for historical spatial data management.[9] Its goal is to represent each entity only once in order to avoid redundancy (multiple records referring to the same entity) and fragmentation (a single entity incorrectly split into multiple records). It is also optimized for comprehensive change identification in order to support our research about frequently changing places. In the DGSD, as in Kantabutra and Owens's Intentionally Linked Entity (ILE) model, the entity is a conceptual object that refers to a single place, even as its spatial, demographic, and political attributes change over time. Place-making events are recorded in a separate historical instance table linked to the entity table through explicitly declared relationships. All named places appear in an entity table. Entities are also linked to attributes, such as feature type, and up to eight kinds of demographic data from three different censuses. Geographic location, recorded as points rather than polygons in the DGSD, is simply one kind of attribute, though the DGSD holds it in a separate point location table.

That is, in distinction to a classic gazetteer data model such as the Alexandria Digital Library (ADL), the DGSD encodes historical events in an offset historical instance table separate from the tables that record entities and attributes.[10] And, unlike an instance-based gazetteer like the CHGIS, which requires a new entry in the main table for each historical change as well as entries in other related tables, the DGSD records only one unique entity for each historical place.[11] Each entry in the historical instance table records a temporally bounded and stable piece of information that refers to a time span during which a given characteristic of a particular entity – such as its name, rank, population, or parent – remained the same. Each entry in the historical instance table is linked with an entry in the entity table. All of the attributes of each entity are temporally referenced to the extent that the source material permits.[12] The DGSD design, with its historical instance table offset from the entity table, offers a potential way forward for designing historical gazetteers of frequently changing places, while the offset attribute table also allows future users to easily integrate additional information about Song jurisdictions. In addition, using this approach, geolocations imported from CHGIS, CCTS, and Hartwell and associated with only one instance of an entity can be readily identified and associated with all of its other instances. For instance, Ping 平 zhou prefecture was named Wangkou 王口 stockade and Huaiyuan 懷遠 county at different times during the Song. However, since it remained conceptually the same place throughout the era, it is a single DGSD entity associated with seven entries in the historical instance table and a single geolocation in the point location table.

HGIS ANALYSIS CASE 1: THE POLITICS OF TERRITORY IN SONG DYNASTY CHINA[13]

During the Song era, imperial authority expanded, while the aristocratic class dissolved and the military apparatus atrophied, replaced by a meritocratic civil bureaucracy. The cultivation of new strains of fast-ripening rice, the diking and draining of southern wetlands, and the colonization of the tribal far south allowed the population of the empire to triple; and it gave rise to the most commercial and urban economy to exist anywhere on earth prior to the eighteenth century.[14] Meanwhile, the pastoralists to China's north founded formidable regimes that joined vast cavalries and tribal structures with Chinese-style bureaucracy. By the early twelfth century, half of the empire had been occupied by the Jurchen people of Manchuria; by the late thirteenth century, the Mongols had toppled the remainder of the empire. Analysis and mapping using the DGSD reveals that the spatial organization of the empire changed substantially in reaction to these events; and it also demonstrates that historical spatial data analysis and HGIS have matured to the point that spatial analysis, at least when it is performed using a resource developed with historical understanding in mind, can be integrated with documentary research to yield new historical insights.

Our core research and data design question – why was the Song political landscape so unstable? – was inspired by a well-known work of social science history, completed before historical spatial data modeling, visualization, and analysis made it possible to answer empirically. Sociologist Charles Tilly argued that the spatial organization of state power emerged when governments sought to balance the often contradictory requirements of war making and revenue extraction. Emergent territorial jurisdictions allowed regimes to collect taxes more efficiently. However, spatial organization was unstable because the spatial distribution of state activity that served military priorities differed significantly from the spatial distribution that facilitated revenue production.[15] Military forces had to be located between their likely sites of activities and their major sources of supplies, while civilian officials had to be distributed in correspondence to population geography. Meanwhile, revenue-collecting activities needed to be organized around the geography of trade, wealth, and income. Finally, short-term political imperatives could contradict all of these considerations, so the spatial distribution of state activities often reflected the agendas of politically successful parties.[16] Attempts to reconcile the demands of extraction and war making produced distinctive forms of regional spatial organization, which was then renovated in accordance with new struggles, crises, and priorities.

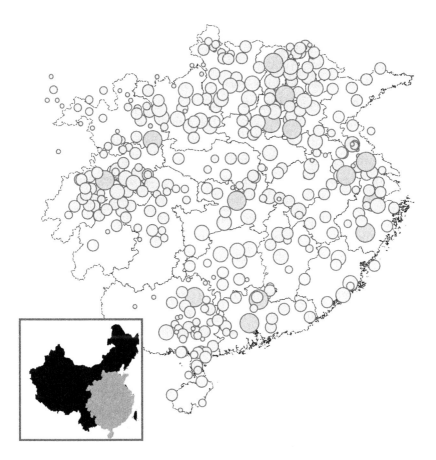

5.2. The distribution of jurisdictions in the Song dynasty roughly correlates to its core-periphery structure, though legacy decisions and anomalies remained. This map depicts the spatial distribution of the county-to-prefecture ratio. Each icon represents a prefecture, with its size based on the number of counties under its jurisdiction. Note the dense clusters of "mini-prefectures" around the northern and western perimeters of the realm. The inset map depicts the relatively small extent of the Song Empire compared to modern China.

This was the dynamic at work in Song China. The documentary record and the DGSD reveal that wealthy tax-bearing jurisdictions only required low expenditures and could function at large size and population: jurisdictions in the imperial core tended to be large unless they were vestiges of the spatial priorities of earlier eras. However, jurisdictions that served as colonial and military outposts in more fractious precincts required a dense imperial field presence relative to their size and population and tended to be small (see figure 5.2). The impulses were contradictory. Almost by definition, jurisdictions that required a significant government presence were unable to raise the revenue to support it based on local resources.

Compounding matters, Song fiscal policy presumed that each prefecture in the realm ought to be financially self-sufficient. The ideal of the bureaucratic state contradicted the reality of local financial autonomy. In many regions of the empire, prefectures were frequently in deficit.[17] When financial crisis became unsustainable, prefects had no alternative but to petition the court to revise the spatial organization of their districts, which could be expanded to create a larger tax base or contracted to reduce defense and administrative costs.[18] A great many territory-making decisions rested explicitly on revenue considerations. However, prefectures were also the core unit for military organization, and one of the main demands on prefecture revenue was for defense funding and provisioning armies. Prefecture revenue paid the salaries of the Prefectural Army troops stationed within their borders, and civil prefects directed military affairs.[19] In the year 1066, prominent statesman Ouyang Xiu 歐陽修 (1007–1072) attributed Song defeat in the war against the Tangut Xi Xia regime to the northwest to the fact that Song armies were stationed in close to two hundred small and decentralized forts and garrisons governed by twenty-four prefectures in five provinces.[20]

As the discussion above demonstrates, Song spatial change varied regionally because fiscal and military priorities had such different geographical implications. It had a distinctive history of temporal change as well. While HGIS is generally conceived as a methodology for revealing spatial variation, a historical gazetteer like the DGSD that is designed with spatial change event tracking in mind can be equally valuable for exploring and explaining temporal variation in spatial transformation. The following section is based upon SQL query, not analysis using GIS software, but it is equally a part of HGIS research.

As the timeline in figure 5.3 depicts, most Song spatial change clustered in three distinct eras. The mid-tenth-century Song founders capitalized on the successes of predecessor regimes that had developed pro-

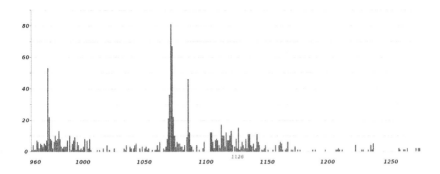

5.3. The timeline depicts the episodic character of spatial renovation in Song dynasty China. The 1,000-plus instances of Song spatial change are clustered into three eras, each of which lasted for several decades. Short-term politics, catastrophic events, and long-term structural issues all contributed to the transformation of the Song landscape.

cedures for wresting court control over resources from the tax-farming warlords who governed much of China in the ninth century. Making hundreds of adjustments to the spatial landscape during its founding decades, the Song regime created a unified spatial organization appropriate to a single imperial entity: it had a northern defense perimeter, separate political and commercial cores, and a remote southern frontier. One-third of all spatial change during this era transpired on the southern frontier, where the Song court consolidated remote, miasmic, and impoverished jurisdictions where civil officials refused to serve. The year 1005, when the Song court signed a peace treaty with its Khitan Liao neighbors to the north, marks the end of the founding generation, and spatial change essentially ceased the same year.

The eleventh century saw territorial ramifications resulting from real hostilities and imagined threats from pastoralist and tribal neighbors. The need to invest in a wartime landscape on the steppes required consolidating jurisdictions in the imperial core if they were secure and tendered little tax revenue while establishing new ones that could assist the court in capturing new sources of wealth or meeting its military objectives. During the New Policies reform era of the 1070s, provincial authority and revenue-sharing mechanisms expanded. As shown in figure 5.4, the most marginal jurisdictions in north China were abolished, with the demotions there supporting colonization initiatives and new

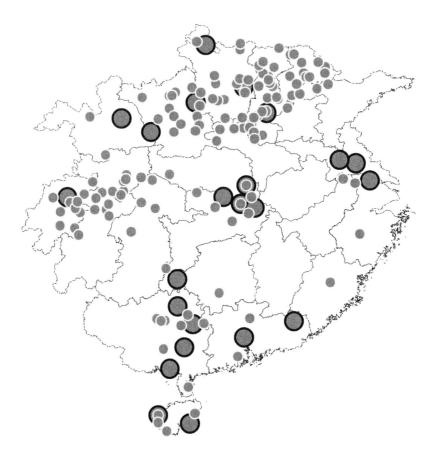

5.4. The Song spatial landscape was transformed during the 1070s reform era and the subsequent reaction. The state presence declined on the North China plain, in Sichuan, and in Guangnan, while the Yangzi watershed remained stable. Counties were abolished at a much higher rate than prefectures. This map depicts the counties (small icons) and prefectures (large icons) that were merged or demoted between 1067 and 1101.

jurisdictions on the periphery. Although two-thirds of the abolished jurisdictions were subsequently restored, the eleventh century still closed with a political landscape that had shifted toward a new southern center of gravity.

In 1127 the Song regime lost the northern half of its territory to Jurchen Jin invaders. A long and destructive war devastated farms and cities in the Song heartland, and at the end, a new international border cut through the middle of lands once controlled by the Song. An arc of new prefectures protected the new border, while an innovative policy allowed for jurisdictions to be temporarily demoted in the parts of the empire where the depredations of armies led to demographic collapse. As refugees moved into the far south, many jurisdictions that had been abolished two centuries before were restored. However, once a peace treaty was signed in 1142, the spatial landscape became almost completely stable for the last century of the Song reign.

Historical spatial analysis based upon the DGSD reveals that, as Charles Tilly would have predicted, Song state power varied spatially, since military geography, population geography, economic geography, and political factionalism each made different demands upon imperial organization. Song rulers faced contradictions between different ideal political landscapes as well as military crises and virulent factional politics. Nevertheless, Song spatial change adhered to a general pattern of consolidating jurisdictions located in political and economic cores while expanding them on settlement and military frontiers. However, the court's political capital was only sufficient to renovate the imperial landscape during three relatively brief eras of founding, reform, and revival. These findings are interesting for many topics in Chinese history; and it is our hope that they will help to inspire a new field in the spatial history of state power as well.

HGIS ANALYSIS CASE 2: INTEGRATING ENVIRONMENTAL AND GAZETTEER DATA: THE VIEW FROM THE YELLOW RIVER

The previous section of this essay explains the dynamics of spatial change and the politics of landscape at the scale of the regime and region. The DGSD, based upon data in Song national gazetteers and not upon local history or fieldwork, is well suited for researching spatial patterns of that extent. However, analysis at an imperial scale is not adequate to demonstrate why particular jurisdictions within a given area were maintained or abolished. For that, the DGSD needs to be integrated with other kinds of data. Until now, historians who have sought to move from large-scale reasoning to the explanation of particular cases of spatial change have utilized narrative and documentary historical sources rather than GIS. This has been our approach to investigating Song spatial history as well. However, extant documentary materials refer to only about 10 percent of all the spatial changes in the empire, and in most of those cases, only one document survives from what would have once been a complex paper trail. It is, therefore, important to develop approaches to local and regional spatial history that do not rely solely on documents.

Song officials themselves complained that some changes were made "randomly" and without regard for local circumstances.[21] Nevertheless, while contingency and personal advocacy help to explain the politics of spatial change, GIS is essential for developing a more nuanced and complex history of spatial organization in a particular region. In this section of the essay, we demonstrate that the DGSD, integrated with environmental systems data that provide higher regional resolution and additional spatial information, reveals significant spatial patterns of spatial change in the wake of environmental disaster. This approach suggests the contours of a GIS-based and ecologically informed regional history that incorporates historical gazetteer data.[22]

This section of the essay demonstrates that a catastrophic change in the course of the Yellow River in 1048, its aftermath, and the environmental degradation that preceded it had a significant effect upon the organization of political space. In a finding that reinforces the conclusions introduced in the previous section of this essay, we learned that the course change itself had little effect on the political landscape for twenty years, during a time when the court did not have an interest in renovating the landscape. However, when a reformist government came to power in the 1070s, spatial organizations around the new course and the old course were both transformed, though in distinctively different ways. The course change had been preceded by dramatic land-use intensification around the pastoralist frontiers near the upper course of the river and its watershed. That process impacted the environment downstream and is also amenable to spatial analysis.

The Yellow River is the most sediment-laden river in the world. Today it carries 1.6 billion tons of silt per year. Over 90 percent of that total comes from the middle reaches of the river – the contemporary

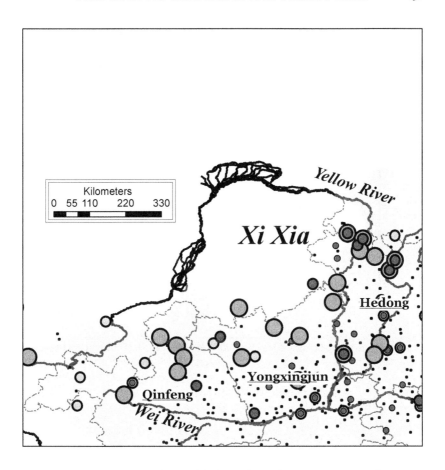

5.5. Song spatial change on and around the loess plateau from 960 to 1126. Newly founded prefectures, represented by light icons, expanded dramatically. Dark-shaded icons are jurisdictions that were demoted or consolidated. The stippled background denotes the extent of the loess plateau. Each prefecture could be associated with as many as two dozen forts and garrisons.

Gansu, Inner Mongolia, Shaanxi, and Henan provinces – which traverse the friable and erosion-prone loess plateau.[23] Owing primarily to instability caused by the heavy silt load, much of the lower course of the river was enclosed between levees as early as the third century BCE. In spite of that, the historical record attests to over fifteen hundred floods prior to the mid-twentieth century along with about thirty major course changes.[24]

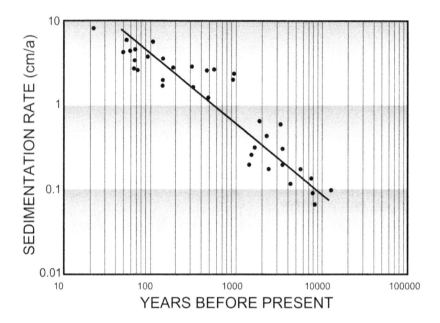

5.6. Change in sedimentation rate in the Yellow River during the Holocene era based on J. Xu, "Naturally and Anthropogenically Accelerated Sedimentation in the Lower Yellow River, China, over the Past 13,000 Years," *Geografiska Annaler. Series A, Physical Geography* 80 (1998): 67–78. Note the spectacular increase around the 1000 year BP mark, which is the time of the Northern Song.

During the tenth and eleventh centuries, the loess plateau was among the most intensively exploited new frontiers of the Song Empire. The region lay astride the border between the territory of the Song Empire and that of the Tangut Xi Xia, opponents in a lengthy rivalry and a four-year war from 1040 to 1044. Soon after taking power in 960, the Song commenced a massive garrison-building exercise and began to establish new prefectures in the loess plateau as well (see figure 5.5). Moreover, in a new innovation, officials called for garrisons to be populated by soldier-farmers who would fund their occupation by tilling and grazing on fragile loess soils.[25] New forts, garrisons, and farming regions were established on both sides of the border. There was a rapid increase in population and exposure of the fragile loess soils that lay beneath primeval forests and grasslands.

Recent work in geomorphology, summarized in figure 5.6, confirms that an abrupt increase in the sediment load carried by the Yellow River occurred about one thousand years ago, precisely the moment that pasture and forest clearing began to expose the soil there at a higher rate than ever before.[26] Scientists already assert that the shift resulted from a rapid increase in human activity on the loess plateau. Cultivation and deforestation on the loess plateau resulted in erosion, which discharged more sediment into the river.[27] Historical sources confirm that flooding, which had been infrequent for eight hundred years, escalated from the ninth and tenth centuries onward.[28]

Early eleventh-century erosion on the loess plateau had severe effects downriver. In the lower reaches of the river, especially from Henan province to the sea, the river drops in elevation by only 93.6 meters. As the river enters the plains, the silt carried from the middle reaches is deposited in the riverbed. In prehistoric times, the river meandered through wetlands and shallow lakes, changing its route whenever older beds filled with sediment. However, in historical times, residents and a state that had invested in cities and farms wished to prevent the river from breaching. They built levees higher and higher, until the riverbed loomed over the surrounding farmland.[29] Flood-prevention activities were not always effective, and even when they were, the plains become waterlogged and saline as a result of changes to the whole ecosystem. Seepage from the dikes increased the surrounding groundwater level and led to the formation of swampland. Salinization and other forms of soil deterioration reduced agricultural output.[30] Once it was constrained by levees, the river was locked into place. While population densities were high, the adjacent creeks and wetlands disappeared, diminishing opportunities for irrigation and making subsequent floods more violent. Water shortages and waterlogging were both common as wetlands and lakes were drained and floods persisted, while silt buildup dictated that wells had to be dug increasingly deep.[31]

The Yellow River maintained a stable course in its lower reaches from 11 to 1048 CE. This was its longest single era of stability in recorded history. Even before the shock of the eleventh-century silt increase, the lower course was old and fragile, and the agrarian ecology surrounding it was badly compromised. The natural ability of the river to control its course declined at the same time that the sediment load rose and the population grew. In 1048 a major breach of the Shanghu 商胡 dike (today a lake in the northeastern Henan city of Puyang 濮陽) led to a massive course change, its first in a thousand years, and one of fifty Yellow River floods during the Northern Song.[32]

In the wake of the 1048 flood, some one million people died or fled. Another million people died in a subsequent flood in 1068, and smaller floods occurred frequently.[33] The region around the new course became waterlogged, salinated, and deforested in the wake of the floods.[34] The area around the millennium-old course had already suffered the same outcomes, and a legacy of ecologically destructive land use compounded flooding there. Cities and market towns declined along tributaries that became dry or clogged with silt.[35]

In order to determine the effects of the course change on the organization of the political landscape, we have conducted a spatial analysis based upon two integrated datasets. The first is the DGSD. The other is a hydrological dataset that we developed that includes the pre- and post-1048 courses of the lower Yellow River, the middle and upper courses, a seventy-five-kilometer buffer on either side of each of those courses, and a larger hinterland around each course. We arbitrarily circumscribed the northern hinterland based on provincial and international boundaries and defined the southern hinterland to approximate the area of the northern one and to encompass similar floodplain terrain. The creation of two equal-area hinterlands allowed us to compare the density of the state presence in two regions. We also cataloged events of change to the political landscape between the course changes of 1048 and 1126.

Spatial and temporal analysis, summarized in figure 5.7 and table 5.1, exposes several previously indiscernible characteristics of the late Northern Song state presence in the lower Yellow River landscape. First, it reveals the spatial distribution of the state presence. The new course and the old course regions have distinctive political landscapes and spatial histories, even though they are both part of a similar north China plain ecology. The old course region – ecologically degraded and of limited strategic significance – supported relatively few counties and

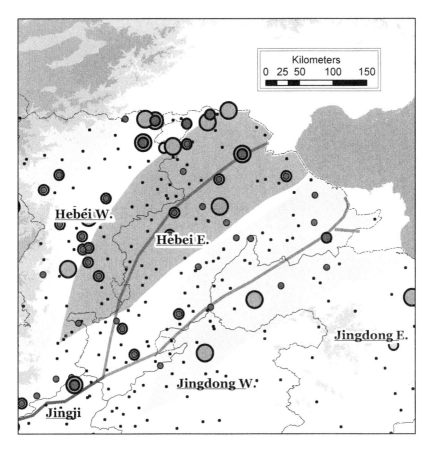

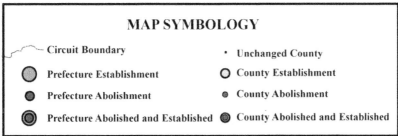

5.7. The pre- and post-1048 courses of the lower Yellow River and associated changes in the political landscape between 1048 and 1126. Buffer zones around the river courses are depicted in gray shades. The old river course is the southerly one, and the new river course is the northerly one.

Table 5.1. The distribution of the state presence and its changes during the study period

	Number of counties	Number of prefectures	Ratio of counties to prefectures	Number of established counties	Number of abolished counties	Percent abolition	Establishment/ Abolition	Prefecture establishment	Prefecture abolition
New core	63	13	4.1:1	12	16	25.4	75%	1	1
New hinter	108	25	4.32:1	17	25	23.1	68%	5	6
Old core	57	6	9.5:1	1	11	19.3	9%	2	0
Old hinter	80	12	6.7:1	2	11	13.75	18%	2	1

Note: These are the same data that figure 5.7 presents in map form.

remarkably few prefectures. The new course, with better prospects for agriculture and close proximity to a tense international border, was a different matter. Within the equalized-area hinterland, the old course had only three-quarters as many counties – the basic tax-bearing unit of Song administration – as the new one and only half as many prefectures – the higher-rank miniatures of the court that managed army garrisons. The difference in the county to prefecture ratio was even more pronounced in the core buffer around each river course. The county to prefecture ratio around the new course was in line with empire-wide averages, while the county to prefecture ratio around the old course was among the highest in the realm.[36] That is to say, not only were counties fewer in number around the old course than the new course, but prefectures were even more sparse. The state and particularly its military arm were less visible. Counties were one-third larger – less densely distributed – around the old course than the new one. From both a fiscal and a military point of view, state investment and intervention around the old course was relatively limited.

Second, spatial analysis reveals the chronology of spatial change. Surprisingly, spatial renovation did not begin for twenty years after the Yellow River course change. Rather than an immediate reaction to a crisis, late Northern Song spatial history around the Yellow River adhered to the pattern introduced in the previous section of this essay: that spatial renovation was associated with particular periods of state activism of relatively short duration. As in the rest of north China, during the 1070s reform decade, many counties were merged and demoted. During the 1080s, many were restored, and the restoration trend continued through the early 1100s. Although the location of the river course correlates with distinctive differences in the political landscape, the catastrophic flood event does not. Court politics and policies dictated the renovation of the political landscape even in the wake of environmental cataclysm. In the Song context, structural and political affairs dictated spatial change more than particular events, even highly impactful ones.

Nevertheless, once changes to the spatial landscape began to occur, the renovations were significant, and the pattern of change differed between the two regions. Prefecture geography remained stable in both regions. However, in the new course region, a quarter of all counties were demoted or merged, though three-quarters of them were subsequently restored. By contrast, in the old course region, less than a fifth of counties were abolished, but almost all of the abolitions persisted.

The course change did influence reform-era administrators considering spatial renovation. In one case, the Hebei county of Qianning 乾宁 in the new course region, the historical record explicitly notes that the jurisdiction was demoted in the early 1070s as a result of continuing devastation in the wake of the Shanghu levee break and restored in 1088 when refugees returned to their homes and the population of the former county surpassed ten thousand households.[37] While we have not yet identified other documents explicitly linking changing political geography and Yellow River catastrophe, it is reasonable to believe that this case is representative. Flooding disrupted settlements equally around the old course and the new course; but long-term environmental degradation affected the old course more severely and probably refugee decisions as well. In addition, beginning in the 1070s, the government initiated ambitious and labor-intensive water-control measures in the new course region; these activities required a more dense state presence there.[38] This, even more than environmental degradation, may explain the differential rate of county restoration in the two regions.

This section of the essay is an early-stage experiment in integrating political geography and demographic data from the DGSD with widely available environmental information. The preliminary results are promising in demonstrating that environmental change, though not catastrophic crisis, affected the political landscape. However, much more remains to be done, particularly to incorporate census data. Further analysis of this phenomenon would also benefit from more mathematically sophisticated spatial analysis that would allow for the evaluation of multiple variables simultaneously – including population, proximity to the international border, and proximity to the old or new course of the river – rather than considering them sequentially and making inferences about their relationship. In order to support more complex spatial statistical analysis, the data that we have utilized thus far also need to be integrated with other spatial data, including soil, terrain, flood events, and transportation routes, and with additional georeferenced demographic and historical information, including tax rates, tax exemptions, population, and battles. Finally, while historical spatial analysis can generate conclusions, it is also a research tool. An important future step in this project is to use the GIS to identify particular jurisdictions that typified larger patterns or diverged from them and search for documentary evidence about them in the historical record.

CONCLUSIONS AND METHODOLOGICAL IMPLICATIONS

This essay explores several interrelated premises about HGIS methodology and about the spatial history of China's Song era. First, it asserts that the distribution of administrative units represents state power manifested as geography. At the spatial scale of the entire empire, variations in the character and density of the state presence are the evidence and the residue of policies about war, taxation, and colonization. Second, it explains that data organization for spatial history has a semantic and that the Digital Gazetteer of the Song Dynasty, the database utilized for this research, is tuned toward analyzing a frequently changing political landscape. Finally, it demonstrates that integrating the gazetteer with ecological information in a GIS makes it possible to study spatial history at the scale of a watershed and suggests possible correlations between geopolitics, ecology, and spatial politics. Support for reasoning at multiple scales is a benefit of HGIS. This essay demonstrates that spatial history methods can help scholars to move between multiple geographies, bridging the divide that has often existed between local history and political history. As historian Richard White points out, "When historians move to the regional, national and transnational scales, not only does the detail usually fall away, but the region and the nation often become mere containers. Spatial analysis matters less and less as the scale increases."[39] In this essay, while remaining within a GIS framework, we have explained phenomena in a consistent way that extends from the river course to the empire.

This work also underscores the need for incorporating events and processes into the HGIS field. As historical geographer Anne Knowles has observed, "Historians seek causal explanations by establishing the temporal sequence of events. Geographers find causation in the spatial proximity or distance of conditions."[40] Incorporating spatial change into gazetteer data models as in the DGSD is one way to integrate temporal and spatial reasoning. Using spatial analysis to evaluate the relative significance of catastrophic events and long-term processes, as in the Yellow River experiment, is another.

NOTES

1. In spite of a sustained interest in historical gazetteers organized by administrative units, the field of historical GIS has not notably considered the spatial history of state power as a research topic. The administrative units of historical gazetteers have more often been used as containers for census data and as the basis for demographic analysis.

2. This and all other claims about the Song political landscape in this essay are derived from our Digital Gazetteer of the Song Dynasty, vol. 1.1 (2010), http://song gis.ucmercedlibrary.info.

3. See, for instance, R. Hartwell, "Demographic, Political and Social Transformations of China, 750–1550," *Harvard Journal of Asiatic Studies* 42 (1982): 365–442.

4. H. Wright, *An Alphabetical List of Geographical Names in Sung China* (Albany, N.Y.: Journal of Sung-Yuan Studies, 1992).

5. China HGIS, http://www.fas.harvard.edu/~chgis; Chinese Civilization in Time and Space Project, http://ccts.sinica.edu.tw; Robert Hartwell China Historical Studies GIS, http://www.fas.harvard.edu/~chgis/data/hartwell.

6. For additional details about the creation of the DGSD and the ingest of point locations from related GIS projects, please consult the DGSD website.

7. For an excellent review of the history of this term, see A. K. Knowles, "GIS and History," in *Placing History: How Maps, Spatial Data and GIS Are*

Changing Historical Scholarship, ed. A. K. Knowles (Redlands, Calif.: ESRI Press, 2008), 1–25.

8. In an earlier article on this topic, Mostern discussed the possibilities for event-based spatial history modeling. See R. Mostern and I. Johnson, "From Named Place to Naming Event: Creating Gazetteers for History," *International Journal of Geographic Information Science* 22 (2008): 1091–1108.

9. V. Kantabutra, J. B. Owens, D. P. Ames, C. N. Burns, and B. Stephenson, "Using the Newly-Created ILE DBMS to Better Represent Temporal and Historical GIS Data," *Transactions in GIS* 14 (2010): 39–58. The DGSD is not a fully realized example of Kantabutra and Owens's Intentionally Linked Entity model. Nevertheless, the intention of the DGSD is similar to the ILE.

10. L. Hill, *Georeferencing: The Geographic Associations of Information* (Cambridge, Mass.: MIT Press, 2006).

11. For a review of historical gazetteer data models, see Kantabutra et al., "Using the Newly-Created ILE DBMS"; and also M. L. Berman, "Modeling and Visualizing Historical Gazetteer Data" (2009), http://www.fas.harvard.edu/~chgis/work/docs/papers/CGA_Wkshp2009_Lex_9apr09.pdf.

12. The China Historical GIS (CHGIS) maintains multiple change events and attributes in its main entity table, recording multiple historical instances as multiple entities. It uses a "part of" table to link

related entities with one another. See P. Bol, "The China Historical Geographic Information System (GIS): Choices Faced, Lessons Learned" (2007), http://www.fas.harvard.edu/~chgis/work/docs/papers/BOL_CHGIS_Lessons_Learned.pdf.

13. This section of the essay summarizes R. Mostern's book *Dividing the Realm in Order to Govern: The Spatial Organization of the Song State (960–1276 CE)* (Cambridge, Mass.: Harvard Asia Center, 2011).

14. Hartwell, "Demographic, Political and Social Transformation."

15. C. Tilly, *Coercion, Capital and European States, 990–1992*, vol. 1 (Cambridge: Blackwell, 1992), 125.

16. Ibid.

17. S. Wang 汪聖鐸, *Liang Song caizheng shi* 兩宋財政史 (Beijing: Zhonghua shuju, 1995), 529–34.

18. W. Bao 包偉民, Songdai difang caizheng shi yanjiu 宋代地方財政史 究 (Shanghai: Shanghai guji chubanshe, 2001), 71–72.

19. Z. Wang 王曾瑜, *Songdai bingzhi chutan* 宋朝兵制初探 (Beijing: Zhonghua shuju, 1983). This discussion is also indebted to C. Hucker, *A Dictionary of Official Titles in Imperial China* (Stanford, Calif.: Stanford University Press, 1985), 46.

20. T. Li 李燾, *Xu zizhi tongjian changbian* 續資治通鑑長編, 5 vols. (1183; Shanghai: Xinhua shudian, 1986), 204.4a–b.

21. Ibid., 365.8756–57, 407.9908–9.

22. G. Cunfer, *On the Great Plains: Agriculture and Environment* (College Station: Texas A&M University Press, 2005); and J. W. Wilson, "Historical and Computational Analysis of Long-Term Environmental Change: Forest in the Shenandoah Valley of Virginia" (Ph.D. diss., University of Maryland, 2005) are two very compelling works of HGIS focused on environmental matters, though with less attention to political geography and state power.

23. L. Gong 龔莉 et al., *Huanghe shihua* 黃河史話 (Beijing: Zhongguo Dabaike Quanshu Chubanshe, 2007), 96–98.

24. Ibid., 87; and M. Ren, R. Yang, and H. Bao, *Zhongguo ziran dili gangyao* (Beijing: Shangwu, 1979), 168, cited in P. C. Huang, *The Peasant Economy and Social Change in North China* (Stanford, Calif.: Stanford University Press, 1985), 59.

25. Gong, *Huanghe shihua*, 157–60; and R. Mostern, "Cartography on the Song Frontier: Making and Using Maps in the Song-Xia Conflict: Evidence from *Changbian* and *Song huiyao*," in *Proceedings of the Third International Symposium on Ancient Chinese Books and Records of Science and Technology* (Beijing: Daxiang chubanshe, 2004), 147–52.

26. J. Xu, "Naturally and Anthropogenically Accelerated Sedimentation in the Lower Yellow River, China, over the Past 13,000 Years," *Geografiska Annaler, Series A, Physical Geography* 80 (1998): 67–78, 72.

27. Y. Saito, Z. Yang, and K. Hori, "The Huanghe (Yellow River) and Changjiang (Yangzi River) Deltas: A Review on Their Characteristics, Evolution and Sediment Discharge during the Holocene," *Geomorphology* 41 (2001): 219–31.

28. L. Zhang, "Changing with the Yellow River: An Environmental History of Hebei, 1048–1128," *Harvard Journal of Asiatic Studies* 69 (2009): 1–36, 4.

29. Gong, *Huanghe shihua*, 99–101.

30. J. Xu, "A Study of Long Term Environmental Effects of River Regulation on the Yellow River of China in Historical Perspective," *Geografiska Annaler, Series A, Physical Geography* 75 (1993): 61–72, 65–66.

31. Gong, *Huanghe shihua*, 151.

32. E. Economy, *The River Runs Black: The Environmental Challenge to China's Future* (Ithaca, N.Y.: Cornell University Press, 2004), 39.

33. Zhang, "Changing with the Yellow River," 2.

34. Ibid., passim.

35. Ibid., 16.

36. Mostern, *Dividing the Realm,* chap. 2.

37. S. Xu 徐松, ed., *Song huiyao jigao* 宋會要輯稿, 8 vols. (1809; Beijing: Zhonghua shuju, 1957), *fangyu* 5.29b–30a.

38. Zhang, "Changing with the Yellow River," 22. Zhang explains that population growth, prosperity, and silk production all flourished in the old course region after 1048. If this – rather than our hypothesis of decline – is correct, it makes the relatively low density of counties and prefectures there even more intriguing. See ibid., 34.

39. R. White, foreword in Knowles, *Placing History,* x.

40. Knowles, "GIS and History," 3.

SIX

Mapping the City in Film

JULIA HALLAM AND LES ROBERTS

IN THIS CHAPTER WE EXAMINE HOW GEOSPATIAL COMPUTING tools such as GIS can contribute to an understanding of the development of local film culture and its contribution to projections of "place," drawing on archival research into Liverpool and Merseyside on film. We will map some of the contradictory and ambiguous spatialities that historically have mediated ideas of "the local" and "the regional" in a range of moving image genres, exploring the correlations between categories of genre, date, and location as assessed in relation to records in a spatial database consisting of over seventeen hundred films shot in Merseyside from 1897 to the 1980s. Significantly, the use of GIS has revealed the ways in which particular styles and genres of filmmaking create their own cinematic maps, initiating new modes of spatial dialogue between the virtual landscapes of the moving image and the architectural, geographic, and imagined spaces within which they are embedded.

A provincial city on the Mersey estuary in England's northwest of around four hundred thousand people, Liverpool is internationally renowned for its football teams (Liverpool and Everton), its music (the 1960s Mersey sound and the Beatles), its infamous slave-trading past, and the three buildings at the Pier Head that dominate its iconic waterfront – the Royal Liver, Cunard, and Port Authority buildings, colloquially known as the "Three Graces." Granted UNESCO world heritage status in 2004 for its innovative enclosed dock systems and grand nineteenth-century neoclassical civic buildings, the once-thriving port, deemed in the nineteenth century the "second city" of the British Empire, has reinvented itself for the twenty-first century as a postindustrial city dependent, at least in part, on heritage and cultural tourism for its continuing economic development and prosperity. The city shared this pattern of growth, decline, and regeneration with many port cities in Europe and North America during the nineteenth and twentieth centuries, their fortunes ebbing and flowing with the shifting tides of global capital and commercial trade.

The films collated in the City in Film database document urban life throughout a century of decline, redevelopment, and reinvention. Visitors passing through the city in the 1890s, many of them European migrants on their way to a new life in the United States aboard the liners that plied the Atlantic trade route between Liverpool and New York, could marvel at the nine miles of busy docklands by traveling the length of the waterfront on the first electric overhead railway in the world. This was a journey taken by Jean Alexandre Promio, a cameraman working for the Lumière Brothers who recorded the first moving images of the docks from one of the railway carriages in one of the first known instances of a "tracking" shot (*Panorama pris du chemin de fer électrique*, Lumière Brothers, 1897). Promio also recorded the modern, architecturally innovative office blocks in the commercial district around the Strand, Water Street, Castle Street, and Dale Street, capturing the busy shoppers on adjacent Lord Street and Church Street (*Church Street*, Lumière Brothers, 1897) and the vestments of civic pride enshrined in the grandeur of St. George's Hall, shot from St. George's Plateau, just outside Lime Street railway station (*Lime Street*, Lumière Brothers, 1897). Based on a reading of the length of the shadows in Promio's images, it seems probable that, like many visitors to the city, Promio arrived at Lime Street and recorded his images, crossing St. George's Plateau as he traveled from the station to the waterfront via the main thoroughfare, Church Street.[1]

Today, the neoclassical hall and the accompanying buildings on the Plateau (the Walker Art Gallery, the William Brown and Picton Libraries in tandem with the Albert Dock, and the Three Graces at the Pier Head) form the core of the maritime mercantile city. Unusually, the city boasts two cathedrals, both built in the twentieth century. The impos-

ing Anglican Cathedral, designed by Giles Gilbert Scott in 1903 in the
Gothic Revival style, is the fifth largest cathedral in the world. Towering
above the commercial district and Liverpool's Chinatown on St. James's
Mount, it took seventy-four years to build and was finally completed in
1978. Facing it, close to the University of Liverpool's Victoria Building
at the other end of Hope Street, is the Metropolitan Cathedral of Christ
the King, a modernist building affectionately known locally as "Paddy's
wigwam," built in the 1960s. Investment in the 1960s sought to improve
road access in and around the city by constructing a second Mersey
tunnel in the midst of the close-knit, inner-city, working-class district
of Scotland Road, close to the first tunnel entrance (opened in 1934) behind St. George's Hall at the bottom of William Brown Street. Other developments included a modern indoor shopping complex opposite Lime
Station on the site of the old fruit and vegetable market; the imposing
tower, topped by a revolving restaurant, now forms part of Liverpool's
iconic skyline. The twenty-first century has witnessed the building of a
new shopping and leisure complex, Liverpool One, opposite the Albert
Docks on the site of the old Customs House (bombed during the Second World War), the development of an arena and conference center
on the former Kings Dock, the opening of a new cruise ship terminal at
the Pier Head, and the construction of the largest newly built national
museum in the UK for over a hundred years, the Museum of Liverpool.[2]

Films made in and about the city focus on many of these developments, charting changes in the urban landscape and the effects of these
often controversial regeneration schemes on the city's many and varied
communities. The mapping database has been developed in part with
museum curators who, inspired by the City in Film project, have begun
the task of georeferencing and digitizing materials and artifacts relating
to the Merseyside area in the collections of National Museums Liverpool. These are being housed in a permanent electronic resource modeled
on a GIS database in the new Museum of Liverpool "history detectives"
gallery (opened in 2011), which enables public access via a map-based
touch-screen interface to images, films, and audio that begin to reveal
the distinctive histories and identities of the people and places of the
Mersey region.

FILM MAPPINGS

Intellectually, the project draws on and develops from work into the relationship between film and place, a relationship that has principally focused on the city as a space in which the activities of filmmaking and filmgoing form a nexus of enquiry informed by interdisciplinary and multidisciplinary perspectives. Following the "spatial turn" in the humanities and social sciences in the 1990s, the term "mapping" has gathered significance.[3] A growing vanguard of researchers is studying the relationship between film, space, and place from disciplines that range from geography, urban studies, architecture, and history to literature, film, media, and cultural studies. What motivates much of the work across this apparently disparate field is an interest in the ways in which the interdisciplinary study of moving images, and the cultures of distribution and consumption that develop in tandem with the production of those images, provides renewed insights into our knowledge of the development of urban modernity and modern subjectivity. In his survey of the emerging field of what may loosely be termed "cinematic cartography," Les Roberts explores the different ways in which "thinking spatially" underpins a growing body of research on film and the moving image, noting that it is becoming increasingly difficult to gauge what is meant by the spatial turn and the ubiquitous trope of mapping, which is found in much contemporary cultural criticism.[4] Echoing Henri Lefebvre's argument that space is culturally and materially reproduced as part of lived everyday reality, Roberts argues that there is a need to situate and embed visual cultures in social and material landscapes and to explore or "map" the interplay between the representational and the material.[5] In film studies, for example, although there has been theoretical concern with genealogical mappings of the discursive terrain that created the conditions that we now know as cinema, the dynamic and dialectical interplay between different generic spatial formations and their role in the material and symbolic production of social space is less well explored.[6] Responding to Giuliana Bruno's suggestion that film is a form of "modern cartography," Roberts identifies some of the different ways that film and cartography have begun to find convergence, theoretically, methodologically, and practically, creating a number of strands in the emerging field of what can be broadly defined as "cin-ematic cartography."[7] These are briefly summarized in the following five paragraphs.

The first of these categories and the one that is most securely ground-ed in the material and symbolic aspects of place is the mapping of film production and reception. In the United States, scholars such as Robert C. Allen and Jeffrey Klenotic have begun to explore the use of Geograph-ical Information Systems (GIS) and digital mapping in historical studies of film distribution and consumption. As Allen points out, despite the "historical turn" that has shaped recent directions in film scholarship, as a discipline "film studies continues to be dogged by ambivalence to-wards the use of empirical methods."[8] Identifying the potential that re-sources such as GIS can offer the film historian, scholars such as Allen are therefore pushing forward research in this area in new, significant, and productive ways. Allen's project Going to the Show uses over 750 Sanborn Fire Insurance maps of 45 towns and cities in North Carolina between 1896 and 1922. Drawing on a dataset featuring information on 1,300 movie venues identified from the maps and an extensive archive of contextual materials, such as newspaper advertisements and articles, photographs, architectural drawings, and city directories, Going to the Show "situates early movie going within the experience of urban life in the state's big cities and small towns. It highlights the ways that race con-ditioned the experience of movie going for all North Carolinians – white, African American, and American Indian."[9] Similarly, Klenotic is using GIS technology to explore the social and geographic contexts of film dis-tribution and exhibition in New Hampshire.[10] Both Allen and Klenotic are part of the HoMER network (History of Moviegoing, Exhibition and Reception), an international group of film scholars established in 2004 whose aim is to "promote understanding of the complex, international phenomena of filmgoing, exhibition, and reception."[11] The development and subsequent availability of database collations of data relating to film practices – whether in terms of production and exhibition, or geogra-phies of consumption and location, or information on genre, studio loca-tions, and patterns of distribution – has meant that cartographic meth-ods of geohistorical analysis are now increasingly recognized as valuable tools for historical research on film.[12]

The second category of "cinematic cartography," film-related tourism, represents an area that has developed into something of a global phenomenon in recent years, prompting the publication not only of movie maps of cities and regions (often as tie-ins to major film releases) but also of a string of film-tourism travel guides that have become a focus of research into movie-mapping and place-marketing. The British Tourism Authority's (BTA) *Movie Map of Britain* (1990) was the first national campaign that sought to capitalize on the economic potential of film-related tourism; the map became BTA's (now Visit Britain) most successful printed product. The organization has since gone on to produce a series of movie maps and has become a global player in the film tourism market. Working with film production and distribution companies, Visit Britain has developed dedicated film tourism offices in Los Angeles and Mumbai and typically plans its location maps with movie studios at least twelve months in advance of the date of a major film release.[13] Film tourism has brought with it growing convergence between the film and tourism industries, with each providing mutually reinforcing promotional tie-ins and product or brand awareness designed to stimulate both the consumption of place (the economic imperative of the tourism, leisure, and cultural industries) and the consumption of film and television productions. A number of recent studies have examined the economic impacts or potential of this form of destination marketing, although studies that address the social, cultural, and geographic impacts of film-related tourism remain comparatively underdeveloped.[14]

By way of contrast, recent approaches in film studies have focused on the ways in which maps are embedded in feature films; as Tom Conley points out, "Since the advent of narrative in cinema – which is to say, from its very beginnings – maps are inserted in the field of the image to indicate where action 'takes place.'"[15] In Sébastien Caquard's discussion of cinematic maps – or "cinemaps" – he argues that early animated maps in films such as Fritz Lang's *M* (1931) predated many of the future functions of modern digital cartography, such as the use of sound, shifts in perspectives, and the combination of realistic images and cartographic symbols. Caquard suggests that professional cartographers can learn much from the study of cinematic techniques used by Lang and other filmmakers in terms of their status as cinematic precursors to modern forms of mediated cartography.[16] Conley also examines the use of maps in feature films focusing on examples from postwar cinema.[17] Conley's approach to what he terms "cartographic cinema" can be defined in terms of its focus on the geographic and representational cartographies contained within the diegesis and on the psychological and affective forms of mapping that are mobilized between film and viewer in terms of his or her subjectivity and psychic positionality.

Similarly focusing on feature films, Bruno's *Atlas of Emotions* provides a detailed theoretical exposition of the ways in which the affective properties of the cinematic medium play host to mappings of the psychic and emotional topographies that are given form in the immaterial architectures that structure the complex interplay between spatial textualities of film and the subjective "navigation" of these spaces by the viewer and spectator. For Bruno, the psychogeographic mobilities and affective geometries that are unleashed by film and other forms of moving image culture prompt renewed critical understanding not only of the ways we might read or "map" the spaces of film but also of how the forms and architectures of urban space might shape theoretical, aesthetic, and practical reengagements with cities themselves: "Mapping is the shared terrain in which the architectural-filmic bond resides – a terrain that can be fleshed out by rethinking practices of cartography for travelling cultures, with an awareness of the inscription of emotion within this motion. Indeed, by way of filmic representation, geography itself is being transformed and (e)mobilized. . . . A frame for cultural mappings, film is *modern cartography*."[18] Conley's cartographic cinema treads a similar theoretical terrain to that of Bruno, noting that even if a film does not feature a map as part of its narrative, "by nature [film] bears an implicit relation with cartography. . . . Films *are* maps insofar as each medium can be defined as a form of what cartographers call 'locational media.'"[19] In a similar vein, Teresa Castro's discussion of the "mapping impulse" refers to a "visual regime," a way of seeing the world that has cartographic affinities.[20] Cinematic cartography here refers less to the presence of maps per se in films than to the cultural, perceptual, and cognitive processes that inform understandings of place and space. Focusing on what she describes as "cartographic shapes," Castro argues that "panoramas" (viewpoints shaping synoptic and spatially coherent

landscapes and vistas), "atlases" (visual archives and spatiovisual as-
semblies), and "aerial views" ("god's-eye" or bird's-eye perspectives from
planes or hot-air balloons) define a cinematic topography in which the
mapping impulse is a central cognitive element. Drawing attention to
the broad and complex theoretical terrain within which mapping and
cartographic practices are embedded, Castro notes that "mapping can
therefore refer to a multitude of processes, from the cognitive operations implied in the structuring of spatial knowledge to the discursive
implications of a particular visual regime."[21]

Finally, the last category in Roberts's suggested five-point typol-
ogy of cinematic cartographies is what the artist and filmmaker Patrick
Keiller has dubbed "film as spatial critique."[22] To date, the most productive resource for research in this area has been archival film materials
from the early days of film (1890s–1910s) and the postwar period (1950s–
1970s). In the case of the latter, archival research into Liverpool on film
illustrates ways in which a spatial reading of films of postwar urban landscapes exposes and articulates some of the contested or contradictory
spatialities emerging during this period as a result of large-scale and
controversial modernist urban planning, which left its destructive stamp
on many cities during the 1960s and 1970s.[23]

In contrast to the emphasis on feature films in all the above approaches, the University of Liverpool's City in Film project is the first attempt to comprehensively map the wide range of genres and production
practices that have contributed to how the local and regional has been
perceived and projected in moving image media.[24] Focusing on factual
productions, over 1,700 items have been cataloged, ranging from actualities, travelogues, newsreel footage, amateur and independent productions, promotional material, and campaign videos and enabling in-depth
analysis and the development of a socially and spatially embedded reading of what Roberts has termed "the archive city."[25] As well as cataloging
the films using conventional data such as title, producer, date, duration,
format, and so on, wherever possible the films have been viewed and
cataloged according to the buildings and locations depicted and their
spatial function and use. This has enabled us to study in some depth the
dynamic ways in which moving images are invested in the everyday production of locality, space, and subjective identities and how particular

genres engage with a historically contingent geography of place. Transferring the City in Film catalog to a GIS platform enables the development of a more refined process of geohistorical analysis as well as the
production of a range of georeferenced contextual materials, including
digitized segments of particular films, interviews with filmmakers, cine
society programmes, company/organizational material, and supporting
documentation. The use of GIS also enables the research team to situate the content of films listed in the catalog using digital mapping tools,
informing understandings of the ways in which the city is visualized by
specific genres and at particular times. Furthermore, the mapping process is enabling a fruitful dialogic tension to emerge between different
perceptions of place and identity as they are articulated in specific genres
and filmmaking practices.

LOCATING THE CITY IN FILM

The use of the name Merseyside to depict a regional area raises the first
problem that this research had to confront, that of the blurred and shifting boundaries between the city and its hinterland. Using Ordnance
Survey maps from the 1890s to the present and historical boundary data,
we can trace how the changing political and administrative boundaries
of the city and its hinterland have shaped the cinematic geography of the
films at different times. One of the questions that quickly emerge when
mapping a city's representation in film is where to draw the boundaries
that define the urban area. What or where is the object that is the "city
in film"? At the start of our research the area bounded by the inner ring
road to the east that demarcates the inner core of the nineteenth-century city from its twentieth-century suburban and industrial hinterland
(Queens Drive) and the natural border of the River Mersey to the west
and south marked out the area that was initially to be the geographical
focus of enquiry. This was in large part a practical consideration – the
need to delimit the amount of potential research material. However, as
the current City in Film map of Liverpool and Merseyside shows, attempts to "geographically fix" a clearly defined urban spatial area have
proved problematic, an indication that many of what can or could be
regarded as "Liverpool films" takes us, by default, to consider a more

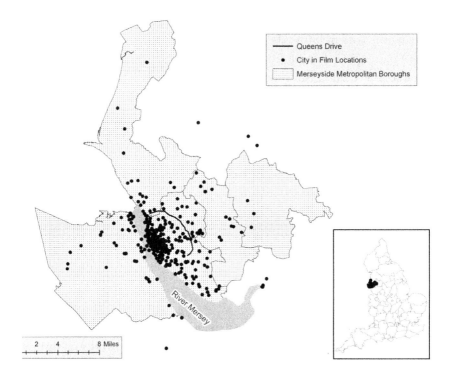

6.1. Map of Merseyside film locations showing the Queens Drive boundary.

regionally defined object of enquiry. As might be expected, the densest cluster of locations is found in and adjacent to the central areas around the Pier Head, William Brown Street, and Hope Street (Vauxhall, Everton, Dingle, and Abercromby Wards), the areas that form the central axis of the city and house its principal civic, commercial, and religious buildings and arts, education, entertainment, and leisure venues, but there are numerous locations in outlying districts beyond the Queens Drive boundary clustered around the airport at Speke, the racecourse at Aintree, and the wealthier suburban areas (figure 6.1).

Since the earliest of moving image representations of Liverpool was filmed from a carriage on the Overhead Railway in 1897 (the Lumière Brothers' *Panorama pris du chemin de fer électrique*), transport has continued to be an important feature of films made in and around the city, a factor that has demanded close analysis of the role of transport infra-

structures in historical representations of the city in film. The radial geometries that connect the urban landscape of Liverpool with the urban,
suburban, and regional geographies of the wider Merseyside area prompt
consideration of the networks and practices of mobility that have shaped
the historical development of the city and region. However, other factors shaping the historical geography of film practice in Liverpool and
Merseyside have also had an important impact on where or, indeed,
how we might draw the boundaries that delimit and define our object of
enquiry. The redrawing of administrative boundaries, for example, can
have the obvious effect of placing or (more crucially) displacing moving
image geographies that formed clearly defined areas of film, place, and
urban identity. A good case in point is the example of Southport, a town
some thirty miles from Liverpool that was formerly part of the county
of Lancashire but that, following the creation of Merseyside in 1974,
is now in Sefton, one of the five metropolitan boroughs of Merseyside
(alongside Knowsley, Liverpool, St. Helens, and Wirral). In conducting
a longitudinal study of archive films of Liverpool, therefore, the shifting civic and geographic status of films historically aligned to different
county and administrative authorities needs to be taken into account.
Like Southport, Bootle, an independent county borough until 1974, is
now part of Sefton. As a consequence of the redrawing of administrative
boundaries, films shot in areas such as Bootle, including many of the
early Mitchell and Kenyon series of actuality films made of the city in
1900–1901 such as *Employees Leaving Alexandra Docks, Liverpool* (1901)
and the first reconstructed actuality film, *Arrest of Goudie* (1901), have
become incorporated within a cinematic geography that brings them
into neighboring alignment with Crosby and Seaforth in the borough
of Sefton.[26] Prior to the movement of the docks to the river mouth at
Seaforth, the historical importance of the dock industries at Bootle has
meant that the town's former imaginaries of place were more closely associated with those of Liverpool, three miles to the south.

    While the geographic relocation of local, place-based films may be
of only marginal significance in terms of the broader meanings and
contextual framings that we might otherwise extract from readings of
archival film material, ethnographic research amongst filmmakers in
Merseyside has drawn critical attention toward the contested nature of

the "place" and identity of local film cultures in the region. Responding to the question as to whether he regards himself as a Merseyside
filmmaker, Jim Morris, a member of Southport Movie Makers, an amateur film club established in 1949, pointed out that his filmmaking colleagues, as well as people in Southport more generally, have tended to
set themselves apart (symbolically and geographically) from "Merseyside," drawing a boundary somewhere around Crosby that excludes the
nearby heavily industrialized dockland areas such as Seaforth, now in
south Sefton:

> When I first came to Southport it was in Lancashire, and then it became
> Merseyside. Well, that didn't bother me . . . but [for another member of the
> club] anywhere south of Crosby he doesn't know; [and] *Liverpool* . . . ? [laughs]
> And that is the attitude of a lot of people in Southport. . . . It is always a sore
> point in Southport. . . . "Sefton," well, I think they perhaps accept Sefton as a
> more suitable title, but "Merseyside"? – I think they associate that word with
> all that is bad.[27]

The imagined geography represented by such views encompasses rural
Formby, an affluent middle-class coastal town to the south of Southport,
but not industrial Bootle and other urban areas nearer to Liverpool.

This example demonstrates some of the problems that arise when
attempting to map and place local film cultures. Film location sites, as
merely points on the map or polygon data, narrate a spatial story that
elides the more fuzzy dynamics of lived and symbolic space. The incorporation of qualitative data in the form of video and audio files of
interviews, oral histories, and other ethnographic-based materials on the
GIS platform provides for a more nuanced reading of a city or region's
film geographies. This anthropological approach to visual cultures of
space and place allows for a greater recognition of the fluid, open, and
contested nature of geographic boundaries. Moreover, to include the
work of Southport-based filmmakers on our GIS film map of Merseyside
is itself to misrepresent the locally refined sense of place that has shaped
and defined the habitus and identity of members from Southport Movie
Makers. By attaching qualitative data to point data on the map, we are
thus able to chart a more representative view of how film geographies
are perceived and articulated by those who both produce and consume
local films.

MAPPING URBAN FILM GENRES

A breakdown by film genre enables a more precise mapping of the shape and form of local production practices over time and the ways in which these processes reflect or create exceptions to national and international trends and developments in terms of the kinds of practices that develop and the types of films made. Mapping the locations that appear in different genres of the city film highlights the extent to which specific production practices construct and project different ideas and spatial perceptions of the city, with particular locations serving to convey, for instance, a "civic vision," as typically can be found in promotional films produced by local councils and municipal authorities.[28] As we discuss below, these may be contrasted with genres in which locations are suggestive of an altogether different sense of place and urban imaginary.

Focusing on the city center area of Liverpool, the patterns observable in locations mapped across film genres demonstrate the ways in which a city's cinematic geographies reflect what can perhaps more accurately be described as *cities* in film: a mosaic of overlapping representations of the city's urban landscape that convey the different meanings attached to specific discourses and practices surrounding the production of city films. If we chart the locations featured in "official" productions, such as newsreels and promotional films, we can form an overall impression of the type of locations and landscapes that shape the cinematic geography of these generic representations.

The map of locations in newsreel productions (figure 6.2) reveals an overall emphasis on spaces associated with industry and commerce (docks, the Royal Liver building, Water Street, hotels), transport links (including the two Mersey road tunnels, the Lime Street railway station, and the Overhead Railway), civic buildings and monuments (Town Hall, Municipal Buildings, St. George's Hall, the Cenotaph, the Wellington Monument), places of worship (the city's Anglican and Metropolitan Cathedrals, St. Nicholas' Church), and education institutions and associated locations (the University of Liverpool and Royal Liverpool Hospital). Strongly reflective of the city's institutions, engineering prowess (Queensway and Kingsway road tunnels), and proud civic identity, the

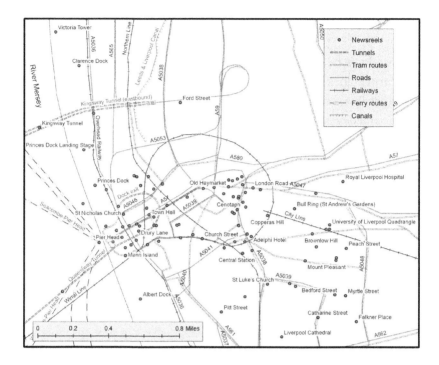

6.2. Liverpool city center map showing locations in newsreel films.

newsreels depict a city shaped by events linked with broader national interests; the local and vernacular are thus less at the forefront in terms of the locations and landmarks represented on-screen.

Following a similar pattern, the locations mapped in promotional films of Liverpool (figure 6.3) also focus on the buildings around the Pier Head, the cathedrals and university, the Lime Street railway station, the Overhead Railway, and the waterfront but at the same time include places of leisure and consumption in the central area (theaters, art galleries, music venues, and the shopping areas of Clayton Square, Church Street, and Whitechapel), the civic and municipal buildings on and around William Brown Street (including the William Brown and Picton Libraries, the Walker Art Gallery, and St. George's Hall), and Chinatown, an acknowledgment, at least in part, of Liverpool's cultural and ethnic diversity. Again with a wider audience in mind, the promotional films offer a sense of the city in which the civic, cultural, and com-

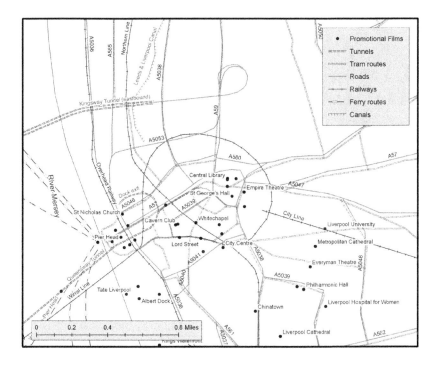

6.3. Liverpool city center map showing locations in promotional films.

mercial opportunities on offer define the topographic specificity of this film genre. Functioning largely as marketing devices to raise industrial, commercial, and touristic awareness of Liverpool, the majority of the promotional films are productions commissioned by the Liverpool City Council and Merseyside Development Corporation.

Turning to films categorized as documentaries (professional and independently produced nonfiction films), we get a different picture again (figure 6.4). What is immediately apparent in comparison to the previous two genres is the sheer number and variety of the locations. Not only are more areas of the city mapped in Liverpool documentaries, but there is also a greater emphasis on districts defined in terms of housing and residential usage, with streets rather than just buildings finding their way onto the map. But in addition to many of the more prominent and established locations that appear in the newsreels and promotional films, there is far more extensive coverage of the local and everyday (schools,

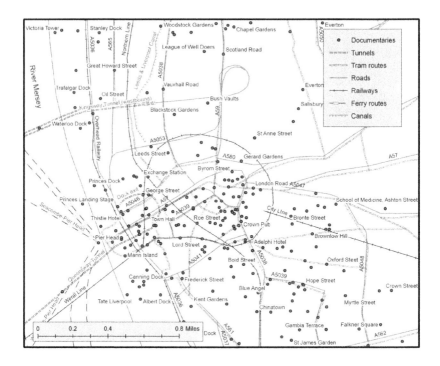

6.4. Liverpool city center map showing locations in documentary films.

pubs, clubs, sports venues, local churches, cafés, and restaurants), with a notable shift toward residential areas, particularly the inner-city tenement housing blocks built to replace the overcrowded eighteenth- and nineteenth-century courts that became a prominent feature of Liverpool's urban landscape from the 1930s (these include Fontenoy Gardens, Gerard Gardens, Vauxhall Gardens, and St. Andrews Gardens, or the "Bullring," as it is more commonly known).

The local and everyday is also well represented in the map of amateur film locations, although this is more apparent the farther one travels out from the city center. A focus on amateur factual production in the Merseyside region from the 1920s displays a pattern that parallels the development of Liverpool's suburban hinterland and the gradual movement of the city's more affluent population from the central areas to the greener environs across the Mersey. From the earliest depictions of the city (e.g., the Lumière Brothers' *Panorama pris du chemin de fer électrique,* 1897, or

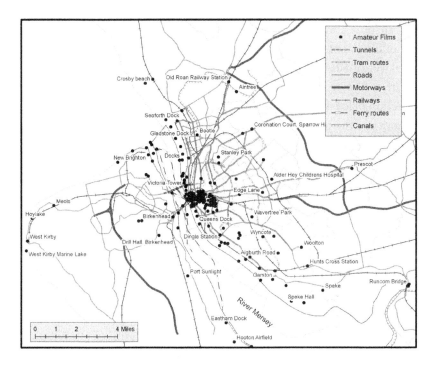

6.5. Regional map showing locations in amateur films.

Mitchell and Kenyon's *Liverpool as Seen from the Front of a Tram,* 1901),
forms of transport and mobility have played a prominent role in the way
Liverpool has been documented on film. A search of the City in Film database shows 201 films featuring locations or spaces whose function is associated with transport, with a further 270 films featuring scenes involving people engaged in different forms of movement and mobility both
within and to and from the city. Transport and mobility thus emerges as
one of the key variables by which we can search and query a GIS spatial
database of Merseyside archive film data. There are films that trace journeys from the suburbs into the city, films of people moving around the
city via various different modes of transport, and films about transport
(trams, the Overhead Railway, bridges, and high-speed roads).[29] The
net total of transport and mobility films in the database is 322, which is
nearly 20 percent of the total number of films listed. It is important to
note that this does not mean that one-fifth of these films are travelogues

or transport films – the statistics reflect a spatial and geographical reading of films, not a reading by genre. However, a large number of these
films were made by amateur filmmakers and members of local cine clubs,
and they feature journeys in and out of the city center. Figure 6.5 shows a
selection of locations documented in amateur films. The overwhelming
majority of the films that fall within the amateur category are made by
filmmakers and cine clubs based outside of Liverpool (especially in the
Wirral). Mapping these more expansive location points highlights the
essentially mobile nature of much amateur filmmaking practice in the
region, demonstrating the extent to which transport geographies and
routes within and beyond the city have remained an important factor in
the documenting of Liverpool on film and, by extension, of the shaping
of ideas of place, locality, and identity.

The ability to map the geographies of amateur filmmaking practice
in Liverpool and Merseyside allows us to pay closer critical attention to
the spatial situatedness of the "archival gaze" and the routes and mobilities that have helped shape and determine the imaginary of Liverpool
and/or Merseyside to which, taken collectively, these films contribute.
Narrowing the search parameters further, films made by Liverpool-
based amateur filmmakers and cine groups active from the 1950s (of
which, compared to their Wirral and other regional counterparts, there
have been comparatively few) are mostly clustered within the central
urban area; there is less visible evidence that these filmmakers were
interested in filming the wider region, other than perhaps anticipated
popular destinations such as Aintree Racecourse to the north or New
Brighton, a seaside resort a ferry journey away across the Mersey. By
contrast, as indicated in figure 6.5, films made by amateur filmmakers
operative across Merseyside display a more far-reaching geographical
spread in terms of the distance traveled between place of domicile and
filmic destination, highlighting the close association between amateur
film and leisure practices such as travel, tourism, and sightseeing. The
focus on forms of transport to and from Liverpool and within the city
center itself suggests (1) the enduring popularity of transport as an amateur film topic and (2) the geographical relationship with Liverpool, its
transport forms, and its landmark gateways (ferry terminals, bridges,
tunnels, railways, etc.) for filmmakers commuting in from the Wirral

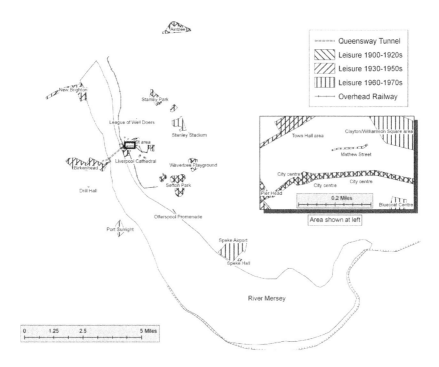

6.6. Map showing changes and growth of leisure and recreation areas in films of Liverpool (1900s–1970s).

and the wider Merseyside region or traveling into the city to participate in (and document) events, festivals, and other activities that have taken place at different times in Liverpool's history.

MAPPING SPATIAL FUNCTIONS AND SPATIAL USE

The inclusion of data relating to the definition or function of the space depicted in each film that was available for viewing on the City in Film database and the information on the way spaces are being used by individuals and groups that appear in the films allows for analysis of, on the one hand, the architectural and topographic characteristics of historical landscapes on film and, on the other, the anthropological and ethnographic qualities attached to specific urban spaces. Figure 6.6 shows cinematic geographies of leisure and recreation at three different periods from the 1900s to the 1970s.

From the early days of film in Liverpool we see that the football stadia for the two city clubs, Liverpool and Everton, are already a well-established feature on the map of leisure sites on film, with early recordings of matches such as the Liverpool Derby in 1902 taking place in the area on the map to the north of the city center labeled Stanley Park (*Everton v. Liverpool*, Mitchell and Kenyon, 1902). Similarly, to the north, the racecourse at Aintree appears in 1903 as part of *Bootle May Day Demonstration and Crowning of the May Queen* (Mitchell and Kenyon, 1903). In the south of the city, Sefton and Princes Parks appear in one of the earliest amateur films shot in the city; called simply *Liverpool Streets and Parks,* the film was made in 1925 by members of the Saxton family. Sefton Park also appears in newsreel films, one of which shows the unveiling of the park's famous statue of Peter Pan in 1928. In the city center the area around Pier Head began to show signs of attracting leisure and tourist activity, not least on account of the new landmark buildings that had been constructed on the site during this period. Built between 1907 and 1918, the Royal Liver, Cunard, and Port of Liverpool buildings are by far the most recognized iconographic symbols of Liverpool and its waterfront today. The other prominent leisure sites in early film of the city were the areas around Lime Street and William Brown Street, which boasted the grand neoclassical buildings of St. George's Hall, Picton Library, and Walker Gallery, the city center streets of Church Street and Lord Street, principally associated with shopping and retail, and churches associated with society weddings such as St. Luke's, now an empty shell due to bomb damage in World War Two.

By the 1930s the most notable additions to the leisure map were destinations across the Mersey: the resort of New Brighton on the northern tip of the Wirral peninsula, and Birkenhead, a short ferry ride from Pier Head. The area around Pier Head is by now the most frequently depicted location, with leisure activities extended to the adjacent Canning and Albert Dock area, including the Custom House, which was later demolished as a result of damage caused by wartime air raids. Films that depict rare footage of the Custom House include *Local Scenes/Rodney Street* and *Mauretania Leaving Liverpool,* both of which were made by amateur filmmakers in the 1930s.

By the 1950s film activity by students at the University of Liverpool reflected geographies of leisure centered not only around the university district itself but also through the city center more generally as part of the annual Panto Week festivities, which formed the main subject matter of the Basement Film Unit, the student film club at the university whose productions were known as "Sphinx Reels." The Anglican Cathedral, the largest cathedral in the United Kingdom, also started to appear as a site of leisure in films made during the 1950s. Although the cathedral was not finally completed until 1978, the completion of the tower in 1942 conferred the status of iconic city landmark on the building, ensuring its continuing popularity as a tourist destination alongside its important religious and civic functions.

From the late 1890s until its closure in 1956 the Overhead Railway remained a popular attraction and place of leisure. Running along the length of the docks, the Overhead featured in many films shot on and around the waterfront, with filmmakers capturing views both of and from the elevated railway. The closure and eventual demolition of the Overhead Railway coincided with a number of other significant changes in the cultural geography of Liverpool around this period. The rise of youth culture and the emergent Merseybeat scene in the 1960s would firmly place Mathew Street, location of the Cavern Club, where the Beatles first attracted significant attention, on the cultural map of Liverpool. This is also reflected in the cinematic geography of the 1960s, with downtown music venues such as the Cavern, the Downbeat Club, the Blue Angel, and the Mardi Gras appearing in documentaries such as *And the World Listened,* a Pathé production from 1965 sponsored by Liverpool Corporation. Locations such as the Bluecoat Arts Centre, the Everyman Theatre, and the Liverpool Art School provide further indicators of the cultural vibrancy and attraction of the Liverpool arts scene during the 1960s.

Coincidental to or perhaps in part as a consequence of the closure of the Overhead Railway in the late 1950s was the growing popularity of journeys along the Manchester Ship Canal and River Mersey. Although the canal appeared in films from the 1930s onward, it was not until the 1960s, with the emergence of amateur films such as *Journey down the Ship*

Canal (J. L. Hayden, 1967), *Manchester Ship Canal* (Harry Barker, ca. 1960), *Voyage along the Manchester Ship Canal* (Malcolm Watts, 1960s), and others that the canal featured as a site primarily associated with leisure activity.

With the opening of the Roman Catholic Metropolitan Cathedral in 1967, both the cathedral and nearby Hope Street (which connects the Metropolitan with the Anglican Cathedral) emerged as sites of attraction for filmmakers. In the city center, the area around Clayton and Williamson Squares also became a popular leisure and recreation location around this time due in no small part to the opening of St. John's Precinct shopping center and its tower in 1971 (complete with a tower-top revolving restaurant), which inaugurated the gradual transformation of the city center district into spaces almost exclusively defined by retail and leisure consumption.

While the locations described above represent places and spaces either designed for or functioning as sites of leisure and recreation, the type of activities that take place in these or any other locations in the city may reflect a wide range of uses and forms of urban or social engagement. For example, there are many films documenting military parades or political demonstrations that took place in parks and other public spaces. The ability to query the attribute data by spatial use as well as function therefore allows consideration of the architecturally less tangible dynamics of *social space:* the practices and symbolic structures of those who inhabit the urban landscape and who invest it with meaning.

By way of illustration, figure 6.7 shows a selection of sites of festivals and parades from the 1900s to the 1970s. As might be expected, from the early 1900s the Pier Head and adjacent docks (Princes and Albert) played host to a large number of parades that were captured on film. These are mostly related to military and maritime events: the arrival of important dignitaries and heads of state, ranks of troops descending the floating roadway to embark on waiting ships, or crowds gathered to wave off cruise liners carrying loved ones or emigrants bound for America or Canada. The Pathé newsreel *The Immortal 55th* (1926), for instance, documents a military parade and other activities linked to the Civic Week festivities in October 1926. As well as locations on and around Pier Head and the river, events in the film take place at St. George's Plateau

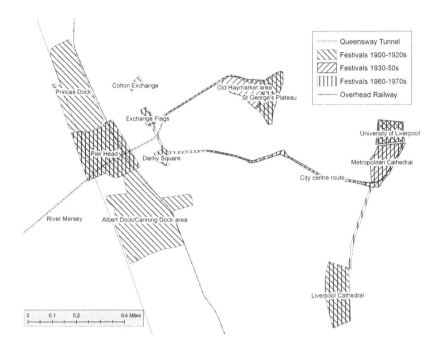

6.7. Map showing changes and growth of areas linked to festivals
and parades in films of Liverpool (1900s–1970s).

between Lime Street and William Brown Street, another key location
for festivals and parades in Liverpool.

One of the earliest filmic documents of parades in the city is *The
Liverpool Pageant: Celebrating the 700th Anniversary of the Foundation
of Liverpool.* This took place in Wavertree Playground (not shown on
the map) and, as the title suggests, marked the celebration of the seven
hundredth anniversary of the granting of the royal charter by King John
in 1207.

In the eighteenth century, Exchange Flags, the square behind the
Town Hall was the epicenter of trade and commerce; it was here that the
notorious business deals were done that underpinned the slave trade, a
major source of the city's wealth. In the early decades of the twentieth
century the square was an important site for parades and civic events
and is featured in many newsreels and actualities, including films made
by Mitchell and Kenyon in 1900–1901, such as *St George's Day Procession*

in Liverpool (1901), *Trafalgar Day in Liverpool* (1901), and *Visit of Earl Roberts and Viscount Kitchener to Receive the Freedom of the City, Liverpool* (1902). Today the square is little more than a space of transit serving no real symbolic function for the city, although the statue at its center, commissioned in 1813 by the antislavery campaigner William Roscoe to commemorate Admiral Lord Nelson, continues to serve as a reminder of its infamous trading past.

The other significant location for festivals and parades was the aforementioned St. George's Plateau. Of the many films that include footage of this area, it is films of military parades and marches that are the most typical as well as Armistice Day events held at the cenotaph located in front of St. George's Hall. In addition, there are several films of the horse parades that were regularly held here, for example, the Pathé newsreels *Annual May Parade of Horses* (1923) and *Horses in Fancy Dress* (1926). Titles of newsreels such as *St David's Day 1917* (Pathé, 1917) and *St David's Day Celebrations* (Pathé, 1917) illustrate the importance of this location for symbolically marking and celebrating the identity and presence of Liverpool's Welsh community, one of the earliest and largest of ethnic groups that migrated to the city.

Moving into the 1930s, the completion of the construction of the Queensway Tunnel between Liverpool and Birkenhead, at the time the longest underwater tunnel in the world, provided the subject matter for a large number of films, including many that documented the opening ceremony on 18 July 1934. Opened by King George V and attended by local dignitaries from both cities, the event took place in the area around the tunnel entrance at Old Haymarket and William Brown Street as well as at the Birkenhead end, King's Square. Given the importance of the tunnel to the commercial and industrial growth of Merseyside and the sheer scale of the engineering feat involved in its construction, the project was to attract much attention from news reporters and filmmakers. The opening ceremony was widely reported in the newsreels, but there is also extensive archive footage shot by amateur filmmakers.[30]

Footage of the Panto Week parades organized by students from the university mapped another important site of festivities in Liverpool. The annual procession of students set out from the university at Brownlow Hill and followed a route through the city center. Of the known archive footage of these events, including newsreel items, student productions such as *Sphinx Reel No. 6, 1956: Pantomania* (Basement Film Unit, 1956) and *Sphinx Reel No. 7, 1957: Panto 1957* (Basement Film Unit, 1957) provides perhaps the best coverage of the events and of the geographical range of the procession.

Notable additions to cinematic geographies given over to festivals and parades in the 1960s and 1970s include, as with the Basement Film Unit productions, routes through the city center in the shape of the homecoming celebratory parade following Liverpool Football Club's Football Association Challenge Cup win in 1965. This event was covered in the British Movietone production *Ee-Aye-Addio – the Cup's Back Home* (1965), showing the rapturous reception of the team, led by their captain, Ron Yeats, and legendry manager, Bill Shankly, from many thousands of supporters lining the streets of the city. The Hope Street area was another location that featured in films from this period in the form of the Hope Street Pageant, which took place in 1977 in celebration of Queen Elizabeth's silver jubilee and her visit to Liverpool in June of that year. This event was documented in *Hope Street Glory*, a Granada Television production narrated by the Liverpool poet Roger McGough.

Finally, returning to Pier Head, by the 1970s there was a decline in the use of the area for festivals and parades, as evidenced in archive filmic records. This mirrors the more general economic and industrial decline of the docks and waterfront area, which had, by the 1970s and 1980s, reached its nadir. Indeed, responding to the growing mood of militancy and social unrest that was felt throughout the city at the time, in the 1980s the Pier Head was more likely to play host to trade union rallies and political demonstrations, as documented in *Unemployment March, 1980*, filmed by students from Prescot College of Further Education. St. George's Plateau was also a place where political demonstrations were frequently held, videos and recordings of which were made in the 1980s by filmmakers who formed part of a growing independent film sector on Merseyside clustered around a communally run production resource known as Open Eye.[31] The greater availability of video enabled local people to talk back to television news and current affairs programming; broadcast footage of the notorious Toxteth riots was counterbalanced by a documentary made by Liverpool Black Media (*They Haven't Done*

Nothin', 1985), while the collectively owned Community Productions Group recorded protests against unpopular legislation such as the tendering of National Health Service cleaning and laundry services to private contractors (*Love Me Tender*, 1985) and the effects of urban regeneration schemes on local people (*Disappearing Communities*, 1989). In these films, the people of the city, so often subjected to the gaze of others in city films, record their stories and their protests in the places where they live and work, a deterritorialization of filmic space in which the symbolic public spaces of civic and institutional authority are inhabited by the participatory actions and collective endeavor of its citizens.

CONCLUSION: CINEMATIC CARTOGRAPHY

As we have demonstrated, mapping a city in film in the way outlined in this chapter enables researchers to (1) navigate the spatial histories attached to landscapes in film; (2) develop new frameworks of analytical enquiry in relation to film, place, and memory; and (3) rethink and reformulate some of the questions critically addressing the place of archival images of cities and other locations in the wider cultural landscapes of memory, heritage, and local/national placemaking.

This chapter has sought to formulate some initial discussions as to the ways in which GIS resources can inform critical understandings of the relationship between film practice and the historic built environment. While offering a unique practical tool that is able to push forward research in this area in significant ways, GIS also presents hitherto unexplored and challenging theoretical possibilities insofar as it initiates new forms of spatial dialogue between the virtual landscapes of the moving image and the architectural, geographic, and imagined spaces within which they are embedded. The layering of these geographies in the form outlined in this essay contributes to the development of an explicitly spatial and synchronic mode of historiographical engagement with a city's image-spaces. This coincides with what Lev Manovich suggests is an epistemological shift toward the adoption of the *database* as the new symbolic form that can shape critical analysis of film texts and practices (spatial, vertical, paradigmatic), as opposed to the dominant *narrative* model (diachronic, linear, cause and effect), the syntagmatic form of which inhibits the kind of layered geospatial historiographical analyses advanced in this chapter.[32] Privileging metaphors such as "navigation," "mapping," "sorting," "searching," and "excavating" over those of more passive activities such as "spectating," "gazing," "viewing," and "watching," an emerging field of *cinematic cartography* is both a product of and a response to the shifting cultural, spatial, and intellectual terrain toward which much discussion and analysis in this area is increasingly turned.

NOTES

With thanks to the UK Arts and Humanities Research Council for funding the Mapping the City in Film project.

1. R. Koeck, "Liverpool in Film: J. A. L. Promio's Cinematic Urban Space," *Early Popular Visual Culture* 7 (2009): 63–81.

2. Museum of Liverpool, http://www.liverpoolmuseums.org.uk/mol/about/building.aspx.

3. B. Warf and S. Arias, eds., *The Spatial Turn: Interdisciplinary Perspectives* (Abingdon: Routledge, 2009); L. Roberts, "Mapping Cultures – a Spatial Anthropology," in *Mapping Cultures: Place, Practice, Performance,* ed. L. Roberts (Basingstoke: Palgrave, 2012), 1–25.

4. L. Roberts, "Cinematic Cartography: Projecting Place through Film," in Roberts, *Mapping Cultures,* 68–84. For a selection of some of the recent literature on film, space, and place, see N. AlSayyad, *Cinematic Urbanism: A History of the Modern from Reel to Real* (London: Routledge, 2006); G. Bruno, *Atlas of Emotion: Journeys in Art, Architecture and Film* (New York: Verso, 2002); C. Brunsdon, *London in Cinema: The Cinematic City since 1945* (London: British Film Institute, 2007); S. Caquard and D. R. F. Taylor, eds., "Cinematic Cartography," special issue, *Cartographic Journal* 46 (2009); T. Conley, *Cartographic Cinema* (Minneapolis: University of Minnesota Press, 2007); T. Cresswell and D. Dixon, eds., *Engaging*

Film: Geographies of Mobility and Identity (Lanham, Md.: Rowman and Littlefield, 2002); E. Dimendberg, *Film Noir and the Spaces of Modernity* (Cambridge, Mass.: Harvard University Press, 2004); W. Everett and A. Goodbody, eds., *Space and Place in European Cinema* (Oxford: Peter Lang, 2005); J. Hallam, "Mapping Urban Space: Independent Filmmakers as Urban Gazetteers," *Journal of British Cinema and Television* 4 (2007): 272–84; R. Koeck and L. Roberts, eds., *The City and the Moving Image: Urban Projections* (London: Palgrave, 2010); M. Konstantarakos, ed., *Spaces in European Cinema* (Exeter: Intellect, 2000); M. Lefebvre, *Landscape and Film* (London: Routledge, 2006); C. Lukinbeal and L. Zonn, eds., "Cinematic Geographies," special issue, *GeoJournal* 59 (2004); J. D. Rhodes and E. Gorfinkel, eds., *Taking Place: Location and the Moving Image* (Minneapolis: University of Minnesota Press, 2011); L. Roberts, *Film, Mobility and Urban Space: A Cinematic Geography of Liverpool* (Liverpool: Liverpool University Press, 2012).

5. H. Lefebvre, *The Production of Space* (Oxford: Blackwell, 1991).

6. For examples of these genealogical mappings, see D. B. Clarke, *The Cinematic City* (London: Routledge, 1997); D. B. Clarke and M. A. Doel, "Engineering Space and Time: Moving Pictures and Motionless Trips," *Journal of Historical*

Geography 31 (2005): 41–60; and for a different perspective on gesture and embodiment in cinema, see P. Valiaho, *Mapping the Moving Image: Gesture, Thought and Cinema circa 1900* (Amsterdam: Amsterdam University Press, 2010).

7. Bruno, *Atlas of Emotion,* 71.

8. R. C. Allen, "Relocating American Film History: The 'Problem' of the Empirical," *Cultural Studies* 20 (2006): 48–88, 49.

9. Going to the Show, http://docsouth.unc.edu/gtts/index.html.

10. J. Klenotic, "Putting Cinema History on the Map: Using GIS to Explore the Spatiality of Cinema," in *Explorations in New Cinema History: Approaches and Case Studies,* ed. R. Maltby, D. Biltereyst, and P. Meers (Oxford: Blackwell, 2011), 58–84.

11. HoMER Project, http://homerproject.blogs.wm.edu.

12. J. Hallam and L. Roberts, eds., *Locating the Moving Image: New Approaches to Film and Place* (Bloomington: Indiana University Press, 2013).

13. L. Roberts, "Projecting Place: Location Mapping, Consumption and Cinematographic Tourism," in Koeck and Roberts, *The City and the Moving Image,* 183–204.

14. See, for example, S. Beeton, *Film-Induced Tourism* (Clevedon, UK: Channel View, 2005); H. Kim and S. Richardson, "Motion Picture Impacts on Destination Images," *Annals of Tourism Research* 30 (2003): 216–37; R. Riley, D. Baker, and C. S. V. Doren, eds., "Movie Induced Tourism," *Annals of Tourism Research* 25 (1998): 919–35. For studies that bring a more critical approach to developments surrounding film-related tourism, see R. Tzanelli, *The Cinematic Tourist: Explorations in Globalization, Culture and Resistance* (London: Routledge, 2007); Roberts, *Film Mobility and Urban Space,* 128–81.

15. T. Conley, "*The 39 Steps* and the Mental Map of Classical Cinema," in *Rethinking Maps: New Frontiers in Cartographic Theory,* ed. M. Dodge, R. Kitchen, and C. Perkins (London: Routledge, 2009), 131–48, 132.

16. S. Caquard, "Foreshadowing Contemporary Digital Cartography: A Historical Review of Cinematic Maps in Films," in Caquard and Taylor, "Cinematic Cartography," special issue, *Cartographic Journal* 46 (2009): 46–55, 54.

17. Conley, *Cartographic Cinema;* Conley, "*The 39 Steps* and the Mental Map"; T. Conley, "Locations in Film Noir," in Caquard and Taylor, "Cinematic Cartography," special issue, *Cartographic Journal* 46 (2009): 16–23.

18. Bruno, *Atlas of Emotion,* 71.

19. Conley, *Cartographic Cinema,* 1–2.

20. T. Castro, "Cinema's Mapping Impulse: Questioning Visual Culture," in Caquard and Taylor, "Cinematic Cartography," special issue, *Cartographic Journal* 46 (2009): 9–15; T. Castro, "Mapping the City through Film: From 'Topophilia' to Urban Mapscapes," in Koeck and Roberts, *The City and the Moving Image,* 144–55.

21. Castro, "Cinema's Mapping Impulse," 14.

22. P. Keiller, "Film as Spatial Critique," in *Critical Architecture,* ed. J. Rendell, J. Hill, M. Fraser, and M. Dorrian (London: Routledge, 2007), 115–23.

23. Hallam, "Mapping Urban Space"; L. Roberts, "Making Connections: Crossing Boundaries of Place and Identity in Liverpool and Merseyside Amateur Transport Films," *Mobilities* 5 (2010): 83–109; L. Roberts, "Dis/embedded Geographies of Film: Virtual Panoramas and the Touristic Consumption of Liverpool Waterfront," *Space and Culture* 13 (2010): 54–74.

24. Mapping the City in Film: A Geo-historical Analysis, http://www.liv.ac.uk/lsa/cityinfilm.

25. Roberts, *Film, Mobility and Urban Space.*

26. V. Toulmin, *Electric Edwardians: The Story of the Mitchell and Kenyon Col-*

lection (London: British Film Institute, 2006), 38–42.

27. Jim Morris, interview by Les Roberts and Ryan Shand, Southport, 4 March 2009.

28. J. Hallam, "Civic Visions: Mapping the 'City' Film 1900–1960," *Culture, Theory and Critique* 53 (2012): 37–58.

29. Roberts, "Making Connections."

30. See ibid.; Hallam, "Civic Visions."

31. J. Hallam, "Mapping the 'City' Film 1930–1980," in Hallam and Roberts, *Locating the Moving Image,* forthcoming.

32. L. Manovich, "Database as Symbolic Form," *Convergence* 5 (1999): 80–99; J. Hallam and L. Roberts, "Mapping, Memory and the City: Archives, Databases and Film Historiography," *European Journal of Cultural Studies* 14 (2011): 355–72.

SEVEN

Conclusions: From Historical GIS to Spatial Humanities: Challenges and Opportunities

IAN N. GREGORY AND ALISTAIR GEDDES

THE ESSAYS IN THIS VOLUME ILLUSTRATE THE DIVERSITY OF topics within and beyond history that can be conducted using historical GIS (HGIS) and the fields of spatial history, humanities GIS, and spatial humanities that are emerging from it. The topics discussed cover rural history, urban history, demography, religious history, and environmental history. Reflecting this diversity, the authors come from disciplines including history, geography, sociology, and media studies. The sources and approaches vary from the highly quantitative analyses of census data – particularly prevalent in Beveridge's essay – to the very qualitative – exemplified particularly by Hallam and Roberts. Schwartz and Thevenin, in particular, illustrate that these two do not have to be mutually exclusive. Although their essay is based primarily on quantitative sources, they also make considerable use of qualitative material that could not be georeferenced, notably, the writing of contemporary journalist Richard Jefferies. The scales used in the book vary from a single city to a country the size of China, and the periods under study vary from the twentieth century to the Song dynasty. Within these, the studies cover time periods that vary from single-date snapshots to analyses covering a century and more.

As well as reflecting the diversity of HGIS, the essays also reflect its current development. As discussed in the introduction, the first three chapters conduct applied pieces of research that explore specific research questions of interest to a wide audience of historians. The second three are more concerned with further developing the field of HGIS by applying it in new ways or by incorporating new types of sources. These essays are more strongly relevant to audiences who are already interested in HGIS or those who are interested in what it may have to offer to their discipline in the future. This is not a criticism, because the field needs to develop its breadth as well as its depth; thus, essays that pioneer new approaches are important.

This chapter explores how HGIS and related fields are likely to develop in the future and the challenges that face them. These issues will be discussed under five main headings: quantitative HGIS, qualitative HGIS, technological developments, moving beyond the discipline of history, and moving beyond the academy.

QUANTITATIVE HGIS

Although quantitative HGIS is better developed than other parts of the field, there are still many areas in which further progress can be made and other challenges where perhaps we should accept that there is likely to be less progress than we might hope.

From an applied perspective, as we have already stated, many projects are reaching – or have reached – a stage where the emphasis has shifted toward historical research with less emphasis on GIS databases and methodologies; in other words, these projects are evolving from HGIS into spatial history. This can be expected to continue but does not mean that there are not still potential improvements and challenges on the GIS side.

Methodologically, the two key issues that stand out are time, and error and uncertainty. These issues affect qualitative sources but are perhaps more pressing with quantitative ones. An improved handling of time would be particularly beneficial from an analytic perspective. While a significant amount of research effort has gone into topics such as standardizing polygons representing administrative units at different dates so that data can be directly compared over time,[1] we still have very poor tools for analyzing change over space and time simultaneously. This means that researchers still have to rely on very spatially aggregate time-series graphs to look at change over time or to compare multiple map snapshots that stress space but are poor at representing temporal change. In an ideal world we would be able to move away from these two extremes to more sophisticated types of analyses that would allow us to explore change over space and time simultaneously. There have been some developments in this that are driven, to a great extent, by the needs of the HGIS community.[2] It should be remembered, however, that within the GISc (Geographical Information Science) community there have been calls for improved temporal functionality for some considerable time.[3] The extent to which progress is likely to be made in the form of technical fixes is open to debate.

Error and uncertainty have also been long-standing research issues within the wider GISc community.[4] They have a particular relevance to humanities sources, where inaccuracy, ambiguity, and incompleteness are common. While progress has been made and further improvements can be expected, there are limitations to what technical fixes developed by GISc can be expected to achieve. Many technical solutions involve increasingly statistical approaches that quantify uncertainty and its effects and are thus a long way from the types of approaches typically used within the humanities.[5] The more traditional humanities solutions – close reading and careful interpretation of results and patterns – are also relevant and should not be overlooked. Metadata are also important here.

A final issue with quantitative HGIS is that the major challenge in conducting research used to be building databases. Many very rich data resources now exist, and, rather than building more, a major emphasis should be placed on using existing ones. There are technical and institutional barriers to this, but there is currently great potential in using, repurposing, and integrating these resources to conduct new research that provide opportunities to make rapid progress on applied research questions.

QUALITATIVE HUMANITIES GIS

An issue that clearly emerges from the last two chapters of this volume is that GIS has much to offer to the study of qualitative sources in disciplines within and beyond history, but there is still much work to be done before this reaches the same level of maturity as some of the more quantitative work. The rise of the use of qualitative sources within HGIS is a particularly exciting one and one where HGIS has much to offer to the wider GISc community, where qualitative GIS is still in a relatively early stage of development.[6] Within the humanities, quantitative history is – and is likely to remain – a relatively small field; thus, if GIS is only able to handle quantitative data, its impact will be limited. If, on the other hand, GIS is able to cope with qualitative sources, then not only will it become applicable to a much wider range of fields within historical research, but it will also become usable across many other subjects within the humanities – potentially in any humanities discipline where geography is seen as relevant. These disciplines could include – but are not limited to – literary studies, linguistics, classics, religious studies, media studies, and the performing arts. They could also include the more cultural areas within human geography that have traditionally been hostile to GIS because of its quantitative nature.

Many challenges remain in making progress with qualitative sources, but solutions seem achievable, and rapid progress can be expected. The first challenge is simply to create effective spatial databases of qualitative sources. The development of attribute data in a range of nontraditional formats such as still images, movies, and sound will definitely continue within and beyond GIS. Georeferencing these collections is clearly a major challenge, and it is here that the development of appropriate infrastructures may have a large role to play. Most qualitative sources can be satisfactorily georeferenced to point locations. It is much quicker and easier to develop a list of place-names with their associated point coordinates than it is to develop the large databases of changing administrative boundaries required for many quantitative sources. Lists in this form are the simplest type of gazetteer, and many of these currently exist, with some of them, such as Geonames, being freely available.[7] Developing, extending, and disseminating these resources has the potential to pay handsome dividends for humanities GIS, as they have the potential to allow us to georeference any source that has place-names and can sensibly be represented in point form. Assuming that the place-names in the source match the gazetteer versions reasonably well, this process is quick and easy. Gazetteers include place-names, but they should also be able to deal with more complex issues such as spelling variations, disambiguating different places with the same name, multilingual issues, and so on.[8]

Once these datasets are available, the time and cost of georeferencing any dataset that includes place-names becomes greatly reduced, opening up the possibility of georeferencing a wide range of attribute data sources within and beyond the humanities.

A further extension in the use of qualitative data that is also showing encouraging signs is the use of texts within GIS. Unstructured texts such as essays, books, official reports, and newspapers are the most widely used source within the humanities. Until recently these seemed to lie beyond the scope of GIS; however, it is becoming apparent that techniques from corpus linguistics can be used to extract place-names from corpora, the technical name for a large body of text, usually in digital form. Combining these techniques to extract place-names with the abilities of gazetteers to georeference place-names quickly and easily has the potential to allow unstructured texts to be converted into GIS databases.[9] The development of these techniques is taking place in parallel with the increasing availability of large historical corpora as a result of large-scale digitization projects such as Early English Books Online, the Proceedings of the Old Bailey Online, and even, potentially, Google Books.[10] Additionally, material that will be relevant to modern historians in the near future will be "born digital," such as, possibly, the Wikileaks material on the Iraq War. Given this possibility, the potential for these techniques to be applied to explore texts in entirely new ways becomes enormous.

A further potentially useful infrastructure is the development and availability of online historical map collections, particularly where these are georeferenced.[11] The material that these types of collections hold is a rich source of potential research in its own right. It can also be used as background information for more specific sources and to help with georeferencing sources and features that may not appear in gazetteers.

While all of these infrastructural developments are important, the main question is not "what can be built?" but "what new analyses can be done and what contributions to knowledge will they make?" We are still in the early stages of answering this, perhaps even in understanding how best to go about it. As large humanities databases become available, questions still remain about how best to explore or analyze these given the apparent contradictions between the potential size and complexity of such databases, on the one hand, and the emphasis on close reading and nuanced understanding in humanities scholarship, on the other. Add to these the need to understand geographical complexity, the limitations of simple GIS maps, and the perceived unsuitability of statistical approaches to the humanities, and in-depth exploration of these types of databases begins to seem like a daunting task. One possible approach to resolving this dilemma is a more receptive attitude toward statistics. The social sciences have shown that statistics can be a very useful tool in helping to summarize complex patterns through techniques such as density smoothing, which is widely used to make complex point patterns more understandable. To return to a theme from the introduction, statistical techniques do not lead to positivism; they are simply a tool to help the researcher to understand complex patterns by summarizing them in the form of summary statistics, diagrams, or maps.[12]

In moving from humanities GIS toward spatial humanities, exemplar projects that actually tackle these challenges and then publish results are required, even if they are pilot projects or work that is still some way from full completion. There is a growing list of publications of this type, but more is required.[13] These developments need to be accompanied by a cultural change within the humanities that makes humanities scholars more receptive to the potential and impact of digital approaches generally. In the latter of these, an undoubted cultural shift is going on, as shown by the rise of digital humanities on both sides of the Atlantic.[14] This is a trend that can be expected to continue, indeed, it must continue, if the humanities are going to remain relevant in the digital world.

TECHNOLOGICAL DEVELOPMENTS

GIS software was not developed with humanities applications in mind, and its future development will not be driven by the requirements of academics in the humanities. The challenge is thus to take what is usually provided by commercial companies primarily for business markets and use these as appropriately as possible. Unfortunately, this means that when it comes to developing the core tools, humanities academics are following and adapting other people's agendas rather than leading the agenda. Most humanities academics wanting to use GIS would like software that is affordable, is relatively easy to use, does the basic operations well, and provides all of the required functionality. Regrettably, such software does not exist.[15] At one end of the market are the major commercial GIS software packages such as ArcGIS that offer a wide and sophisticated suite of tools.[16] If these packages are not available through a site license, they can be prohibitively expensive, and even if they are available, they often have a long learning curve associated with them. At the other end are packages such as Google Earth, which is free and very easy to use but provides such limited functionality that it cannot be classed as full GIS software.[17] In between these extremes there is very little available. One possible solution to this is that open source GIS software packages are reaching maturity; a good example is Quantum GIS.[18] These open source packages are free but arguably harder to use than commercial packages, and they provide less functionality, although they do the basic GIS operations. One possible further advantage of open source software packages is that their functionality can be extended by programmers, thus providing the potential for functionality to be developed specifically for the requirements of the humanities.

An alternative approach to using and adapting existing software would be to develop a custom written software package or packages specifically for humanities GIS purposes. This must be approached with caution and realism, as solutions like this tend to require large amounts of resources, have long lead times, are highly dependent on a small number of individuals (usually one key person), and rarely achieve as much user acceptance as they perhaps deserve. Within the HGIS sphere the Great American History Machine and the *Time*Map project both provide examples of potentially excellent products that never really achieved their potential at least in part because of the difficulties of going from good software to a package widely accepted by users.[19] This problem has affected not only the GIS community but also other fields within history and computing.[20]

A more practical solution to the difficulties of using GIS software is to provide better training in existing software tools available to humanities scholars. Ideally this training would be included in postgraduate courses; however, at present the demand is probably too limited within a single institution. The solution is the provision of short courses, and these are becoming increasingly prevalent.[21]

The core technology of GIS, involving vector and raster data models and the operations that can be performed on them, has been stable since the 1980s. The major advances in this area have been in user interfaces and in the development of more sophisticated techniques to manipulate data in this form. Around this, however, the technology has developed rapidly and will continue to do so. Mapping technologies such as Google Earth and Google Maps have become mainstream parts of the Internet, along with more specialist HGIS Internet mapping applications such as Social Explorer and Hypercities.[22] The full implications of these, and indeed many other types of Internet technologies, have yet to be realized in the humanities and indeed the broader academy. Their major implication is that it is now possible to "publish" GIS and other data and research online in an interactive form. This poses two questions. First, a traditional academic publication involves the author presenting an argument to a reader along with evidence to support that argument. If we can publish large and complex georeferenced databases using these types of technologies, which frequently have taken large amounts of academic effort to create, then to what extent can these be considered academic publications? While they are based on large amounts of scholarly work, they often require readers to develop their own argument from the evidence, and even if an argument is provided by the author, to what extent is this required, given that readers are expected to explore the evidence themselves in more detail than in a conventional publication? The second question is related to peer review. It is easy to publish these resources, but how can a measure of quality be provided for readers and credit given to the author/creator? As yet we are a long way from having effective peer review systems for these types of products. This causes a range of problems – not least associated with promotion and tenure – that are inhibiting the development and dissemination of potentially valuable resources. Solutions will involve a major cultural shift across the entire academy and are thus unlikely to happen quickly.

While the academy wrestles with these issues, the technology continues to evolve at a rapid rate. The most recent development is the move into location-based services (LBS) and augmented reality (AR), where georeferenced content is disseminated in the field using devices such as tablet computers and smart phones.[23] There is clearly enormous potential to use these with humanities GIS–based projects, but how these contribute to scholarship and pedagogy remains to be seen.

MOVING BEYOND THE DISCIPLINE OF HISTORY

A theme that has occurred often in this book is that GIS enables any datasets to be integrated as long as they can be georeferenced to locations on the Earth's surface. If it is possible to use this technique to cross the boundaries between "data silos," it should also be possible to use it to cross subject and disciplinary boundaries. One of the most obvious areas where there is the potential to do this but where surprisingly little progress has been made to date is within humanities GIS itself. The two subjects within the humanities where the use of GIS is best developed are history and archaeology.[24] Despite both fields being interested in the past, they remain very separate. This may reflect their different origins – in representing census-style data for history and survey data for archaeology – but both fields have developed way beyond these beginnings. There must be the potential to break down the divisions between the two to learn lessons from each other and to develop scholarship that draws on traditions and sources from both disciplines. Unfortunately, once these divisions have grown up this can be harder than it should be. As GIS use develops in other disciplines within the humanities it is in everyone's interest that such divisions do not develop; instead, there should be a strong interdisciplinary approach.

As well as divisions between subjects, the divide between quantitative and qualitative approaches is one of the most pronounced within academia, and, in geography in particular, it is sometimes highly divisive.[25] The ability to integrate different types of sources also opens up the intriguing possibility of crossing this divide. In general, quantitative data give us comprehensive but abstracted sources that are very good at describing patterns but are less good at explaining why these patterns are as they are. Qualitative sources tend to be more selective but more in-depth and are much more effective at developing explanations. Bringing these two together to both describe and explain patterns offers truly exciting new potential that is enabled by GIS but will require a strongly interdisciplinary approach to implement.

Further developing the theme of crossing disciplinary divides, the humanities have much to learn from other fields that have a longer tradition of GIS use, particularly in the social sciences but also in the earth sciences. While approaches from these disciplines do need to be adopted in a critical manner that questions their suitability for the sources and approaches used in the humanities, there is much to be learned from these fields, the approaches that they have taken, and the lessons that they have learned along the way. There is also the need for better collaboration between the humanities and disciplines such as geographical information science, computer science, library science, and corpus linguistics. The methodological expertise from these disciplines has much to offer to the humanities, and some of the technical and methodological challenges that confront humanities GIS use also provide research challenges within these disciplines.

Finally, from an applied perspective, as Southall shows in his essay, there is the potential to conduct research that crosses the divide between disciplines that study the past and disciplines that study the present. Most humanities disciplines concentrate on the past, but there is a clear potential to collaborate with sociologists, geographers, economists, demographers, health researchers, and a range of others who typically concentrate on the present. This enables questions such as "how did conditions from the past affect the present?" and "how did we get to where we are now?" to be asked.

MOVING BEYOND THE ACADEMY

Whatever the limitations of maps, people like them and enjoy interacting with them. This has enabled projects like Social Explorer, A Vision of Britain through Time, Locating London's Past, and Mapping the Lakes to present complex information to much broader audiences than conventional academic publishing could ever succeed in reaching.[26] All of these projects have their origins in academic research, but all have been highly successful in disseminating their material far more widely to audiences that include journalists, politicians and other decision makers, businesspeople, genealogists, heritage professionals, and the general public. These groups have a wide range of interests in GIS-based materials, including subjects associated with their local area; topics relevant to an area that they have visited; place-specific events, culture, literature, and heritage and their legacies (which include liabilities, pollution, and subsidence as well as more positive themes); and national and regional trends such as segregation that have a geographical component. To date, most of these projects have been largely driven by the opportunities that academics have spotted, but there is clearly the potential to work in partnership on these types of products.

Nonacademic sectors also have much to offer to the academic community. Many people and organizations from outside the academic sector are generating georeferenced data – or data that could usefully be georeferenced – for a wide range of purposes. These vary from user-generated content on sites such as Flickr to data from museum, library, and archive catalogs.[27] There is enormous potential to use these types of resources in ways that benefit both sectors, as they can provide inputs for academic study, and academics can repurpose and present them in new ways that will benefit other audiences.

CONCLUSIONS

Historical GIS, humanities GIS, spatial history, and spatial humanities are four terms that put a different emphasis on an evolving field that started with a very quantitative approach to history but has evolved to have the potential to cover many aspects of digital research into the geographies of the past. There are still challenges to be overcome, but the field is reaching maturity, especially in the more quantitative side, although the qualitative is catching up fast. The field is highly interdisciplinary, covering not only many different topics in history but also different disciplines within the humanities and technical fields such as GISc and digital humanities. This interdisciplinarity is a strength, but it does raise challenges, as the researcher has to have expertise in GIS and in geographical thinking as well as the topic under study. It also means that the literature tends to be very fragmented among different journals on different topics. However, as the essays in this volume make clear, there are strong and cohesive threads that run through the field and that are leading to the creation of a broad, inclusive field with much to offer to the academic study of the past as well as to many other fields within and beyond the academy.

NOTES

1. See I. N. Gregory and P. S. Ell, "Breaking the Boundaries: Integrating 200 Years of the Census Using GIS," *Journal of the Royal Statistical Society Series A* 168 (2005): 419–37; and J. P. Schroeder, "Target-Density Weighting Interpolation and Uncertainty Evaluation for Temporal Analysis of Census Data," *Geographical Analysis* 39 (2007): 311–35.

2. See C. Weaver, D. Fyfe, A. Robinson, D. Holdsworth, D. J. Peuquet, and A. M. MacEachren, "Visual Analysis of Historic Hotel Visitation Patterns," *Information Visualization* 6 (2007): 89–103; and D. A. Fyfe, D. W. Holdsworth, and C. Weaver, "Historical GIS and Visualization: Insights from Three Hotel Guest Registers in Central Pennsylvania, 1888–1897," *Social Science Computer Review* 27 (2009): 348–62.

3. See the introduction for a definition of GISc and how it differs from GIS. G. Langran and N. R. Chrisman, "A Framework for Temporal Geographic Information," *Cartographica* 25 (1988): 1–14 provides an early example of work in this area.

4. See, for example, D. Unwin, "Geographical Information Systems and the Problem of 'Error and Uncertainty,'" *Progress in Human Geography* 19 (1995): 549–58; and A. Agumya and G. J. Hunter, "Responding to the Consequences of Uncertainty in Geographical Data," *International Journal of Geographical Information Science* 16 (2002): 405–17.

5. See, for example, Q. Guo, Y. Liu, and J. Wieczorek, "Georeferencing Locality Descriptions and Computing Associated Uncertainty Using a Probabilistic Approach," *International Journal of Geographical Information Science* 22 (2008): 1067–90; or the essays in G. M. Foody and P. M. Atkinson, eds., *Uncertainty in Remote Sensing and GIS* (Chichester: John Wiley, 2002).

6. M. Cope and S. Elwood, eds., *Qualitative GIS: A Mixed Methods Approach* (London: Sage, 2009).

7. Geonames, http://www.geonames .org.

8. See L. L. Hill, *Georeferencing: The Geographic Associations of Information* (Cambridge, Mass.: MIT Press, 2006); R. Mostern and I. Johnson, "From Named Place to Naming Event: Creating Gazetteers for History," *International Journal of Geographical Information Science* 22 (2008): 1091–1108; H. R. Southall, R. Mostern, and M. Berman, "On Historical Gazetteers," *International Journal of Humanities and Arts Computing* 5 (2011): 127–45.

9. See the following three essays for different approaches to this issue: I. N. Gregory and A. Hardie, "Visual GISting:

Bringing Together Corpus Linguistics and Geographical Information Systems," *Literary and Linguistic Computing* 26 (2011): 297–314; C. Grover, R. Tobin, K. Byrne, M. Woollard, J. Reid, S. Dunn, and J. Ball, "The Use of the Edinburgh Geoparser for Georeferencing Digitised Historical Collections," *Philosophical Transactions of the Royal Society A* 368 (2010): 3875–89; M. Yuan, "Mapping Text," in *The Spatial Humanities: GIS and the Future of Humanities Scholarship,* ed. D. J. Bodenhamer, J. Corrigan, and T. M. Harris (Bloomington: Indiana University Press, 2010), 109–23.

10. Early English Books Online, http:// eebo.chadwyck.com/home; Proceedings of the Old Bailey, London's Central Criminal Court, 1674–1913, http://www.old baileyonline.org; Google Books, http:// books.google.com.

11. The David Rumsey Map Collection, http://www.davidrumsey.com provides a good example.

12. A. S. Fotheringham, "Trends in Quantitative Methods I: Stressing the Local," *Progress in Human Geography* 21 (1997): 88–96.

13. See Meeks and Mostern as well as Hallam and Roberts in this volume and other examples, including D. Cooper and I. N. Gregory, "Mapping the English Lake District: A Literary GIS," *Transactions of the Institute of British Geographers* 36 (2011): 89–108; and E. Barker, S. Bouzarovski, C. Pelling, and L. Isaksen, "Mapping an Ancient Historian in a Digital Age: The Herodotus Encoded Space-Text-Image Archive (HESTIA)," *Leeds International Classical Studies* 9 (2010): 1–36.

14. C. L. Borgman, "The Digital Future Is Now: A Call to Action for the Humanities," *Digital Humanities Quarterly* 3, no. 4, http://digitalhumanities.org/dhq /vol/3/4/000077/000077.html.

15. See Tom Armitage's section on "Open & 'Free' Geo Software and Data" at http://digimap.blogs.edina.ac.uk/2013/06 /19/geoforum-2013-liveblog.

16. ESRI, http://www.esri.com.

17. Google Earth, http://earth.google .com.

18. Quantum GIS, http://www.qgis .org.

19. D. Miller and J. Modell, "Teaching United States History with the Great American History Machine," *Historical Methods* 21 (1988): 121–34; *Time*Map: Time-based interactive mapping, http:// www.timemap.net.

20. O. Boonstra, L. Breure, and P. Doorn, *Past, Present and Future of Historical Information Science* (Amsterdam: NIWI-KNAW, 2004).

21. See the Digital Humanities Summer Institute (DHSI), http://www.dhsi .org, and the Historical GIS Research Network, http://www.hgis.org.uk for examples.

22. Social Explorer, http://www .socialexplorer.com; Hypercities, http:// hypercities.com.

23. A. Brimicombe and C. Li, *Location-Based Services and Geo-Information Engineering* (London: Wiley, 2009).

24. For history, see, for example, I. N. Gregory and P. S. Ell, *Historical GIS: Technologies, Methodologies and Scholarship* (Cambridge: Cambridge University Press, 2007); and A. K. Knowles, ed., *Placing History: How Maps, Spatial Data and GIS Are Changing Historical Scholarship* (Redlands, Calif.: ESRI, 2008). For archaeology, see, for example, J. Connolly and M. Lake, *Geographical Information Systems in Archaeology* (Cambridge: Cambridge University Press, 2006); and H. Chapman, *Landscape Archaeology and GIS* (Stroud: History Press, 2006).

25. D. Sui and D. DeLyser, "Crossing the Qualitative-Quantitative Chasm I:

Hybrid Geographies, the Spatial Turn and Volunteered Geographical Information (VGI)," *Progress in Human Geography* 36 (2012): 111–24.

26. Social Explorer, http://www.socialexplorer.com; A Vision of Britain through Time, http://www.visionofbritain.org.uk; Locating London's Past, http://www.locatinglondon.org; Mapping the Lakes: A Literary GIS, http://www.lancs.ac.uk/mappingthelakes.

27. M. F. Goodchild, "Citizens as Sensors: The World of Volunteered Geography," *GeoJournal* 69 (2007): 211–21; Flickr, http://www.flickr.com.

EIGHT

Further Reading: From Historical GIS to Spatial Humanities: An Evolving Literature

IAN N. GREGORY

AS WAS STATED IN THE INTRODUCTION, THE USE OF GIS TO study the past has evolved rapidly over the last decade or so, and we now stand at a position where the field is becoming both deeper and broader. As the field develops, so too does the literature, which has become increasingly voluminous but also increasingly disparate, making it difficult to keep track of developments in the field and to see what other researchers working on different topics but with similar challenges are doing. This chapter attempts to summarize this literature. It starts with publications that provide an overview of the field, moves on to databases and methods, and then turns to applied research before finishing by introducing the emerging fields of humanities GIS and spatial humanities. The chapter describes the current literature. It is not meant to be fully comprehensive and does not include earlier chapters in this book unless completely necessary. It also only includes conventional academic publications, thus ignoring web resources (other than articles in electronic journals), of which there are many. For a more comprehensive list of publications and a list of web resources, see the Historical GIS Research Network website (http://www.hgis.org.uk). Suggestions for updates to this site are always welcome.

Although there were a few papers written on HGIS in the 1990s, the growing momentum and maturity of the field was marked by a special edition of *Social Science History* (vol. 24, no. 3), published in 2000 and edited by A. K. Knowles. Since then, this literature has grown rapidly and now includes a significant number of books from high quality university presses and articles in many of the leading journals. Many of the early papers, such as most of those in the 2000 volume of *Social Science History,* talked about the construction of databases and the potential that these systems would have once they were completed. By the mid-2000s significant works of applied scholarship started to appear in many fields, with urban history, environmental history, historical demography, and medieval history being particularly rich seams. As was discussed in the introduction, two trends are apparent. First, it is becoming increasingly common to talk of spatial history rather than historical GIS, reflecting a move from a technological focus to the applied. Second, from its origins in social science history, the use of GIS is spreading across the discipline and into new humanities subjects. At present its use in these disciplines is perhaps where it was in history several years ago, with the emphasis more on creating databases and their potential for scholarship rather than on finished articles. Nevertheless, this is clearly a rapidly developing and exciting growth area that is often referred to as humanities GIS or spatial humanities.

HISTORICAL GIS

Perhaps the first book that could be called a historical GIS book, although it predates the term by some years, is M. Goerke, ed., *Coordinates for Historical Maps* (St. Katharinen: Max-Planck Institut für Geschichte, 1994); however, this is really only of interest as it illustrates just how far the field has developed. After the 2000 volume of *Social Science History,* three publications appeared in quick succession that further defined the field. I. N. Gregory, *A Place in History: A Guide to Using GIS in Historical Research* (Oxford: Oxbow, 2003) outlined what GIS had to offer to historians at a technical level (see http://www.ccsr.ac.uk/methods /publications/ig-gis.pdf). A. K. Knowles, *Past Time, Past Place: GIS for History* (Redlands, Calif.: ESRI Press, 2002) and a special edition of *History and Computing* (vol. 13, no. 1 [2001]), edited by P. S. Ell and I. N. Gregory, presented collections of essays on the state of the field at that time. Edited volumes have continued to be produced at an increasing pace, with the work that they contain developing considerably. A special edition of *Historical Geography* (vol. 33) appeared in 2005, and *Placing History: How GIS Is Changing Historical Scholarship* was published in

2008 (Redlands, Calif.: ESRI Press); both are edited by A. K. Knowles. A special edition of *Social Science Computer Review* (vol. 27, no. 3), edited by T. J. Bailey and J. B. M. Schick; a Dutch volume, Tijd en Ruimte: Nieuwe toepassingen van GIS in de alfawetenschappen (Time and space: New applications of GIS in the humanities) (Utrecht: DANS), edited by O. Boonstra and A. Schuurman; and a double issue of the International Journal of Humanities and Arts Computing (vol. 3, nos. 1–2) that was largely devoted to historical GIS appeared in 2009. Most recently, M. Dear, J. Ketchum, S. Luria, and D. Richardson, eds., GeoHumanities: Art, History, Text at the Edge of Place (New York: Routledge, 2011) contains a section of nine chapters on spatial histories.

There is an increasing trend for new collections to be more focused on particular aspects of historical GIS and/or spatial history. These include a 2008 special edition of the *Journal of the Association of History and Computing* (vol. 11, no. 2), which was concerned with teaching using historical GIS; a 2010 special section of *Social Science History* (vol. 34, no. 2) devoted to using historical GIS to study railways and political economy; a 2011 special issue of the *Journal of Interdisciplinary History* (vol. 42, no. 1), edited by J. Marti Henneberg, that again looks at railways and society; and a 2011 special issue of *Social Science History* (vol. 35, no. 4), focused on historical GIS and urban history and edited by D. A. DeBats and I. N. Gregory.

There has also been a developing literature that explores what GIS has to offer to historical research, including I. N. Gregory, K. K. Kemp, and R. Mostern, "Geographical Information and Historical Research: Current Progress and Future Directions," *History and Computing* 13 (2001): 7–24; P. Doorn, "A Spatial Turn in History," GIM *International* 19, no. 4 (2005), http://www.gim-international.com/issues/articles/id453-A_Spatial_Turn_in_History.html; I. N. Gregory and R. G. Healey, "Historical GIS: Structuring, Mapping and Analyzing the Geographies of the Past," Progress in Human Geography 31 (2007): 638–53; I. N. Gregory and P. S. Ell, Historical GIS: Technologies, Methodologies and Scholarship (Cambridge: Cambridge University Press, 2007); and two chapters in Knowles, Placing History, the first by A. K. Knowles, "GIS and History," 1–26, and the second by D. J. Bodenhamer, "History and GIS: Implications for the Discipline," 219–34.

There is also literature on teaching historical GIS and teaching history with it. This includes R. Churchill and A. Hillier, "Teaching with GIS," in Knowles, *Placing History*, 61–94; D. J. Bodenhamer and I. N. Gregory, "Teaching Spatial Literacy and Spatial Technologies in the Digital Humanities," in *Teaching Geographical Information Science and Technology in Higher Education*, ed. D. J. Unwin, K. E. Foote, N. J. Tate, and D. DiBiase (Chichester: John Wiley, 2011), 231–46; and J. B. Owens and L. Woodworth-Ney, "Envisioning a Master's Degree Program in Geographically-Integrated History," Journal of the Association of History and Computing 8, no. 2 (2005), as well as the 2008 special issue of the Journal of the Association of History and Computing.

GENERAL GIS BOOKS

It should not be forgotten that there is also a large literature on GIS generally that, while not directly aimed at the historical community, is very relevant to it. Good introductions include N. R. Chrisman, *Exploring Geographical Information Systems,* 2nd ed. (New York: John Wiley, 2002); M. N. DeMers, *Fundamentals of Geographic Information Systems* (New York: John Wiley, 2000); F. Harvey, *A Primer of GIS: Fundamental Geographic and Cartographic Concepts* (New York: Guildford, 2008); D. I. Heywood, S. Cornelius, and S. Carver, *An Introduction to Geographical Information Systems,* 4th ed. (Harlow, UK: Prentice Hall, 2012); D. J. Martin, *Geographical Information Systems and Their Socio-economic Applications* (New York: Routledge, 1996); and R. Nash Parker and E. K. Asencio, GIS *and Spatial Analysis for the Social Sciences: Coding, Mapping, and Modelling* (New York: Routledge, 2008). For a fuller description of GIS as an academic field, see the essays in the two volumes of P. A. Longley, M. F. Goodchild, D. J. Maguire, and D. W. Rhind, eds., *Geographical Information Systems: Principles, Techniques, Management and Applications,* 2nd ed. (New York: John Wiley, 2005), while for more of an overview on the uses of GIS, see the same four authors' book *Geographical Information Systems and Science,* 3rd ed. (New York: John Wiley, 2010). N. Schuurman, GIS: *A Short Introduction* (Malden, Mass.: Blackwell, 2004) provides a more critical look at the epistemology of GIS. J. Pickles, ed., *Ground Truth: The Social Implications of Geographic Information Systems* (New

York: Guildford Press, 1995) was the first attempt to critically explore GIS and caused a considerable controversy at the time. Many of the views expressed in this volume have since moderated, in part as a consequence of the GIS community responding to them, as essays by some of the same authors in Longley et al., *Geographical Information Systems* illustrate.

TIME IN GIS

A major issue that GIS is frequently criticized for is its perceived poor handling of time, something that is regarded as particularly important for historical applications. The mainstream GIS community has been exploring the issue of time for many years. One of the earliest books in this field that still expresses the issues well is G. Langran's *Time in Geographical Information Systems* (London: Taylor & Francis, 1992). Slightly more recently, D. J. Peuquet's *Representations of Space and Time* (New York: Guildford, 2002) presents an update of how the field has (and has not) developed over the ensuing ten years. The same author also has a chapter in Longley et al., *Geographical Information Systems* that summarizes many of these themes.

   Chapter 6 of Gregory and Ell, *Historical GIS,* discusses the relevance of time in GIS to historical GIS. One area that is particularly relevant here is the use of "areal interpolation" techniques, which allow data collected using different sets of boundaries, such as those at different dates, to be compared. I. N. Gregory and P. S. Ell's "Breaking the Boundaries: Integrating 200 Years of the Census Using GIS," *Journal of the Royal Statistical Society, Series A* 168 (2005): 419–37, and "Error Sensitive Historical GIS: Identifying Areal Interpolation Errors in Time Series Data," *International Journal of Geographical Information Science* 20 (2006): 135–52 describe this application. Their paper "Analysing Spatio-temporal Change Using National Historical GISs: Population Change during and after the Great Irish Famine," *Historical Methods* 38 (2005): 149–67 provides an applied example of this approach. Alternative examples of approaches that exploit time in historical GIS, this time to explore complex temporal patterns in point data, are provided by D. A. Fyfe, D. W. Holdsworth, and C. Weaver, "Historical GIS and Visualization: Insights from Three Hotel Registers in Central Pennsylvania, 1888–1897," *Social Science Computer*

Review 27 (2009): 348–62; and C. Weaver, D. Fyfe, A. Robinson, D. Holds-worth, D. J. Peuquet, and A. M. MacEachren, "Visual Analysis of Historic Hotel Visitation Patterns," *Information Visualization* 6 (2007): 89–103.

It is important to remember that interest in exploring and analyz-ing data over space and time simultaneously predates GIS and has been of interest to researchers working outside the GIS community. One of the best discussions of the importance of doing this is D. B. Massey, *For Space* (London: Sage, 2005) and its predecessor, "Space-Time, 'Science' and the Relationship between Physical Geography and Human Geogra-phy," *Transactions of the Institute of British Geographers* 24 (1999): 261–76. Earlier papers exploring this theme from very different perspectives in-clude J. Langton, "Systems Approach to Change in Human Geography," *Progress in Geography* 4 (1972): 123–78; and R. D. Sack, "Chronology and Spatial Analysis," *Annals of the Association of American Geographers* 64 (1974): 439–52.

HGIS DATABASES

Although many of the earlier papers in the field include a discussion of the databases that were created as part of a project or an analysis, few present a frank discussion of the issues and problems that building such a database can cause. Two notable exceptions to this are L. Siebert, "Us-ing GIS to Document, Visualize, and Interpret Tokyo's Spatial History," *Social Science History* 24 (2000): 537–74; and C. Gordon, "Lost in Space, or Confessions of an Accidental Geographer," *International Journal of Humanities and Arts Computing* 5 (2011): 1–22, which include commend-ably honest accounts of building and using HGIS databases of Tokyo and St. Louis, respectively.

Much of the remaining literature is primarily concerned with data-bases that describe national historical GIS projects. These include M. De Moor and T. Wiedemann, "Reconstructing Territorial Units and Hier-archies: An Example from Belgium," *History and Computing* 13 (2001): 71–97; I. N. Gregory, C. Bennett, V. L. Gilham, and H. R. Southall, "The Great Britain Historical GIS: From Maps to Changing Human Geogra-phy," *Cartographic Journal* 39 (2002): 37–49; C. A. Fitch and S. Ruggles, "Building the National Historical Geographic Information System," *His-*

torical Methods 36 (2003): 41–51; and A. Kunz, "Fusing Time and Space: The Historical Information System HGIS Germany," *International Journal of Humanities and Arts Computing* 1 (2007): 111–22. These systems are primarily polygon based and designed to hold census and related data for the past two centuries or so. An alternative approach, based on over a millennium of Chinese data represented using point locations, is provided by M. L. Berman, "Boundaries or Networks in Historical GIS: Concepts of Measuring Space and Administrative Geography in Chinese History," *Historical Geography* 33 (2005): 118–33; and P. K. Bol, "Creating a GIS for the History of China," in Knowles, *Placing History,* 27–60. A. K. Knowles, ed., "Reports on National Historical GIS Projects," *Historical Geography* 33 (2005): 293–314 provides concise summaries of these and other systems. One issue that is usually not well handled in historical GIS databases that represent administrative boundaries is uncertainty in the locations of these boundaries. B. Plewe, "The Nature of Uncertainty in Historical Geographical Information," *Transactions in GIS* 6 (2002): 431–56 describes a solution to this.

It is becoming increasingly obvious that place-name gazetteers, basically database tables that provide coordinate locations for place-names, are an effective way of rapidly georeferencing large amounts of historical material. R. Mostern and I. Johnson, "From Named Place to Naming Event: Creating Gazetteers for History," *International Journal of Geographical Information Science* 22 (2008): 1091–1108; R. Mostern, "Historical Gazetteers: An Experiential Perspective, with Examples from Chinese History," *Historical Methods* 21 (2008): 39–46; and H. R. Southall, R. Mostern, and M. Berman, "On Historical Gazetteers," *International Journal of Humanities and Arts Computing* 5 (2011): 127–45 provide three accounts of this. These build on earlier perspectives when gazetteers were seen more as a way of adding metadata for digital libraries. See, for example, L. L. Hill, "Guest Editorial: Georeferencing in Digital Libraries," *D-Lib Magazine* 10, no. 5 (2004) and other essays in this issue (http://www.dlib.org/dlib/may04/05contents.html).

HISTORICAL GIS ON THE INTERNET

There are a wealth of sites that place historical GIS resources on the Internet (the Historical GIS Research Network, http://www.hgis.org

.uk/resources.htm, provides links to many of them); however, here we are only concerned with the published literature that describes these resources. A. Wilson, "Sydney *TimeMap:* Integrating Historical Resources Using GIS," *History and Computing* 13 (2001): 45–69 describes a museum exhibit system for Sydney, while on a wider scale, H. R. Southall, "A Vision of Britain through Time: Making Sense of 200 Years of Census Reports," *Local Population Studies* 76 (2006): 76–84 describes how material from the Great Britain Historical GIS and elsewhere was put on the Internet. These two papers are primarily concerned with disseminating historical resources in a way that makes use of, and perhaps stresses, their spatial component. An alternative approach to putting historical GIS on the Internet is provided by B. C. Ray, "Teaching the Salem Witchcraft Trials," in Knowles, *Past Time, Past Place,* 19–33, which describes a system that includes not only primary sources but also secondary material and the results of some of Ray's own analyses on the Salem witchcraft trials. This is taken a stage further by W. G. Thomas and E. L. Ayres, "An Overview: The Differences Slavery Made: A Close Analysis of Two American Communities," *American Historical Review* 108 (2003): 1298–1307 (http://www.historycooperative.org/ahr /elec-projects.html), which is primarily an academic publication reporting on the results of an analysis but also uses the electronic environment to allow the reader to read the article in a nonlinear way and link back to a wealth of related materials that would not conventionally be included in a paper publication. Finally, R. G. Healey and J. Delve, "Integrating GIS and Data Warehousing in a Web Environment: A Case Study of the US 1880 Census," *International Journal of Geographical Information Science* 21 (2007): 575–612 present a paper that shows how data-warehousing techniques can be used to respond to complex queries that may be made by users over the Internet using examples of different way of cross-tabulating and mapping results from individual-level data from the 1880 U.S. census.

URBAN HISTORICAL GIS

Urban studies is one of the areas in which historical GIS has made rapid progress. A number of reasons can be identified for this, including, from a database perspective, that cities are usually relatively small, making the databases reasonably quick to construct, and, from an intellectual point of view, that many research topics associated with cities are inherently spatial. Several studies in North America have taken individual- or household-level records and used them to explore historical patterns of segregation. These include J. Gilliland and S. Olson, "Residential Segregation in the Industrializing City: A Closer Look," *Urban Geography* 31 (2010): 29–58, which studies Montreal based on the 1881 census; K. Schlichting, P. Tuckel, and R. Maisel, "Residential Segregation and the Beginning of the Great Migration of African Americans to Hartford, Connecticut: A GIS-Based Analysis," *Historical Methods* 41 (2008): 132–43; and P. Tuckel, K. Schlichting, and R. Maisel, "Social, Economic, and Residential Diversity within Hartford's African American Community at the Beginning of the Great Migration," *Journal of Black Studies* 37 (2007): 710–36, looking at Hartford, Connecticut. D. DeBats, "Tale of Two Cities: Using Tax Records to Develop GIS Files for Mapping and Understanding Nineteenth Century US Cities," *Historical Methods* 41 (2008): 17–38, and DeBats, "Using GIS and Individual-Level Data for Whole Communities: A Path toward the Reconciliation of Political and Social History," *Social Science Computer Review* 27 (2009): 313–30 compare Alexandria, Virginia, with Newport, Kentucky, in the mid-nineteenth century. A. E. Hillier, "Spatial Analysis of Historical Redlining: A Methodological Exploration," *Journal of Housing Research* 14, no. 1:137–67 and her chapter "Redlining in Philadelphia," in Knowles, *Past Time, Past Place,* 79–93 explores how mortgage redlining, the 1930s practice of declaring some areas as risky to make loans to – a practice often associated with race – affected loans in Philadelphia. E. Diamond and D. Bodenhamer, "Investigating White-Flight in Indianapolis: A GIS Approach," *History and Computing* 13 (2001): 25–44, and J. Stanger-Ross, "Neither Fight nor Flight: Urban Synagogues in Post-war Philadelphia," *Journal of Urban History* 32 (2006): 791–812 both investigate the relationship between religious change and broader urban changes. R. C. Allen, "Getting to *Going to the Show*," *New Review of Film and Television Studies* 8 (2010): 264–76 explores how GIS can be used to understand the role of cinema in U.S. cities in the early twentieth century, with race again being a major issue. Moving away from North America, Z. Frank, "Layers, Flows and Intersections: Jeronymo José de Mello and Artisan

Life in Rio de Janeiro, 1840s–1880s," *Journal of Social History* 41 (2007): 307–28 looks at the impact of economic change on artisans in the city; and L. Murray and E. Grahame, "Sydney's Past, History's Future: The Dictionary of Sydney," *Public History Review* 17 (2010): 89–111 describes a broad infrastructure for studying Sydney's past, focusing on a much wider range of sources than many of the studies above.

A very different approach to urban historical GIS is developed by K. Yano, T. Nakaya, Y. Isoda, Y. Takase, T. Kawasumi, K. Matsuoka, T. Seto, D. Kawahara, A. Tsukamoto, M. Inoue, and T. Kirimura, "Virtual Kyoto: 4D-GIS Comprising Spatial and Temporal Dimensions," *Journal of Geography* 117 (2008): 464–78, who focus on creating a three-dimensional model of historic Kyoto and how it has changed over time that will provide a platform for various subsequent analyses.

Three books have also been published in this area that move from answering specific research questions to broader spatial histories of urban areas. These are C. Gordon, *Mapping Decline: St. Louis and the Fate of the American City* (Philadelphia: University of Pennsylvania Press, 2008), which explores urban decline in St. Louis through the twentieth century; and J.-L. Pinol and M. Garden, *Atlas des Parisiens: De la revolution à nos jours* (Paris: Parigramme, 2009), which explores Paris over the past two centuries. These are both well-illustrated books that combine good use of maps and color with high-quality scholarship. J. Stanger-Ross, *Staying Italian: Urban Change and Ethnic Life in Postwar Toronto and Philadelphia* (Chicago: University of Chicago Press, 2010) presents a more conventional academic monograph, focusing on ethnic experiences within these two cities.

ENVIRONMENTAL AND AGRICULTURAL HISTORY

Environmental history is another area in which significant progress has been made in applying GIS techniques to historical research, in particular with two books that make significant revisions to established scholarship. G. Cunfer's *On the Great Plains: Agriculture and Environment* (College Station: Texas A&M University Press, 2005) uses GIS effectively to help challenge the orthodoxy that overplowing caused the Dust Bowl on the U.S. Great Plains in the 1930s; while B. Donahue's *The*

Great Meadow: Farmers and the Land in Colonial Concord (New Haven, Conn.: Yale University Press, 2004) examines conventional but untested beliefs about early agriculture in New England.

A very different paper on agricultural history is A. W. Pearson and P. Collier, "The Integration and Analysis of Historical and Environmental Data Using a Geographical Information System: Landownership and Agricultural Productivity in Pembrokeshire c. 1850," *Agricultural History Review* 46 (1998): 162–76, which provides an early, but still effective, description of what GIS is and what it has to offer to historical research, as well as providing a study of agricultural patterns in rural Wales in the mid-nineteenth century. Other work in this area includes W. Bigler, "Using GIS to Investigate Fine-Scale Spatial Patterns in Historical American Indian Agriculture," *Historical Geography* 33 (2005): 14–32; P. C. Brown, "Corporate Land Tenure in Nineteenth Century Japan: A GIS Assessment," *Historical Geography* 33 (2005): 99–117; R. Hunter, "Methodologies for Reconstructing a Pastoral Landscape: Land Grants in Sixteenth Century New Spain," *Historical Methods* 43 (2010): 1–13; G. Gong and J. Tiller, "Exploring Vegetation Patterns along an Undefined Boundary: Eastern Harrison County, Texas, Late Spring, 1838," *Social Science Computer Review* 27 (2009): 363–79; N. Levin, E. Elron, and A. Gasith, "Decline of Wetland Ecosystems in the Coastal Plain of Israel during the 20th Century: Implications for Wetland Conservation and Management," *Landscape and Urban Planning* 92 (2009): 220–32; and J. W. Wilson, "Historical and Computational Analysis of Long-Term Environmental Change: Forests in the Shenandoah Valley of Virginia," *Historical Geography* 33 (2005): 33–53.

DEMOGRAPHY

Demographic studies are another area in which historical GIS has made significant contributions to wider fields, perhaps reflecting GIS's origins in quantitative approaches. Some of these studies blur the distinction between the historical and the contemporary by exploring long-term change up to the present day. These include a range of British papers that explore long-term changes in mortality patterns, including D. Dorling, R. Mitchell, M. Shaw, S. Orford, and G. Davey Smith, "The Ghost of

Christmas Past: Health Effects of Poverty in London in 1896 and 1991,"
British Medical Journal 321 (2000): 1547–51, which compares London in
the 1890s with the 1990s; I. N. Gregory, "Comparisons between the Geographies of Mortality and Deprivation from the 1900s to 2001: Spatial
Analysis of Census and Mortality Statistics," *British Medical Journal*
339 (2009): 676–79, which does the same for all of England and Wales,
comparing the 1900s with 2001; P. Norman, I. Gregory, D. Dorling, and
A. Baker, "Geographical Trends in Infant Mortality in England and Wales,
1971–2006," *Health Statistics Quarterly* 40 (2008): 18–29 provides a more
continuous comparison over the last thirty-five years; and P. Congdon,
R. M. Campos, S. E. Curtis, H. R. Southall, I. N. Gregory, and I. R. Jones,
"Quantifying and Explaining Changes in Geographical Inequality of
Infant Mortality in England and Wales since the 1890s," *International
Journal of Population Geography* 7 (2001): 35–51 looks at a longer time
series using more widely spaced intervals.

Moving farther back in time, I. N. Gregory, "Different Places, Different Stories: Infant Mortality Decline in England & Wales, 1851–1911,"
Annals of the Association of American Geographers 98 (2008): 773–94 cre-
ates a continuous time series for these six decades that enables him to
challenge the orthodoxy that infant mortality decline was driven by
public health improvements.

Using HGIS to explore mortality and health is much less well developed in other countries, perhaps reflecting Britain's statistics on the
subject. An exception to this is E. M. Carter, "Malaria, Landscape and
Society in Northwest Argentina in the Early Twentieth Century," *Journal of Latin American Geography* 7 (2008): 7–38.

Moving to fertility, G. W. Skinner, M. Henderson, and Y. Jianhua,
"China's Fertility Transition through Regional Space," *Social Science
History* 24 (2000): 613–52 presents an effective analysis of fertility change
in China since the 1960s using continuous time series data. This paper
was one of the earliest applied analyses in historical GIS and still represents an extremely imaginative use of GIS to study long-term change.

Migration would also seem like an area with much potential for historical GIS work; however, to date this has been more limited than might
be expected. P. A. Longley, R. Webber, and D. Lloyd, "The Quantitative Analysis of Family Names: Historic Migration and the Present Day

Neighbourhood Structure of Middlesbrough, United Kingdom," *Annals of the Association of American Geographers* 97 (2007): 31–48 uses surname distributions to map patterns of migration into a town in the northeast of England, a technique that could be applied much more widely. I. N. Gregory, J. Marti Henneberg, and F. J. Tapiador, "Modeling Long-Term Pan-European Population Change from 1870 to 2000 Using Geographical Information Systems," *Journal of the Royal Statistical Society Series A* 173 (2010): 31–50 looks at long-term population change in Europe but not at migration per se.

TRANSPORT AND MOBILITY

Transport is another area that clearly has much potential for GIS-based analyses. The 2010 special issue of *Social Science History* contains three papers on the impact that the development of the rail network had on population in the nineteenth century in different places. J. Atack, F. Bateman, M. Haines, and R. A. Margo, "Did Railroads Induce or Follow Economic Growth? Urbanization and Population Growth in the American Midwest, 1850–1860," 171–97 looks at the United States; I. N. Gregory and J. Marti Henneberg, "The Railways, Urbanization, and Local Demography in England and Wales, 1825–1911," 199–228 looks at England and Wales; and R. M. Schwartz, "Rail Transport, Agrarian Crisis, and the Restructuring of Agriculture: France and Great Britain Confront Globalization, 1860–1900 229–55 compares France and Britain. Moving back in time, M. E. O'Kelly's "The Impact of Accessibility Change on the Geography of Crop Production: A Re-examination of the Illinois and Michigan Canal Using GIS," *Annals of the Association of American Geographers* 97 (2007): 49–63 looks at the impact of the Erie Canal on agriculture; and G. R. Dobbs, "Backcountry Settlement Development and Indian Trails: A GIS Land-Grant Analysis," *Social Science Computer Review* 27 (2009): 331–47 looks at how the arrangement of indigenous trails influenced urban settlement patterns in eighteenth-century North Carolina.

Looking at mobility, D. A. Fyfe and D. W. Holdsworth, "Signatures of Commerce in Small-Town Hotel Guest Registers," *Social Science History* 33 (2009): 17–45; and D. A. Fyfe, D. W. Holdsworth, and C. Weaver in *Social Science Computer Review* use signatures in hotel registers to explore how travelers moved around the northeastern United States in the early twentieth century.

ECONOMIC AND SOCIAL HISTORY

Work in this broad area is more limited, but two papers in particular stand out. In both cases they make use of the ability of a GIS to integrate a wide variety of disparate sources to develop new insights into the topic under study. Thomas and Ayres, "An Overview: The Difference Slavery Made," *American Historical Review* 108 (2003): 1298–1307 presents a detailed analysis of two American counties, one on either side of the Mason-Dixon Line, to investigate a wide variety of factors associated with the local economy and society to investigate the extent to which slavery was a root cause of the Civil War. A. K. Knowles and R. G. Healey, "Geography, Timing, and Technology: A GIS-Based Analysis of Pennsylvania's Iron Industry, 1825–1875," *Journal of Economic History* 66 (2006): 608–34 brings together a wide variety of variables associated with the development of the iron industry over a long time period and, by stressing the importance of temporal and spatial differences, is able to challenge more general studies in this area. A third paper, R. G. Healey and T. R. Stamp, "Historical GIS as a Foundation for the Analysis of Regional Economic Growth: Theoretical, Methodological, and Practical Issues," *Social Science History* 24 (2000): 575–612 presents an earlier perspective on this type of work that stresses the database construction challenges and the opportunities that these open up in this field.

ANCIENT AND MEDIEVAL HISTORY

The above discussion suggests that historical GIS research has largely concentrated on the nineteenth and twentieth centuries. This seems to fit with early criticisms that the technology works best in a data-rich environment. While there is some truth in this, the progress that has been made using GIS to study medieval and even earlier histories suggests that there is also much potential to apply it to periods when sources are very limited, fragmentary, and difficult to use. This is generally because

GIS allows the researcher to make better use of these sources. A leading example of this is the work of B. M. S. Campbell and colleagues, who use the early fourteenth-century *Inquisitiones Post Mortem* – effectively the wills of rich landowners – to explore medieval land use across England. K. Bartley and B. Campbell, "*Inquisitiones Post Mortem*, GIS, and the Creation of a Land-Use Map of Medieval England," *Transactions in GIS* 2 (1997): 333–46 describes how the database underlying this research was created, while B. M. S. Campbell, *English Seigniorial Agriculture 1250–1450* (Cambridge: Cambridge University Press, 2000) and B. M. S. Campbell and K. Bartley, *England on the Eve of the Black Death: An Atlas of Lay Lordship, Land and Wealth, 1300–49* (Manchester: Manchester University Press, 2006) presents the research that developed from this resource.

GIS has also been used at a more local scale to explore medieval towns and settlements, as described by K. Lilley, C. Lloyd, and S. Trick, "Mapping Medieval Urban Landscapes: The Design and Planning of Edward I's New Towns of England and Wales," *Antiquity* 79, no. 303 (2005) (http://www.antiquity.ac.uk); and K. Lilley, C. Lloyd, S. Trick, and C. Graham, "Mapping and Analyzing Medieval Built Form Using GPS and GIS," *Urban Morphology* 9 (2005): 5–15.

Finally, GIS has been used to explore medieval and ancient maps and what they reveal both about the map maker or makers and the areas that they were mapping. C. D. Lloyd and K. D. Lilley, "Cartographic Veracity in Medieval Mapping: Analyzing Geographical Variation in the Gough Map of Great Britain," *Annals of the Association of American Geographers* 99 (2009): 27–48 explores a medieval map of Britain; and R. J. A. Talbert and T. Elliot, "New Windows on the Peutinger Map of the Roman World," in Knowles, *Placing History*, 199–218 explores an even older map of the Roman world, the original of which is believed to date from around AD 300.

TOWARD HUMANITIES GIS AND SPATIAL HUMANITIES

In addition to the progress that GIS has made in history, there is also an increasing trend for it to be used in other disciplines within the humanities, leading to the development of humanities GIS and spatial history. D. J. Bodenhamer, "Creating a Landscape of Memory: The Potential of

Humanities GIS," *International Journal of Humanities and Arts Comput-*
ing 1 (2007): 97–110 and the collection of essays in D. J. Bodenhamer,
J. Corrigan, and T. M. Harris, eds., *The Spatial Humanities: GIS and the*
Future of Humanities Scholarship (Bloomington: Indiana University
Press, 2010) represent the first serious attempts to frame this field. The
potential uses of geographical data have, however, been recognized for
much longer than this, with the use of spatial data as metadata being
seen as particularly important, as shown by D. M. Smith, G. Crane, and
J. Rydberg-Cox, "The Perseus Project: A Digital Library for the Humanities," *Literary and Linguistic Computing* 15 (2000): 15–25.

As the majority of sources used by humanities scholars are unstructured texts, the major challenges at present are first to work out how to
convert these into a form suitable for GIS, which typically requires its
attribute data to be in tabular form, and second, and more importantly,
to explore what these texts have to offer to advance the disciplines that
they are applied to such that, as with history, the research becomes of
interest to people with no inherent interest in GIS or perhaps even in geography. At least three groups of researchers have taken on the challenge
of how to convert texts to GIS format. These are C. Grover, R. Tobin,
K. Byrne, M. Woollard, R. Reid, S. Dunn, and J. Ball, "Use of the Edinburgh Geoparser for Georeferencing Digitized Historical Collections,"
Philosophical Transactions of the Royal Society A 368 (2010): 3875–89;
I. N. Gregory and A. Hardie, "Visual GISting: Bringing Together Corpus Linguistics and Geographical Information Systems," *Literary and*
Linguistic Computing 26 (2011): 297–314; and M. Yuan, "Mapping Text,"
in Bodenhamer, Corrigan, and Harris, *The Spatial Humanities,* 109–23.

At least two papers have explored the potential that mapping texts
offers to develop new scholarship, albeit applied to very different topics. D. Cooper and I. N. Gregory, "Mapping the English Lake District:
A Literary GIS," *Transactions of the Institute of British Geographers* 36
(2011): 89–108 explore eighteenth-century literature associated with the
English Lake District, while E. Barker, S. Bouzarovski, C. Pelling, and
L. Isaksen, "Mapping an Ancient Historian in a Digital Age: The Herodotus Encoded Space-Text-Image Archive (HESTIA)," *Leeds Interna-*
tional Classical Studies 9 (2010): 1–36 explore the writing of a historian
in the ancient world.

There is also the potential to use other types of sources within GIS. J. Hallam and L. Roberts (who also have a paper in this volume), "Mapping, Memory and the City: Archives, Databases and Film Historiography," *European Journal of Cultural Studies* 14 (2011): 355–72 explore how movies can be used within GIS to gain a better understanding of urban history using the example of Liverpool. J. Robinson, "Mapping the Place of Pantomime in a Victorian Town," in *Victorian Pantomime: A Collection of Critical Essays,* ed. J. Davis (Basingstoke: Palgrave Macmillan, 2010) explores how GIS can be used to explore theater history.

Thus it is clear that while the spatial humanities are in a relatively early stage, perhaps comparable with where historical GIS was around a decade ago, pioneering work in the development of databases is occurring, and rapid progress can be expected as this develops.

Contributors

IAN N. GREGORY is Professor of Digital Humanities at Lancaster University. His research interests started by focusing on using GIS within quantitative history but have since spread to using GIS across all humanities disciplines and particularly with textual sources. He is author or coauthor of three books: *Troubled Geographies: A Spatial History of Religion and Society in Ireland* (Indiana University Press, 2013), *Historical GIS: Techniques, Methodologies and Scholarship* (Cambridge University Press, 2007), and *A Place in History: A Guide to Using GIS in Historical Research* (Oxbow, 2003). He is currently principal investigator on the European Research Council's Spatial Humanities: Texts, GIS, Places project (www.lancs.ac.uk/spatialhum).

ALISTAIR GEDDES is a Lecturer in Human Geography at University of Dundee, UK. He has a background in quantitative geography and is interested especially in how place and space can be analyzed using GIS in various fields of research by taking account of the reshaping of GIS itself by developments in data, technology, and methodologies. He is a member of the editorial board of the online service for the Statistical Accounts of Scotland (1791–1845) (http://edina.ac.uk/stat-acc-scot).

ROBERT M. SCHWARTZ is E. Nevius Rodman Professor of History at Mount Holyoke College, Massachusetts. His comparative research on railways and uneven development in Great Britain and France includes "Rail Transport, Agrarian Crisis, and the Restructuring of Agriculture: France and Great Britain Confront Globalization, 1860–1900," *Social*

Science History (2010), and "Spatial History: Railways, Uneven Development, and Population Change in France and Great Britain, 1850–1914," *Journal of Interdisciplinary History* (with I. N. Gregory and T. Thevenin, 2011). He has also cowritten a chapter titled "History and GIS: Railways, Population Change, and Agricultural Development in Late Nineteenth Century Wales" (with I. N. Gregory and J. M. Henneberg) for the collection *GeoHumanities: Art, History, Text at the Edge of Place* (Association of American Geographers and Routledge, 2011). His other recent work on the French seigneurial system and rural communities has appeared in a number of collections.

THOMAS THEVENIN is a Professor of Geography with the Théoriser et Modéliser pour Aménager (ThéMA) research laboratory of the Centre National de la Recherche Scientifique and Université de Bourgogne, Dijon, France.

ANDREW A. BEVERIDGE is Professor of Sociology at Queens College and the Graduate School and University Center of the City University of New York. His team developed Social Explorer (http://www.social explorer.com), an award-winning online research tool funded by the United States National Science Foundation for accessing U.S. census data and demographic information from 1790 to the present. Recently he has been working on two major projects involving urban and neighborhood change and a coedited volume, *New York and Los Angeles: The Uncertain Future* (Oxford University Press, 2013). He was awarded the Public Understanding of Sociology Award of the American Sociological Association in 2007. His research has also been funded by the American Council of Learned Societies and the National Endowment for the Humanities. He is a consultant and contributor on analyses of census data for a number of newspapers, including the *New York Times*.

NIALL CUNNINGHAM is a Research Associate with the Centre for Research on Socio-Cultural Change at the University of Manchester, UK, where he works on issues around social and spatial inequality. He is co-author of *Troubled Geographies: A Spatial History of Religion and Society in Ireland* (Indiana University Press, 2013), based on research funded by

the UK's Arts and Humanities Research Council. He is nearing completion of his PhD dissertation on the geographical distribution of political
deaths during the Northern Ireland Troubles between 1969 and 2001.

HUMPHREY R. SOUTHALL is Reader in Geography at the University
of Portsmouth, UK. His original focus was on the origins of the north-
south divide in Britain. He leads the Great Britain Historical GIS project, securing funding from the UK National Lottery, government agencies, and research bodies, as well as generating commercial funding for
the companion open access web site, A Vision of Britain through Time
(http://www.visionofbritain.org.uk). His recent research concerns information architectures for historical geographical information, empha-
sizing geosemantic as well as geospatial approaches and including the
Old Maps Online global search portal (http://www.oldmapsonline.org).
He is coeditor of a collection on gazetteers and their historical and cultural applications (Indiana University Press) that includes his work with
nineteenth-century descriptive gazetteers and on travel writers from a
much longer period.

ELIJAH MEEKS is a Digital Humanities Specialist at Stanford University
(http://dhs.stanford.edu), where he develops software and data models
for humanities faculty. His recent work (with Ruth Mostern) includes
the Digital Gazetteer of the Song Dynasty. He recently completed a PhD
dissertation at the University of California, Merced, focused on the modeling and analysis of historical socioenvironmental systems in China.

RUTH MOSTERN (http://faculty.ucmerced.edu/rmostern/index.html)
is an Associate Professor and Founding Faculty in the School of Social
Sciences, Humanities, and Arts at the University of California, Merced.
An expert in Chinese and world history, she has a long-standing interest
in socially authored, spatial, and interactive modes for reasoning and
communicating about history. She has recently published the Digital
Gazetteer of the Song Dynasty (http://songgis.ucmercedlibrary.info),
coauthored with Elijah Meeks. Based on this research, she has recently
completed a book, *Dividing the Realm in Order to Govern: The Spatial
Organization of the Song State* (Harvard University Press, 2011).

JULIA HALLAM is a Reader in Film and Media and Head of the Communications and Media Department at the University of Liverpool, UK. She has led two projects funded by the UK's Arts and Humanities Research Council exploring the relationship between film and urban space. Her recent project, *Mapping the City in Film: A Geo-historical Analysis,* has been developing new methodologies for multidisciplinary and intermedial analysis of moving image texts using GIS and creating a map of Liverpool films for public exhibition with the Museum of Liverpool. She is coeditor with Les Roberts on *Locating the Moving Image: New Approaches to Film and Place* (Indiana University Press, 2013).

LES ROBERTS is a Lecturer in Digital Cultures in the Department of Communication and Media at University of Liverpool. His research interests are in the cultural production of space, place, and mobility, with a particular focus on film and popular music cultures. Les's recent projects include a GIS-based geohistorical study of Liverpool's urban landscape in film and ethnographic research into popular music, place, and cultural memory. He is author of *Film, Mobility and Urban Space: A Cinematic Geography of Liverpool* (2012), editor of *Mapping Cultures: Place, Practice and Performance* (2012), and coeditor of *Locating the Moving Image: New Approaches to Film and Place* (2013), *Liminal Landscapes: Travel, Experience and Spaces In-between* (2012), and *The City and the Moving Image: Urban Projections* (2010). For information on recent research activities and publications, see www.liminoids.com.

Index

Accuracy, xii, xiii

Address, 94, 96

Administrative boundaries, 151, 192;
changing, 2, 89, 175; redrawing of, 153

Agrarian depression, 5–9, 18

Agricultural census, 18, 30

Agricultural statistics. *See* Statistics:
agricultural

Agriculture, 2–3, 5–7, 9, 17, 28–29, 105, 137,
196, 198

*Alphabetical List of Geographical Names in
Sung China*, 120–21

Ambiguity, xiii, 100, 174

Analysis, 7, 37, 70, 78; of census data, 28,
93; critical, 168; geohistorical, 147, 151,
169; GIS-based, xvii, 2, 79, 198; HGIS,
119, 123, 129, 197; historical, 27; quantitative, ix, 172; of segregation, 38, 43–45,
50–51, 54, 56, 57, 59; spatial, 6, 8, 14, 27,
63–65, 119–20, 124, 129–30, 134, 137–40;
spatial statistical, 138; statistical, 21, 95

ArcGIS, 101, 104, 105, 112, 178

Archaeologists, 98

Archaeology, 180

Areal interpolation, 190

Attributes, 22, 101, 120, 122–23. *See also*
Data: attribute

Augmented reality, 159

Autocorrelation, spatial, 70. *See also*
Moran's I test, local

Baronies (Ireland), 66, 68

Belfast (Northern Ireland), 70, 72, 76,
78–79, 81

Boundaries, 44, 101, 151, 153, 180, 190; between communities, 81; city, 44; communes, 30; computerized, 93; district,
68; enumeration district, 44; geographic, 154; of history, x, xvi; inconsistent,
68; international, 134; parish, 18, 113;
polygon, xi; property, 111; territorial, 66;
tract, 44; zone, 42. *See also* Administrative boundaries

Buffer, 134, 137

Bureau of the Census (U.S.), 36–38, 40,
43, 44, 59

Burgess, Ernest, 40–43, 51

Cantons: (French), 8, 14, 22, 26; (Song
China), 121

Catalog, 99–100, 151; archive, 99, 182;
card, 100; geographical, 99; library;
xi, 99

Census, 2–3, 28, 89, 93, 104, 123, 194;
England and Wales, 94–97, 112; Irish,
xvi–xvii, 63–64, 65–68, 70, 72; Northern
Ireland, 64, 65, 67–68, 79–81, 83; race
classification in, 45–46; U.S. 37–39,
42–45, 193. *See also* Data: census

Census Bureau. *See* Bureau of the Census
(U.S.)

Census tract, 37–38, 40, 43, 44–45, 54

China Historical GIS (CHGIS), 121

China Historical Studies GIS, 121

Cinematic cartography, 146–50, 168–69

Cinematic geography. *See* Geography:
cinematic

Citation analysis, 43

City in Film: catalog, 151; database,
144–45, 159, 161; map, 151; project, 145,
150, 169
Clustering, 70, 72, 75, 78
Communes (French), 8, 12, 22
Complexity, 21, 177
Concentric ring model, 40–42
Conflict, 2, 62–63, 65, 76–77, 79, 82–83, 119
Context, 38, 99; geographic, 62, 147; his-
torical, 28; national, 66; social, 62
Contextual materials, 147, 151
Coordinate, xiii–xiv, 90, 92, 98, 100–101;
geographic, 8, 96; for historical maps,
187; latitude-longitude, 121; point, 175
Corpus linguistics. *See* Linguistics: corpus
Côte-d'Or, Department (France), 7, 18,
21–22, 27–28
Counties: British, 8, 14, 17–18, 98, 100;
Irish, 68, 72; Northern Irish, 79; Song
China, 119–21, 134, 137–38
Culture, 182; of distribution and consump-
tion; 146; film, 143, 154; human, xv;
moving image, 149; performance, ix;
political, 63; travelling, 149; visual, 146,
154; youth, 163

Data: aggregate, 96; attribute, x–xiii, 89–
90, 164, 175–76, 201; census, xvi–xvii,
44, 63–64, 65, 68, 79, 83, 95, 111, 138, 172,
180, 192; geographical, 201; georeferenced, xi, xiv, 8, 27, 92, 182; GIS, 8, 14, 18,
29–30, 89, 91; HGIS, 10; historical, 90,
94–95, 111, 130; point, 154, 190; polygon,
154; qualitative, 154, 176; quantitative,
xi, 175, 180; raster, xi, 90, 105, 113; satellite, 105–106, 109; spatial, x–xiii, xvii, 44,
92, 138, 201; vector, xi–xii, 105, 112; vital
registration, 93
Data model, x, xiii–xiv, 90, 179; of Digital Gazetteer of the Song Dynasty,
123; gazetteer, 123, 140; GIS, 90; vector,
xiii
Data standards, 104
Database, xi, xvii, 6, 168, 186, 192; construction of, x, 91, 174, 187, 194, 199, 200;
georeferenced, 179; GIS, xii–xiii, xv, 1,
145, 173, 176; HGIS, xv–xvi, 1–3, 191–92;

humanities, 176–77; maps, 111; MySQL,
120; national-scale, 2; object-relational,
101; record, 99; relational, 90, 101; spatial, 143, 159, 175; of Troubles-related
killings, xvii, 63, 77–78, 83
Database of Irish Historical Statistics,
63–65
Dataset, xiv, 176, 180; hydrological, 134;
integrated, 134; large-scale, 58; of movie
venues, 147
Deaths, xvii, 79, 81, 94, 205
Demography, ix, 36, 40, 93, 97, 172, 196;
historical, 93, 97, 187; Irish, 66; medical,
xvi, religious, 64
Density: cattle, 18–19, 22, 26; map, 18; pop-
ulation, 11; of state presence, 119, 134, 139
Density smoothing, 177; kernel, 79–81
Digital Gazetteer of the Song Dynasty
(DGSD), 118–26, 129–30, 134, 138–40
Digital humanities, 177, 182
Dioceses (Ireland), 66
Districts (Ireland), 66, 68, 70, 72–76
Dorset County (England), 14, 17–19, 21–22,
25, 27–28, 30

Emotion, inscription of, 149
Empirical approach, xiii, 120
Empirical generalizations, xiii
Empirical methods, 147
Entities, 101, 121–23
Enumeration district, 38, 44, 48
Epistemological shift, 168
Epistemology, ix, 189
Error: -checking, 121; interpolation, 74,
190; and uncertainty, 173–74
Event, 11, 94, 118, 123–24, 134, 137, 139–40,
156, 161, 164–67, 182; flood, 137–38;
place-making, 120, 122
Experience: common, 83; ethnic, 195;
lived, 27; of movie-going, 147; of urban
life, 147
Exploratory spatial statistical technique,
65, 72

Feature, x–xi, 38, 109, 111, 123, 176
Fertility, ix, 197; change, 197; survey, 97
Field survey maps, 106

Film, xvii, 143–46; amateur, xvi; documentaries, 157, 163; feature, 148–50; genre, 155, 157; newsreel, 150, 155–57, 162, 164–67; promotional, 155–56
Film studies, 91, 146–48
Framing, 29; contextual, 153; geographical, 62

Gazetteer, xvi, 100, 118, 120; historical, 113, 118, 123, 126; instance-based, 123; place-name, 175–76, 192
Generalization, xiii, 7
Geographic(al) Information Science (GISci), x, 174, 181, 189, 190, 192, 193
Geographic(al) Information Systems (GIS), ix–xvii, 2, 6, 8, 27–29, 58, 63, 65–66, 79, 89–90, 97, 100, 103–104, 111–12, 113, 117n31, 130, 139, 143, 147, 151, 168, 174–76, 178–82, 186–90, 194–96, 199–02; archaeology and, 98, 180; functionality, 174, 178; historical (see Historical GIS (HGIS)); humanities (see Humanities GIS); issues of time in, 90, 173–74, 190–91; open-source, 178; platform, xiii, 151, 154; qualitative, 175; software, x–xi, 65, 98, 100, 126, 177–78; technology, xv–xvii, 27, 89–91, 92, 104, 147, 179, 199
Geographic(al) thinking, 27, 29, 183
Geographies, 118, 139, 147; cinematic and film, 153–55, 160–61, 167; of human cultures, xv; of leisure, 163; past, xviii, 182; regional, 153; religious, 63, 66, 68, 76, 81–82; transport, 160
Geography, xi, xiv, xvii, 76, 98, 104, 139, 149, 175, 180, 201; cinematic, 151, 153, 155, 163; conversion table, 95; cultural, 163; discipline of, ix, 146, 172; economic, 129; historical, 153; human, 121, 175; imagined, 154; imperial, 119; of local government, 95; military, 129; parish, 113; of place, 154; political, 138; population, 124, 129; prefecture, 137; Song, 120; of sovereignty, 120; of trade, wealth and income, 124
Geolocation, 123
Georeferencing, 108, 112, 145, 175–76, 192. See also Data: georeferenced

Geospatial: technologies, x; tools, 143
Google, 100; Analytics, 93; Books, 176; Earth, x, 178–79; Maps, 179
Great Britain Historical GIS (GBHGIS). See National Historical GIS: Great Britain (GBHGIS)
Great Migration, 35, 37, 43, 194
Grid cells, 82

HGIS. See Historical GIS (HGIS)
Historical GIS (HGIS), ix–x, xiv–xvi, 2, 27, 29, 62, 66, 104–105, 110–11, 113–14, 118–19, 124, 126, 139, 172–73, 182, 186–90, 197, 199, 202; community, 2, 174; and demography, 196–97; and Internet, 179, 192–93; multinational, 97; projects, 1, 91, 92–93, 97, 113; qualitative, 173, 174–75; quantitative, 173–74; research, xii–xiii, 126; researcher, 115; sources, 90; and spatial history, 6, 173; trends, xiv–xv; urban, 193–95
Historical GIS Research Network, vii, 86, 192
Historiography, x, xv, 1, 91, 119
History, x, xiv, xvii, 11, 21, 29, 89, 97, 109, 126, 133, 179; agricultural, 195–96; ancient, 199–00; Chinese, 129; comparative, 5–7, 28; detectives, 145; discipline of, x, xv–xvi, 92, 146, 172–74, 178, 180, 182, 187, 189, 200–201; early modern, ix; economic, 199; environmental, ix, 172, 187, 195; family, 98; Irish, 64, 69; local, 104, 129, 139; Liverpool's, 161; of medicine, 97; medieval, ix, 187, 199–00; political history, 118, 139; property, 111; quantitative, 175, 182; regional, 130; religious, 111, 172; rural, 172; social, 199; social science, x, xv–xvi, 90–91, 124, 187; spatial (see Spatial history); theatre, 202; urban, ix, 172, 187, 188, 202
History of Moviegoing, Exhibition, and Reception network (HoMER), 147
Humanities, x, xii–xv, xvii, 92, 114, 146, 174–82; digital, 177, 182; spatial (see Spatial humanities)
Humanities GIS, xv–xvi, 91, 172, 174–75, 177–78, 180–82, 186–87, 200–201

Immigrant, 36; groups, 40, 42–43, 51, 58
Imprecision, xii–xiii
Inferences, 138
Information: attribute, xvii; on boundary changes, 96; catalog, 98; census, xvii, 3, 89; ecological, 139; environmental, 119, 138; georeferenced, 8, 36, 138; land-use, 106; on liabilities, 111; locational, 77; map, 106; place-names, 109; place-specific, 100; spatial, 130; systems, 121; Technology, xi; textual, xi, 92, 101
Infrastructure, 175–76, 195; academic, 114; data, xv
Intentionally Linked Entity model, 122
Interpolation: areal, 190; spatial, 68, 74
Interpolation error, 74, 190
Interpretation, xiii, 27, 106, 174

Jefferies, Richard, 4–6, 8, 10–12, 14, 16–17, 27–29, 172

Kernel density smoothing, 79–81
Knowledge, spatial, 150

Land Utilisation Survey of Great Britain, 106, 108–11, 113
Landscape, 150, 155; cultural, 168; and farming, 105–106; film, 168; historical, 161; political, 119, 124, 128–30, 134, 137–39; religious, 63; social and material, 146; spatial, 124, 127, 129, 137; urban, 145, 150, 153, 155, 158, 164; virtual, 143, 168
Landscape monitoring, 106
Line, x–xii; color, 51; isopleth, 60; peace line (Belfast), 81–83; railway, 9; regres-sion, 72
Linguistics, 175; corpus, 176, 181, 201
LISA method, 75
Liverpool, xvi–xvii; 28, 143–45, 150–63, 165–67, 202. See also Merseyside
Local Indicators of Spatial Association, 75
Location: concept of, xi–xiv, xvii, 21, 98, 123, 143, 147; on Earth's surface, xi–xii, 180
Locational media, 149
Location-based services (LBS), 179

Logic, territorial, 118
Longitudinal Study (England and Wales), 94–95, 97

Mapping, xiv, xvi, 124, 149, 150, 155, 160; cultural, 149; database, 145; digital, 109, 147, 151; genealogical, 146; impulse, 149–50; Internet, 179; as metaphor, 169; mid-twentieth century, 96; movie-, 148; texts, 201; trope of, 146
Maps: ancient, 200; animated, 148; authority of, xii; cinematic, 143, 148; critiques of, xi; GIS, 177; hand-drawn, 37; historical, 92, 105, 108, 111; medieval, 200; movie, 148; Ordnance Survey, 106, 108, 112, 151; thematic, 28; tithe, 106, 112; topographic, 106
Mason-Dixon Line, 48, 199
Massey, Douglas, 43, 56
Memory, 168
Merseyside, 143, 145, 151, 153–54, 157–58, 160–61, 166–67. See also Liverpool
Metadata, 104, 174, 192, 201
Migration, ix, 35, 42, 70, 76, 197–98. See also Great Migration
Moran's I test, local, 70–72

Name authorities, 97–100
Narrative, xii, 27, 29, 97, 148, 149; histori-cal, 27; model, 168; sources, 130
National Health Service Central Register (U.K.), 94–95
National Historical GIS, 190, 191–92; China (CHGIS), 121; Great Britain (GB-HGIS), xvi, 30, 92–93, 95, 97, 104, 112–15, 191, 193; Irish, 65; United States (U.S.) (NHGIS), 36–38, 44, 93
National mapping agencies, 92
National Survey of Health and Develop-ment (Britain), 96–97
Network, xii; of local record offices, 98; of mobility, 153; rail, xvi, 2, 12, 16, 198; transport, xvi, 3
Newsreel. See Film: newsreel
NHGIS. See National Historical GIS, United States (U.S.) (NHGIS)

Open source: formats, 91; GIS, 178
Optical Character Recognition, 64
Ontology, 101
Ontology-based architecture, 100
Ordnance Survey (Great Britain), 106, 108, 111, 112, 151

Paradigm: ix, xi, xvii
Parishes (British), 3, 8, 10, 14, 19, 21–22, 99, 101, 104, 112
Park, Robert E., 40–42
Pattern, xiv, xvii, 7; of change, 6; geographical, 2; point, 177; of segregation (*see* Segregation: patterns); spatial, 129–30; temporal, 120, 190
Peace line (Belfast), 81–83
Place, 63, 100–101, 118, 123, 145–49, 164, 168; and identity, 151, 153–54, 160; named, 120, 122; sense of, 154–55
Place-names, 90, 100, 109, 175–76, 192
Point, x–xiii, 81; locations, 121, 175, 192; location table, 123; symbols, 82

Polygon: x–xii, xvii, 89–90, 99, 101, 103, 109, 123, 173, 192
Positivism, ix, xiii, 177
Precision, xii–xiii
Prefectures (Song China), 119–21, 123, 126, 129, 132, 137
Proximity, 8, 39, 139; to international border, 137–38; of/to railway stations, 10–11, 14–16, 21–27, 39

Qualitative GIS, 175
Query, point-in-polygon, 104; SQL, 126
QVIZ project, 98, 103–104

Railway, 2–3, 5–6, 8, 10, 14, 17–18, 21, 27, 160, 188; line, 3, 9, 89; Overhead (Liverpool), 144, 152, 155–56, 159, 163
Railway station, 5, 8, 10–11, 14, 19, 144, 155–56
Raster data. *See* Data: raster
Registration districts (Britain), 8, 10–11, 22, 97, 99, 104
Regression, geographically weighted, 19; ordinary least-squares, 21

Relationships, xiii, 63; entity-instance, 122; funding, 114; hierarchical, 101–103; spatial, 7, 22, 26, 28–29, 83, 89, 121
Religion, 2, 62–63, 70, 75
Representation: of geographic features, 10; filmic, 149, 151–53, 155; space-time, 66; surface-based, 81
Roman world, 200

Salem witchcraft trials, 193
Satellite data, 105–106, 109
Scale, 28, 139
Scatterplot (Scattergraphs), xi, 22, 72
Scholarship, x, xii, xv, 1, 147, 180, 187, 195, 201; humanities, xii, 177
Science: computer, 181; earth, xiii, 181; library, 181; social, ix, xiii, 2, 39, 57, 114, 146, 177, 181
Second World War. *See* World War II
Segregation, 2, 35–36, 39; analysis of, xvii, 38, 43–45; conceptualization of, 40; measurement of, 37, 40, 42–45, 48, 50, 52, 54, 56–58; patterns, xvi, 36–39, 43, 51–52, 57, 194; persistence, 36, 38–39, 43–44, 52, 59
Semantic, 139
Sense of place, 154–55
Situatedness, 160
Song dynasty: China, xvi–xvii, 118–21, 123, 172. *See also* Digital Gazetteer of the Song Dynasty (DGSD)
Spatial analysis. *See* Analysis: spatial
Spatial autocorrelation, 70
Spatial data. *See* Data: spatial
Spatial history, xiv–xv, 1–3, 5–7, 27–29, 118–21, 129–30, 137, 139, 172–73, 182, 187–88, 200
Spatial humanities, ix, xv, 172, 177, 182, 186–87, 200–202
Spatial interpolation, 68, 74
Spatial relationships. *See* Relationships: spatial
Spatial statistics. *See* Statistics: spatial
Spatial turn, 146, 188
Stamp, Dudley, L. 106, 108
State power, 118–21, 124, 129, 139

Statistics, 40, 64, 65, 93, 160, 177; agricul-
    tural, xvi, 9, 28; historical, 93; spatial, 8,
    21, 27, 65
Subjectivity, 146, 149
Surface, 81; continuous, xi; Earth's, x, xii,
    xiv, 118, 180; raster, xii; smoothed, 81
Sutton database, 77–79

Technologies, geographical, xv; Internet,
    179; mapping, 179; spatial, x
Temporal, change, 28, 65, 68, 126, 173; pat-
    tern, 120, 190; reasoning, 140
Text, xi, 21, 99, 120, 168, 176, 201
Tilly, Charles, 124, 129
Time: change over, xvi–xvii, 7, 14, 69,
    89–90, 121–22, 173, 195; in GIS, 190–91;
    lead, xv, 178; series, 64, 197; space and, 5,
    118, 173–74, 191; travel, 21
Topology, polygon, 112
Transport, ix, 39, 79, 152, 159–60, 198; rail,
    5, 7–8, 16–17, 22, 25–28
Travel, 160; time, 21

Travelogues, 150, 159
Troubled Geographies project, 62, 64–65,
    76, 78–79, 82, 83
Troubles (Northern Ireland), xvii, 62, 65,
    70, 76, 82; fatalities associated with, 3,
    63, 89

Uncertainty, 173–74, 192
Urban, planning, 150
User-generated content, 182

Virtual landscape, 143, 168
Vision of Britain Through Time, 93, 100,
    112, 181
Visualization, 8, 124

Web resources, 186
World, digital, 177
World War II, 35, 65, 105, 145, 162

Yellow River (China), 130–31, 133–34:
    course change, 119, 137–38

CPSIA information can be obtained
at www.ICGtesting.com
Printed in the USA
LVOW04s1728051215

465441LV00022B/64/P